Working with German

Level 1

Coursebook

Peter Lupson
Curriculum Manager for Modern Languages,
Croxteth Community Comprehensive School,
Liverpool

Doug Embleton
Managing Director, The Language Service Ltd

Elspeth Eggington
Freelance Linguist

Stanley Thornes (Publishers) Ltd

First published in 1989 by:
Stanley Thornes (Publishers) Ltd
Ellenborough House
Wellington Street
CHELTENHAM GL50 1YW
England

This edition published in 1996.

97 98 99 00 01 / 10 9 8 7 6 5 4 3 2

ISBN 0–7487–2450–8

A catalogue record for this book is available from the British Library.

New illustrations by Shaun Williams
Typeset by Columns Design and Production Services Ltd, Reading
Printed and bound in Great Britain by Redwood Books, Trowbridge, Wiltshire

Introduction

Working with German Level 1 is designed for anyone needing to use the language for practical purposes, in particular for commerce and industry, or holiday and travel. It is based on common situations likely to occur in German-speaking countries.

Each chapter illustrates particular language functions which are developed by means of dialogues and individual or group situational exercises. The chapters are graded structurally and new grammar points are explained at the end of each chapter, together with useful phrases relating to specific situations. There are also additional grammar exercises relating to the new grammar in each chapter.

Students gradually acquire practice in skills they are likely to need when working with the language, for example, fax and letter writing, making telephone calls, translating and summarising. Each chapter has relevant listening and reading comprehensions.

Recorded material is available on cassette for use with this course, and items on cassette are indicated in the book by the symbol [cassette symbol]. Transcripts of the listening comprehensions and dictations are provided at the end of the book together with a glossary of grammatical terms, a list of irregular verbs and a vocabulary list. The definitions given in the vocabulary list relate to the context in which the word is used in the book.

The 1996 revised edition has these new features:

- Additional listening comprehensions for each chapter
- New reading texts using up-to-date authentic materials
- Slight adjustment to the order in which some grammar topics are presented, allowing a more even distribution throughout the course
- Completely revised grammar explanations, with a glossary of the main grammatical terms
- New grammar exercises
- Three additional consolidation chapters (*Zusätzliche Aufgaben*) giving further practice in the main skill areas

Students who have completed this book can proceed to *Working with German Level 2* in which more advanced language skills are developed in the context of specific work-orientated situations.

Contents

Acknowledgements

The authors would like to thank the following for their help: P Steinert-Herrmann, J and M Merten and D, S & S, Lancs.

For the use of photographs and realia thanks are due to:
Austernkeller Restaurant, München (page 75); Bavaria-Verlag Bildagentur (page 112, photo by Kneer); Bild-Archiv des Bundesministeriums für das Post- und Fernmeldewesen (page 123, photo by Thilo Nass); Der Weinmann Tscharke, Düsseldorf (page 90); Deutsche Bahn (pages 32, 33, 36, 37, 38, 39, 40); Deutsche Bank (page 118); Deutsche Bundespost (page 125); Eugen Paternolli (page 5); Foto Goertz Service, Düsseldorf (page 90); Gasthof-Hotel »Krone“ and Hotel »Krone am Park“, Alzenau (page 59); Greg Smith (pages 89, 106, 110, 119, 120, 124); Hotel Central, Hof (page 59); Hotel Coenen, Mönchengladbach (page 51); Hotel Restaurant Adler, Pfullendorf (page 59); Hotel Schultenhof, Gladbeck (page 69); Mössing, Düsseldorf (page 90); Shell International Petroleum Company Ltd (page 135); Stadtparfümerie Pieper (page 90); Stief Pictures (page 152, photo by Paul Wudtke); Tankstelle Wolfgang Klupiec, Krefeld-Linn (page 134); Werbe- und Wirtschaftsförderungsamt der Stadt Düsseldorf (page 23, photo by Ulrich Otte; pages 87, 143, photos by Olaf Raymermann; page 145)

Every attempt has been made to contact copyright holders, but we apologise if any have been overlooked.

Original material was recorded by Elke Dehmel, Friedrich Dehmel and Wolfgang Winkler. New material was recorded by Stephen Grothgar, Michael Hülsman, Brigitte Kahn and Sabine Michael. Thanks are due to Graham Williams of The Speech Recording Studio.

Kapitel 1

Besuch aus Deutschland

Bei Anglia Chemicals (1)

The Buyer and the Production Director of a German company, Sasshofer AG in Mönchengladbach, have come to visit a British company, Anglia Chemicals plc.

Herr Weidmann	Guten Tag. Ewald Weidmann und Lotte Meyer aus Mönchengladbach.
Empfangsdame	Guten Tag, Herr Weidmann, guten Tag, Frau Meyer. Mr Newby erwartet Sie.
	(*Receptionist phones Mr Newby.*)
Empfangsdame	Er kommt gleich.
Herr Weidmann	Danke sehr.
Mr Newby	Guten Tag, Frau Meyer, guten Tag, Herr Weidmann. Mein Name ist Michael Newby. Es freut mich, Sie kennenzulernen.
Herr Weidmann	Guten Tag, Mr Newby, es freut uns auch.

Practice

1 Wie heißen Sie?

Guten Morgen. Ich heiße Lotte Meyer, und ich komme aus Krefeld. Ich arbeite bei der Firma Sasshofer in Mönchengladbach. Ich bin Einkaufsleiterin.

Guten Abend. Mein Name ist Ewald Weidmann. Ich wohne in Neuß bei Düsseldorf, und ich bin Produktionsleiter bei der Firma Sasshofer.

Now give similar information about yourself. Some of the following phrases will be useful:

- Ich heiße . . . /Mein Name ist . . .
- Ich komme aus (England, Irland, Wales, Schottland. Amerika, Australien, Kanada . . .)
- Ich bin (Sekretärin, Geschäftsführer/Geschäftsführerin, Fahrer/Fahrerin, Student/ Studentin, Elektroniker/Elektronikerin, Einkaufsleiter/Einkaufsleiterin bei der Firma . . .)

2 The following conversation takes place between two people on a flight to Germany.

Herr Müller Guten Tag. Müller.
Frau Williams Tag. Mein Name ist Williams. Es freut mich, Sie kennenzulernen.

Herr Müller Sind Sie Deutsche?
Frau Williams Nein, ich bin Schottin.
Herr Müller Ach so, das ist interessant. Und woher kommen Sie?
Frau Williams Ich komme aus Edinburgh. Ich bin Exportleiterin bei der Firma Tartan Textiles. Und Sie, was sind Sie von Beruf?
Herr Müller Ich bin Verkaufsleiter bei der Firma Edelmetall in Oberhausen bei Duisburg.
Frau Williams Und wo wohnen Sie?
Herr Müller Ich wohne in Duisburg.

Now complete this dialogue by adding the appropriate statement or question at →.

→ ____________________

Guten Tag. Mein Name ist Gerhard Schmidt.

→ ____________________

Ich komme aus Deutschland.

→ ____________________

Ich bin Programmierer.

→ ____________________

Ich wohne in Berlin.

Bei Anglia Chemicals (2)

Michael Newby takes his two German visitors on a tour of Anglia Chemicals. He introduces them to some of his colleagues, including David Jones, the Sales Director.

David Jones	Guten Tag. Es freut mich, Sie kennenzulernen. Sind Sie zum ersten Mal in England?
Frau Meyer	Ja, ich bin zum ersten Mal hier, aber Herr Weidmann kommt oft nach England.
David Jones	Ich wünsche Ihnen einen guten Aufenthalt.
Ewald Weidmann	Sie sprechen sehr gut Deutsch. Lernen Sie es hier bei Anglia Chemicals?
David Jones	Nein, meine Frau ist Deutsche. Sie kommt aus Dortmund. Wir sprechen Deutsch zu Hause.
Frau Meyer	Entschuldigen Sie, sind Sie vielleicht Waliser? Ihr Name ist walisisch, nicht wahr?
David Jones	Ja, das stimmt, aber ich selbst bin Engländer.

Practice

1 On the train to a business appointment in London you notice that the passenger next to you has been reading a German newspaper. You begin a conversation with him in German. What do you say to him?

Sie	(Ask if your fellow traveller is German.)
Reisender	Nein, ich bin Österreicher. Ich heiße Paternolli.
Sie	(Ask where he comes from.)
Reisender	Ich wohne in Dornbirn, aber ich arbeite in Feldkirch.
Sie	(Ask what he does for a living.)
Reisender	Ich bin Ingenieur.
Sie	(Ask if this is his first visit to England.)

Reisender	Ja, ich bin zum ersten Mal hier.
Sie	(Wish him a pleasant stay.)
Reisender	Danke sehr.

Herrn Paternollis Visitenkarte

2 Your company has advertised a job for which a German speaker is required. Look at this information sent by one of the applicants.

Your company is sending you to work in Germany, and you need to apply for a work permit. Give the same information as above.

Vorname	Hans-Dieter
Familienname	Schulz
Staatsangehörigkeit	deutsch
Wohnort	Frankfurt
Beruf	Ingenieur

You may need some of these words:

- britisch, australisch, englisch, irisch, kanadisch, amerikanisch
- Direktor/Direktorin, Sekretärin, Stenotypist/Stenotypistin, Lehrling, Programmierer/Programmiererin, Verkaufsleiter/Verkaufsleiterin, Produktionsleiter/Produktionsleiterin, Telefonist/Telefonistin Student/Studentin

3 The following people are participants at an international conference. Answer the following questions, using the words in the box below.

Example Ist Herr Richoux Deutscher? Nein, Franzose.

(*a*) Ist Frau Smith Amerikanerin?

(*b*) Ist Herr Jones Ire?

(*c*) Ist Frau Müller Deutsche?

(*d*) Ist Herr Schäfer Deutscher?

(*e*) Ist Frau Klein Italienerin?

(*f*) Ist Herr Duchêne Belgier?

Österreicher
Schweizerin
Australier
Französin
Kanadier
Britin

4 Here is a family tree of David Jones' immediate family:

David Jones ist Engländer. Er hat eine Frau. Sie heißt Marlies und ist Deutsche. Er hat auch einen Sohn und eine Tochter. Der Sohn heißt Mark, und die Tochter heißt Sara.

Now write a few sentences about Heinz Preissler.

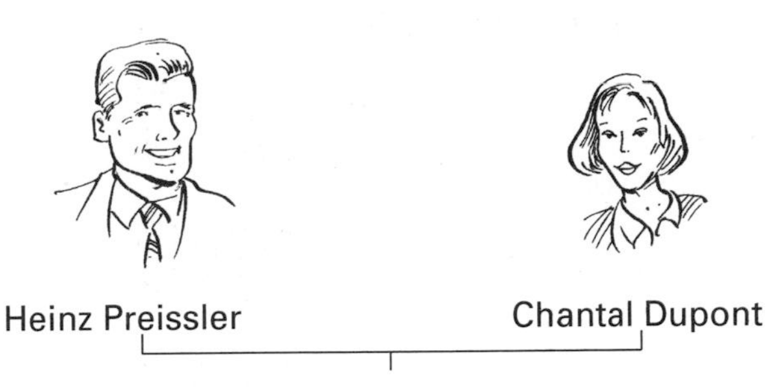

5 Spelling (*buchstabieren*)

You may at some time have to spell aloud in German. Listen to the pronunciation of the alphabet in German, then repeat each letter.

A Ä B C D E F G H I J K L M N O Ö P Q R S T U Ü V W X Y Z

Now give this personal information:

(*a*) Wie buchstabieren Sie Ihren Familiennamen?
(*b*) Wie buchstabieren Sie Ihren Vornamen?
(*c*) Wie heißt Ihre Firma/Ihre Schule/Ihre Universität? Buchstabieren Sie das.
(*d*) Wie heißt die Stadt, wo Sie wohnen? Buchstabieren Sie das.
(*e*) Und Ihr Lehrer/Ihre Lehrerin?

Practise these German abbreviations:

(*f*) DB Deutsche Bundesbahn
(*g*) EU Europäische Union
(*h*) BRD Bundesrepublik Deutschland
(*i*) ZDF Zweites Deutsches Fernsehen
(*j*) GmbH Gesellschaft mit beschränkter Haftung
(*k*) AG Aktiengesellschaft
(*l*) SPD Sozialdemokratische Partei Deutschlands
(*m*) FDP Freie Demokratische Partei
(*n*) CDU Christlich-Demokratische Union
(*o*) ADAC Allgemeiner Deutscher Automobil-Club
(*p*) VW Volkswagen

6 What would you say if you wanted to:

(*a*) ask someone their name
(*b*) tell them you are pleased to meet them
(*c*) ask what job they do
(*d*) ask where they come from.

7 Study this information about Frank Lohmann:

Frank ist Deutscher und wohnt in Köln. Frank arbeitet als Fahrer bei der Firma Schmidt-Möbel.

Now make up similar descriptions for these people:

Name	Beruf	Firma	Staatsangehörigkeit	Wohnort
Stefan	Elektroniker	Schmidt AG	Schweizer	Bern
Petra	Sekretärin	Deutsche Textilien GmbH	Österreicherin	Salzburg
Sabine	Telefonistin	Jung und Sohn GmbH	Deutsche	Kiel
Jürgen	Ingenieur	Schäfer-Autowerke AG	Deutscher	Mannheim

8 Your boss has been to a trade fair and returned with a selection of business cards. He asks you to extract a few details from them. Answer his questions.

(*a*) Was ist Dieter Stütz von Beruf?
(*b*) Wie heißt der Verkaufsleiter von Fecken-Kirfel GmbH & Co.?
(*c*) Wo arbeitet Françoise Oudard?
(*d*) Ist Gerhard Hinzsch Einkaufsleiter?
(*e*) Ist die Deutsche Bahn eine 'AG' oder eine 'GmbH'?

Later he asks another colleague for some more information. Her German is not very good so she asks you to check her information.

(*f*) Gerhard Hinzsch has a new telephone number.
(*g*) Franz Dieter Stütz works in Sales.
(*h*) Axel Eppmann has a direct telephone line.
(*i*) Petra Steding's firm manufactures metal goods.
(*j*) Bärbel Meyer works in Purchasing.

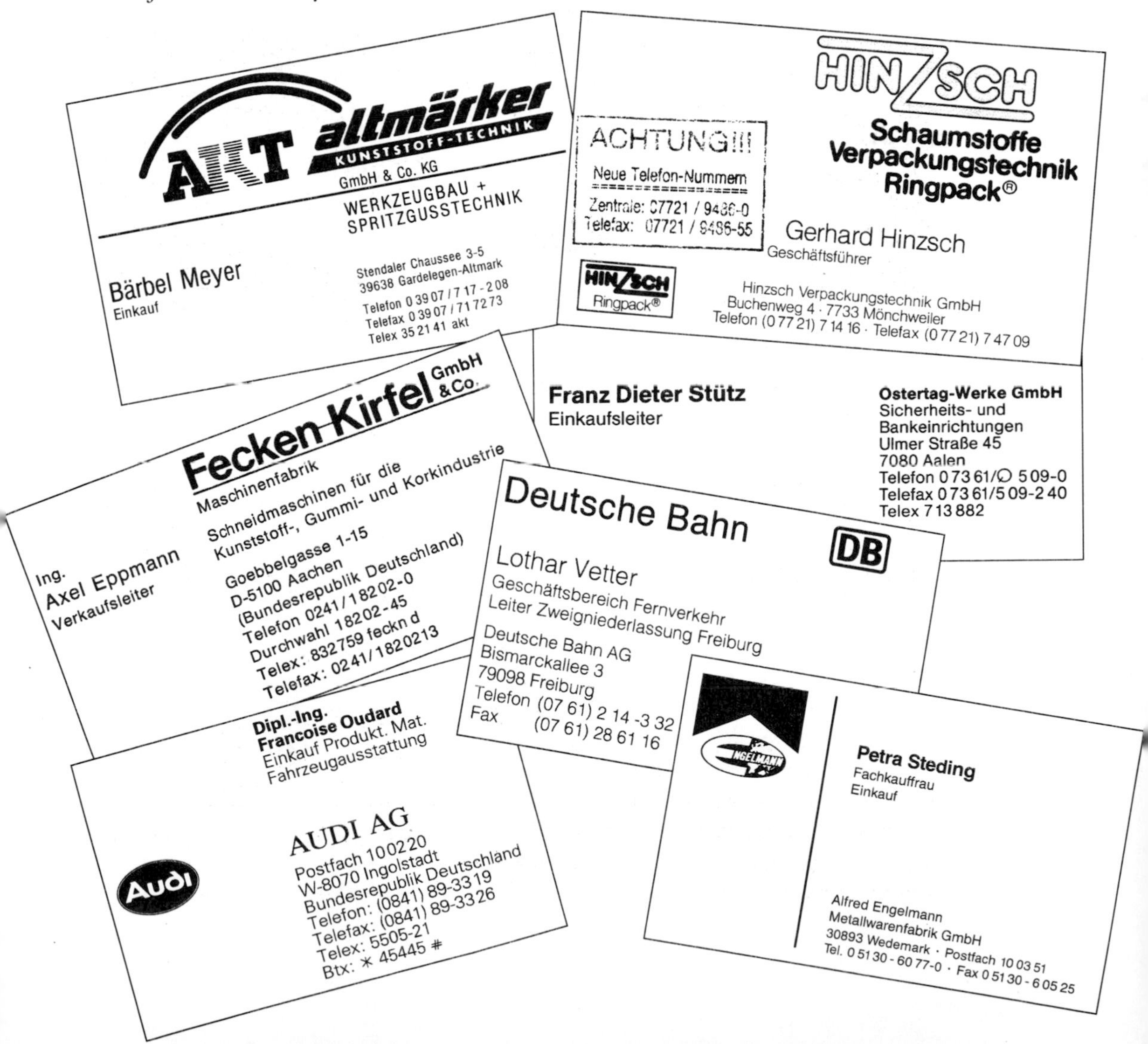

9 Listening comprehension

You will hear a conversation between two businessmen who have met for the first time over lunch at a trade fair in Germany. Listen to what they say and then answer the following questions:

(*a*) Where does Richard Hill live?
(*b*) Where does he work?
(*c*) What is his job?
(*d*) What does Wilhelm Jaeger do?
(*e*) Why is Richard Hill's German so good?

10 Reading

Study this information about Wolfgang Schüßler and Gudrun Schneider:

Ich heiße Wolfgang Schüßler. Ich bin Student in Berlin und bin noch ledig (unverheiratet). Ich studiere Architektur, aber ich arbeite auch als Taxifahrer. Meine Mutter und mein Vater sind auch in Berlin. Ich wohne also zu Hause.

Mein Name ist Gudrun Schneider. Ich komme aus der Schweiz, aber ich wohne jetzt in Deutschland. Ich bin verheiratet. Mein Mann heißt Karl und ist Deutscher. Wir haben ein Kind. Ich arbeite als Sekretärin bei Nordchemikalien in Hamburg. Die Firma ist französisch. Ich spreche also oft Französisch in der Firma. Ich spreche aber auch Deutsch und lerne Englisch. Mein Mann arbeitet auch bei Nordchemikalien als Vertreter.

Now answer the following questions in German:

(*a*) Hat Wolfgang eine Frau?
(*b*) Arbeitet Wolfgang?
(*c*) Wo wohnt er?
(*d*) Ist er Architekt?
(*e*) Wie heißt Gudruns Mann?
(*f*) Ist Gudrun Deutsche?
(*g*) Was ist Gudrun von Beruf?
(*h*) Lernt Gudrun Französisch?

11 Listening comprehension

While travelling by train Michael Newby frequently converses with fellow travellers. Here are some snatches from their conversations. Listen to the cassette and note down what they say about themselves under the following headings: Name, Place of work, Occupation, Family, Foreign languages spoken.

Summary

Useful phrases

1	Greeting people	Guten Morgen Guten Tag Es freut mich, Sie kennenzulernen
2	Introducing oneself and others	Ich heiße . . . Mein Name ist . . .
3	Saying where someone comes from	Ich komme aus . . . Ich wohne in . . . Ich bin Deutscher/Deutsche Österreicher/Österreicherin Schweizer/Schweizerin Amerikaner/Amerikanerin Australier/Australierin Engländer/Engländerin Ire/Irin Schotte/Schottin Waliser/Waliserin

4 Giving information about one's work Ich bin Betriebsingenieur/Betriebsingenieurin
Chefsekretärin
Dolmetscher/Dolmetscherin
Einkaufsleiter/Einkaufsleiterin
Geschäftsführer/Geschäftsführerin

Language forms

1 The present tense

(a) Regular verbs

To express what is happening *now*, you must remove the *en* ending from the infinitive of the verb (the form listed in the dictionary, e.g. *kommen* (to come) and add endings to the remaining stem. These endings match the person or people carrying out a particular action:

kommen (to come)

*ich komm**e*** (I come/am coming)	*wir komm**en*** (we come/are coming)
*du komm**st*** (you come/are coming)	*ihr komm**t*** (you come/are coming)
*er/sie komm**t*** (he/she comes/is coming)	*Sie komm**en*** (you come/are coming)
	*sie komm**en*** (they come/are coming)

Examples

*Ich komm**e** aus Dortmund.*
I come from Dortmund.
(*Note*: *ich* is always written with a small *i* unless it is the first word in a sentence.)

Herr Weidmann kommt jetzt.
Mr Weidmann is coming now.

(*Note*: If a person's name is mentioned, the ending is just the same as with the pronoun relating to that person, e.g. with *Herr Weidmann* or *er* the ending is *t*: *Herr Weidmann komm**t**/Er komm**t**.*)

Wir kommen aus Berlin = We come from Berlin.

Different words for 'you'

In the above list, there are three words for 'you':

du the word to use when speaking to one relation, close friend, or pet

ihr the word to use when speaking to more than one relation, close friend, or pet

Sie the word to use when speaking to one – or more than one – person who is in authority over you (e.g. your boss at work) or to any adult/s with whom you are not on familiar terms.

(*Note*: When writing German, always spell *Sie* with a capital letter.)

(b) Verbs whose stem ends with *t* or *d*

When the *en* is removed from the infinitive, and the remaining stem ends with *t* or *d*, an extra *e* is added to the stem with the following persons (because the word would otherwise be hard to say):

erwarten (to expect)

*du erwart**est*** (you expect/are expecting)

*er/sie erwart**et*** (he/she expects/is expecting)

*ihr erwart**et*** (you expect/is expecting)

Example

*Guten Tag, Frau Meyer. Mr Newby erwart**et** Sie.*
Hello, Mrs Meyer. Mr Newby is expecting you.

(c) Irregular verbs

There are a number of verbs that do not follow the above pattern. They are known as 'irregular' (or 'strong') to contrast with 'regular' (or 'weak'). Two of the most common are *haben* (to have) and *sein* (to be).

haben (to have)	*sein* (to be)
ich habe (I have)	*ich bin* (I am)
du hast (you have)	*du bist* (you are)
er/sie hat (he/she has)	*er/sie ist* (he/she is)
wir haben (we have)	*wir sind* (we are)
ihr habt (you have)	*ihr seid* (you are)
Sie haben (you have)	*Sie sind* (you are)
sie haben (they have)	*sie sind* (they are)

2 How to form questions

(a) Inversion of subject and verb

To turn a statement into a question, simply switch round the subject and verb.

Examples

Statement:	*Sie sprechen Deutsch.* You speak German.
Question:	*Sprechen Sie Deutsch?* Do you speak German?
Statement:	*Er ist zum ersten Mal in Manchester.* He is in Manchester for the first time.
Question:	*Ist er zum ersten Mal in Manchester?* Is he in Manchester for the first time?

(b) Statement followed by *oder?* or *nicht wahr?*

The word *oder* means 'or'. Added to a statement, it is short for the implied question 'or not'?

The words *nicht wahr?* literally mean 'not true'. Added to a statement, they are short for the implied question 'isn't that true?'

In English both *oder?* and *nicht wahr?* can be translated by such expressions as 'isn't he/she?', 'aren't I/you/we/they?', 'can't/don't/won't I/you/he/she?' etc.

Examples

Er ist zum ersten Mal in Manchester, oder?
He's in Manchester for the first time, isn't he?

Sie sind zum ersten Mal in Manchester, nicht wahr?
You're in Manchester for the first time, aren't you?

3 Negation

(a) '*Nein*' followed by a statement

Lernen Sie Deutsch in der Firma?
Are you learning German in the company?

Nein, ich lerne es zu Hause. Meine Frau ist Deutsche.
No, I'm learning it at home. My wife is German.

(b) Using *nicht*

Nicht is the word for 'not'. It is the most common way of forming the negative to say that something is not the case.

The two most frequent positions of *nicht* in a sentence are:

(i) If a subject or object follows the verb, *nicht* usually stands at the end of the sentence.

Examples

Ich verstehe Sie ***nicht***. I don't understand you.
(verb) (object)

Arbeiten Sie im Moment ***nicht****?* Aren't you working at the moment?
(verb) (subject)

(ii) If there is no subject or object after the verb, then *nicht* follows the verb.

Example

Ich komme ***nicht*** *aus Krefeld.* I don't come from Krefeld.
(verb)

4 Stating one's nationality or profession

(*a*) When stating your nationality or profession in German, omit 'a' or 'an'.

Examples

Ich bin Österreicher. Sind Sie Australier?
I'm (an) Austrian. Are you (an) Australian?

Ich bin Verkaufsleiter.
I'm a sales manager.

(*b*) The feminine of nationalities and professions is usually formed by adding *in* to the word.

Examples

*Ich bin Österreicher**in**. Sind Sie Australier**in**? Ich bin Verkaufsleiter**in**.*

There are exceptions to this rule:

*Ich bin Deutsch**er*** (male) *Ich bin Deutsch**e*** (female).

Additional exercises

1 Which form of the verb in brackets is the correct one?

(*a*)	Woher ____ Sie?	(kommst/kommen/kommt)
(*b*)	Ich ____ aus England.	(kommt/kommen/komme)
(*c*)	Wo ____ Sie?	(wohne/wohnst/wohnen)
(*d*)	Ich ____ in Berlin.	(wohne/wohnt/wohnen)
(*e*)	Herr Müller ____ Sie.	(erwarten/erwartet/ erwartest)
(*f*)	Wo ____ ihr?	(arbeitest/arbeiten/arbeitet)
(*g*)	Wir ____ bei der Firma Anglia Chemicals.	(arbeiten/arbeite/arbeitest)
(*h*)	____ du Deutsch hier in der Firma?	(lernt/lernen/lernst)
(*i*)	Nein, ich ____ es zu Hause.	(lernst/lerne/lernen)
(*j*)	John und Ann ____ Deutsch in Heidelberg.	(studiert/studieren/studierst)

2 Replace the infinitive by inserting the correct form of the verb.

(*a*) Ich (heißen) Ewald Weidmann.
(*b*) Mr Newby (kommen) gleich.
(*c*) Wo (wohnen) Sie?
(*d*) (lernen) sie (*she*) Deutsch hier in der Firma?
(*e*) (arbeiten) Sie in Deutschland oder in Österreich?
(*f*) Wo (arbeiten) du?
(*g*) Gudrun und Karl Schneider (sein) verheiratet.
(*h*) Ich (sein) Studentin in Hamburg.
(*i*) Was (sein) Sie von Beruf?
(*j*) (haben) Frau Meyer ein Kind?

3 Turn the following statements into questions by inverting subject and verb.

(*a*) Er arbeitet bei der Firma Sasshofer.
(*b*) Sie (*you*) studieren in Salzburg.
(*c*) Frau Schneider lernt Englisch.
(*d*) Wolfgang ist Geschäftsleiter.
(*e*) Herr Desch erwartet Mr Jones.
(*f*) Sie (*they*) sprechen Deutsch.

4 Turn the statements in Exercise 3 into questions by adding *oder?* or *nicht wahr?*

5 Make the following sentences negative using *nicht*.

(*a*) Ich arbeite in Deutschland.
(*b*) Herr Walter erwartet Sie.
(*c*) Er lernt Englisch zu Hause.
(*d*) Ich bin verheiratet.

6 Translate the following sentences into German.

(*a*) Hans Schmidt is Austrian. He comes from Graz.
(*b*) Maria Braun is Swiss. She lives in Bern.
(*c*) My name is Kylie Ramsey. I am Australian.
(*d*) Ann Taylor is an engineer.
(*e*) Fritz Stingl is a sales manager.
(*f*) Ludwig Leitner is a representative.
(*g*) Clint Mitchum is American. He's an interpreter.

Kapitel 2

Wann fahren Sie?

Am Telefon

The negotiations between Sasshofer AG and Anglia Chemicals plc were a great success, and a promising business relationship has begun. Very shortly after the visit of the Germans to England, Michael Newby is invited by his opposite number, Herbert Walter, to visit Sasshofer AG. The respective secretaries make the necessary arrangements on the telephone.

Telefonist	Sasshofer AG. Guten Tag.
Andrea Morgan	Guten Tag. Hier Anglia Chemicals. Ich möchte bitte Frau* Steiner sprechen.
Telefonist	Augenblick bitte. Ich verbinde.
Frau Steiner	Steiner. Guten Tag.
Andrea Morgan	Guten Tag, Frau Steiner. Hier Andrea Morgan von der Firma Anglia Chemicals. Ich bin die Sekretärin vom Geschäftsführer, Mr Michael Newby.
Frau Steiner	Ach ja. Mr Newby kommt bald zu Besuch, nicht wahr?
Andrea Morgan	Ja richtig.
Frau Steiner	Gut. Wann kommt Mr Newby nach Deutschland?

*It is normal business practice to call all women (from the age of about 18 onwards) *Frau*, whether or not they are married.

Andrea Morgan	Er möchte am vierten Oktober kommen und drei Tage in Mönchengladbach bleiben. Geht das?
Frau Steiner	Moment bitte . . .
	(*Frau Steiner has meanwhile checked in her diary and established that 4 October is convenient.*)
Frau Steiner	Ja, das geht. Soll ich ein Hotelzimmer für ihn reservieren?
Andrea Morgan	Ein Einzelzimmer, bitte.
Frau Steiner	Mit Bad oder Dusche?
Andrea Morgan	Mit Bad, bitte.
Frau Steiner	Fliegt er nach Düsseldorf?
Andrea Morgan	Ja, er fliegt von Manchester ab. Er kommt um zehn Uhr am Flughafen an. Dann fährt er mit der Bahn weiter. Der Zug ist um halb zwölf in Mönchengladbach.
Frau Steiner	Ja gut. Herr Walter holt ihn dann vom Bahnhof ab.
Andrea Morgan	Danke für Ihre Hilfe.
Frau Steiner	Gern geschehen. Auf Wiederhören.
Andrea Morgan	Auf Wiederhören.

Practice

1 Listen to the following questions and answers and pick out the date mentioned in each one. The first one has been done for you.

(*a*) Wann kommt Herr Schmidt? Am 4. Mai
(*b*) Wann fliegt Herr Johnson nach Deutschland?
(*c*) Wann besuchen Sie die Firma Sasshofer?
(*d*) Wann kommen Sie nach Düsseldorf?
(*e*) Wann fährt Frau Young nach Mönchengladbach?
(*f*) Wann kommen Sie zu Besuch?

2 Making arrangements

An English secretary telephones Switzerland to discuss the arrangements for her boss's forthcoming visit to the Maschinenfabrik Rieter AG in Winterthur. Take the part of the secretary.

Rieter AG	Wann möchte Mr Hodgkins in die Schweiz kommen?
Sie	(Say he would like to come on 14 June and to stay in Winterthur for two days. Ask if that is possible.)
Rieter AG	Moment mal . . . Ja, das geht. Soll ich ein Hotelzimmer für ihn reservieren?
Sie	(Say yes please.)

Rieter AG	Ich empfehle das Hotel Reinhart. Da gibt es Einzel- und Doppelzimmer mit Bad oder mit Dusche. Was soll ich reservieren?
Sie	(Say a single room with a bathroom.)
Rieter AG	Fliegt Herr Hodgkins nach Zürich?
Sie	(Say yes, he is flying from Manchester to Zürich and then continuing his journey by rail. He will arrive at the airport at 15.30.)

3 Here are the plans of some of the personnel of Sasshofer and Anglia Chemicals. Working in pairs, take the part of Frau Steiner or Andrea Morgan and answer each other's queries on staff arrangements.

Herr Schmidt's visit to Altrincham	Friday 4 November	Miss Thompson's visit to Germany	Wednesday 6 July
Mr Johnson's flight to Düsseldorf	Thursday 9 June	Frau Meyer's flight to England	Sunday 8 May
Mr Turner's visit to Sasshofer	Monday 1 February	Herr Weidmann's visit to England	Saturday 5 March

Example Wann kommt Herr Schmidt nach Altrincham? Am Freitag, dem vierten November.

(*a*) Wann fliegt Mr Johnson nach Düsseldorf?
(*b*) Wann besucht Mr Turner die Firma Sasshofer?
(*c*) Wann kommt Miss Thompson nach Deutschland?
(*d*) Wann fliegt Frau Meyer nach England?
(*e*) Wann ist Herr Weidmann in England?

4 The arrangements for Mr Newby's visit are later confirmed by fax. Read the fax, then answer the questions.

> **Betr.: Besuch von Mr M Newby vom 4.–7. Oktober.**
> Wir möchten folgendes bestätigen: Mr Newby kommt um 10.00 Uhr am Flughafen Düsseldorf (Flug-Nr. LH 322). Wir haben vom 4.–7. ein Einzelzimmer mit Bad im Hotel Coenen für ihn reserviert. Wir erwarten ihn am Montag, d. 4. Oktober um 11.30 Uhr.

(*a*) How is Mr Newby travelling to Düsseldorf?
(*b*) At what time will he arrive there?
(*c*) At what time will he arrive in Mönchengladbach?
(*d*) What *two* things do we know about his hotel accommodation?

5 Listening comprehension

You work for a company in Germany which is organising some seminars for its foreign representatives. They phone your company individually with their travel plans which they leave on the answerphone. Listen to the cassette, and using the following headings, make a note of their travel plans and the questions that they ask: Date of arrival, Method of transport, End of visit, Their questions.

6

(a) Your colleague is trying to work out his leave for the coming year. Use the table below to answer his questions. The list includes holidays and festivals in Germany; the highlighted dates are also public holidays.

Example

- Wann ist Karfreitag?
- ■ Am vierzehnten April.

(b) You want to arrange a meeting with a German company. Fix a date with your German counterpart that is convenient for both of you. Note that British and German public holidays are not always the same.

Example

- Ich will am 6. Juni die Firma besuchen.
- ■ Ja, der 6. Juni geht/Nein, das geht nicht, ich bin in Frankreich.

Fest- und Gedenktage

Neujahr	1. 1.	Mariä Himmelfahrt	15. 8.
Heilige Drei Könige	6. 1.	Erntedankfest	1. 10.
Valentinstag	14. 2.	Tag der deutschen Einheit	3. 10.
Aschermittwoch	1. 3.	Reformationstag	31. 10.
Palmsonntag	9. 4.	Allerheiligen	1. 11.
Karfreitag	14. 4.	Allerseelen	2. 11.
Ostersonntag	16. 4.	Volkstrauertag	19. 11.
Ostermontag	17. 4.	Buß- und Bettag	22. 11.
Weißer Sonntag	23. 4.	Totensonntag	26. 11.
Maifeiertag	1. 5.	1. Advent	3. 12.
Muttertag	14. 5.	Mariä Empfängnis	8. 12.
Christi Himmelfahrt	25. 5.	2. Advent	10. 12.
Pfingstsonntag	4.6.	3. Advent	17. 12.
Pfingstmontag	5.6.	4. Advent	24. 12.
Fronleichnam	15.6.	1. Weihnachtstag	25. 12.
		2. Weihnachtstag	26. 12.

7 Ewald Weidmann, of Sasshofer AG, has arranged a meeting with some business colleagues. He wishes to check on their arrival times, and also on the arrangements of other members of the company. How will his secretary answer his questions?

Example Wann kommt Frau Scharf an? 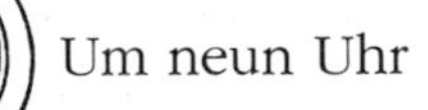 Um neun Uhr

(*a*) Wann kommt Herr Zimmerman an? 

(*b*) Wann holen wir Hans-Jürgen Braun vom Bahnhof ab? 

(*c*) Wann kommt Frau Fischer zu Besuch? 

(*d*) Wann erwarten Sie Mr Hodgkins? 

(*e*) Wann fährt Herr Schmidt nach Österreich? 

(*f*) Wann fliegt der Produktionsleiter nach England? 

8 The tables below and on page 22 outline the travel plans of some of your colleagues who will be attending business meetings next week at your parent company in Germany, and elsewhere. Using the information in the table, advise the parent company of their plans.

Example Doug Jones fliegt am Samstag nach Deutschland.

Doug Jones	fliegen	Samstag		Deutschland
Kate Wilson	fahren	Montag	Bahn	Heidelberg
Sue Evans und John Ward	ankommen	Dienstag		Flughafen
Mike Wood	fahren	Mittwoch	Bahn	Hamburg

der Geschaftsführer	fliegen	Freitag		Köln
Steve Webster	fahren	Sonntag	Auto	Karlsruhe
Jo Parker	kommt	Dienstag	Zug	Berlin
Cath Bonner	fahren	Montag	Bus	Bonn
Andrew James und Linda Miller	fahren	Mittwoch	Zug/Taxi	Messe
Simon Collins	fliegen	Samstag		Potsdam

9 Pair-work

Some useful questions and answers:

- Der wievielte ist heute? Heute ist (der vierte Januar).
- Der wievielte ist morgen/übermorgen? Morgen ist (der fünfte Januar).
- Der wievielte ist Samstag? Samstag ist (der achte August).
- Wann haben Sie Geburtstag? Am (zwanzigsten August).

Ask a partner these questions, then make up other questions if you need more practice.

10 Dictation

Listen to the cassette and write down the dates as they are dictated to you.

11

(*a*) You will be visiting Düsseldorf on business and need to reserve a hotel room. Phone the *Hotel Bergerhof* and:
- (i) specify the type of accommodation you will require *(Einzelzimmer, Doppelzimmer, Bad, Dusche)*
- (ii) say on which day you will arrive
- (iii) say how many days you will be staying
- (iv) ask if these arrangements will be possible
- (v) thank the telephonist for his/her help.

(*b*) You are a telephonist at the *Hotel Bergerhof* in Düsseldorf. You receive a call from England. Ask the caller:
- (i) what type of accommodation he/she requires
- (ii) when he/she will be arriving
- (iii) how long he/she will be staying.
- (iv) Then tell the caller that these arrangements will be possible.
- (v) Close the conversation.

12 Listening comprehension

You will hear a telephone conversation between two businessmen who are arranging to meet at the *Igedo Messe*, a fashion fair in Düsseldorf. Listen to what they say then answer the questions that follow.

(*a*) When is the fair taking place?
(*b*) How are the two men travelling to Düsseldorf?
(*c*) From which cities and on which days are they leaving?
(*d*) What will Herr Schneider be doing in Duisburg?
(*e*) How is he getting to Düsseldorf on the Monday?
(*f*) At what time will he arrive there?
(*g*) Where will Herr Bauer be meeting him?

Igedo Messe

13

You want to meet a business acquaintance at a conference (*auf einer Tagung*) in Zürich. You phone him/her to make the necessary arrangements. What do you say to your acquaintance?

Sie (Say you are going to the conference in Zürich on Friday. Ask if he/she is going too.)
Bekannte(r) Ja, sicher.
Sie (Ask when he/she is travelling.)
Bekannte(r) Ich fahre am Donnerstag mit der Bahn von Basel.
Sie (Ask when his/her train arrives in Zürich.)
Bekannte(r) Um halb zehn.

Sie	(Say you will meet him/her at the station. Say that your train from Winterthur arrives at half past eight.)
Bekannte(r)	Also gut. Bis Donnerstag.
Sie	(Say goodbye.)

Summary

Useful phrases

1	Expressing a desire	Ich möchte bitte Frau Steiner sprechen
2	Asking someone to wait	Augenblick bitte Moment bitte
3	Enquiring/replying about possibility	Geht das? Ja, das geht
4	Thanking someone and responding to thanks	Danke für Ihre Hilfe Gern geschehen!
5	Enquiring about travel times	Wann kommt er nach Deutschland? Wann fahren Sie? Wann kommen Sie in Düsseldorf an?
6	Giving travel information	Er fliegt von Manchester nach Düsseldorf Er fährt mit der Bahn weiter Er kommt um neun Uhr am Flughafen an Ich fahre nächsten Montag nach Düsseldorf Ich fliege am Sonntag von München Um halb neun bin ich in Düsseldorf
7	Asking how someone is and replying	Wie geht es Ihnen? Danke gut, und Ihnen?
8	Arranging to meet	Ich hole Sie vom Bahnhof ab Bis dann!
9	Expressing confirmation	Also gut! Ganz bestimmt! Abgemacht!
10	Enquiring about accommodation arrangements	Soll ich ein Hotelzimmer reservieren?
11	Recommending something	Ich empfehle das Hotel Reinhart
12	Saying goodbye (on telephone)	Auf Wiederhören

Language forms

1 The nominative case

The nominative case expresses the subject of the verb.

(a) How to say 'the'

There are three words for 'the' in German which accompany the subject of a sentence. Each identifies a different gender.

der (masculine) die (feminine) das (neuter)

Examples

Der *Verkaufsleiter wohnt in Krefeld. Er heißt Herbert Zung.*
The sales manager lives in Krefeld. His name is Herbert Zung.

Die *Geschäftsführerin heißt Anna Neubauer.*
The managing director is called Anna Neubauer.

Das *Brandenburger Tor ist in Berlin.*
The Brandenburg Gate is in Berlin.

Note Don't be surprised to find that many words that we understand as being neuter in English, e.g. 'chair' and 'door', are masculine or feminine in German!

The plural word for 'the', irrespective of gender, is *die*.

(b) How to say 'a'

The words for 'a' which accompany the subject of a sentence are also gender-linked. They are:

ein (masculine) *eine* (feminine) *ein* (neuter)

Examples

Ein *Einkaufsleiter aus England besucht die Firma Sasshofer.*
A senior buyer from England is visiting the Sasshofer company.

Eine *Hotelreservierung ist absolut notwendig.*
A hotel reservation is absolutely necessary.

Ein *Einzelzimmer ist ganz billig.*
A single room is quite cheap.

2 Word order

(a) One verb in a sentence

The verb always stands as the second element in a sentence.

Example	*Mr Newby*	***fliegt***	*nach Deutschland.*
	1	2	
	(subject)	(verb)	
	Mr Newby	is flying	to Germany.
	(subject)	(verb)	

Notice how this happens even where the English word order might suggest differently.

Example

Sogar im Sommer	***ist***	*das Geschäft*	*schlecht.*
1	2	3	
	(verb)	(subject)	
Even in summer	business	is	bad.
	(subject)	(verb)	

(b) Two verbs in a sentence

If there are two verbs in a sentence, the second verb goes to the end of the sentence.

Example

Mr Newby	***will***	*nach Deutschland*	***fliegen*** *.*	(German word order)
	1		2	
Mr Newby	wants	to fly	to Germany.	(English word order)
	1	2		

(c) Separable verbs

These are verbs with prefixes such as *ab*, *an*, *auf*, *aus*, *mit*, *nach* and *zu*.

Examples

ab*holen* (to meet – at station etc.)

an*kommen* (to arrive)

In sentences in which the only verb is a separable verb, the prefix separates from the rest of the verb and goes to the end of the sentence.

Examples

abholen: *Er* ***holt*** *Sie vom Bahnhof* ***ab*** *.*
He'll meet you from the station.

ankommen: *Sie* ***kommt*** *um neun Uhr* ***an*** *.*
She's arriving at 9 o'clock.

(d) The time-manner-place rule

The order of facts in a German sentence follows the rules: time-manner-place. This can be remembered as the when?-how?-where? sequence.

Example

Ich fahre	*am Donnerstag*	*mit der Bahn*	*nach Wien.*
	Time	Manner	Place
I'm travelling	to Vienna	by train	on Thursday.
	Place	Manner	Time

3 Numerals 0–100

Cardinal numbers	**Ordinal numbers**	**Cardinal numbers**	**Ordinal numbers**
0 Null			
1 eins	1st erste	16 sechzehn	16th sechzehnte
2 zwei	2nd zwei*te*	17 siebzehn	17th siebzehnte
3 drei	3rd dritte	18 achtzehn	18th achtzehnte
4 vier	4th vier*te*	19 neunzehn	19th neunzehnte
5 fünf	5th fünf*te*	20 zwanzig	20th zwanzig*ste*
6 sechs	6th sechs*te*	21 einundzwanzig	21st einundzwanzig*ste*
7 sieben	7th sieb*te*	30 dreißig	30th dreißig*ste*
8 acht	8th ach*te*	40 vierzig	40th vierzig*ste*
9 neun	9th neun*te*	50 fünfzig	50th fünfzig*ste*
10 zehn	10th zehn*te*	60 sechzig	60th sechzig*ste*
11 elf	11th elf*te*	70 siebzig	70th siebzig*ste*
12 zwölf	12th zwölf*te*	80 achtzig	80th achtzig*ste*
13 dreizehn	13th dreizehn*te*	90 neunzig	90th neunzig*ste*
14 vierzehn	14th vierzehn*te*	100 hundert	100th (ein)hundert*ste*
15 fünfzehn	15th fünfzehn*te*		

4 The date

Days of the week

Montag – Monday
Dienstag – Tuesday
Mittwoch – Wednesday
Donnerstag – Thursday
Freitag – Friday
Samstag (or Sonnabend in northern Germany) – Saturday
Sonntag – Sunday

am Montag – on Monday
am Dienstag – on Tuesday

Months of the year

Januar – January	Juli – July	*Note* In Austria:
Februar – February	August – August	Jänner – January
März – March	September – September	Feber – February
April – April	Oktober – October	
Mai – May	November – November	
Juni – June	Dezember – December	

im März – in March
im April – in April
der erste Mai – 1st May
der zweite Mai – 2nd May
am ersten Mai – on 1st May
am zweiten Mai – on 2nd May
Note the abbreviated forms:
der 6. Mai – 6th May
am 17. Mai – on 17th May

5 The time

Wie spät ist es?/Wieviel Uhr ist es? What time is it?

(a) On the hour
Es ist ein Uhr/zwei Uhr/drei Uhr/vier Uhr
It is one/two/three/four o'clock

(b) Past the hour
Es ist ein Uhr fünf/zehn/fünfzehn/zwanzig
It is 1.05/1.10/1.15/1.20
or
Es ist fünf/zehn/Viertel/zwanzig **nach** eins
It is five/ten/quarter/twenty past one
Es ist halb zwei
It is half past one
Note The Germans say it is a half *towards* two.

(c) Towards the hour
Es ist zwölf Uhr fünfunddreißig/vierzig
It is 12.35/12.40
or
Es ist fünf/zehn/Viertel/zwanzig **vor** eins
It is five/ten/quarter/twenty to one

Additional exercises

1 Complete the gaps in the sentences below with either *der, die* or *das.*

(*a*) ______ Geschäftsführer heißt Herr Newby.
(*b*) ______ Frau heißt Ingrid.
(*c*) ______ Engländer kommt aus London.
(*d*) ______ Sekretärin ist verheiratet.
(*e*) ______ Kind ist zu Hause.
(*f*) ______ Zug kommt um neun Uhr an.
(*g*) ______ Hotel Coenen ist in Mönchengladbach.
(*h*) ______ Firma Anglia Chemicals ist in England.

2 Complete the gaps in the following sentences with either *ein* or *eine.*

(*a*) ______ Dusche kostet extra.
(*b*) ______ Einzelzimmer ist für Frau Kohl reserviert.
(*c*) In fünf Minuten kommt ______ Zug aus Bremen an.
(*d*) In Düsseldorf findet heute ______ Messe statt.
(*e*) Wir haben ______ Kind.

3 Arrange the words in the following sentences in the correct order. Start the sentence with the word or words in italics, and ensure that the verb is in the correct position.

(*a*) nach fliegt Deutschland *Mr Newby*
(*b*) reservieren Sie für Einzelzimmer *wir* ein.
(*c*) Düsseldorf Sie kommen *wann* nach?
(*d*) gut sprechen Deutsch *Sie.*
(*e*) in der Firma oft Französisch *ich* spreche.
(*f*) ich in wohne Deutschland *jetzt.*
(*g*) studieren in Architektur London *wir.*
(*h*) Sie *was* Beruf von sind?
(*i*) in Bonn *um elf Uhr* der Zug ist.
(*j*) ich empfehle *das Hotel Reinhart.*

4 Extend the following sentences by adding *will* or *möchte.*

Examples
Er fliegt nach Deutschland.
Er *will* nach Deutschland *fliegen.*

(*a*) Sie kommt um neun Uhr.
(*b*) Ich lerne Deutsch.
(*c*) Herr Becker besucht die Firma Bosch.

(*d*) Die Verkaufsleiterin reserviert ein Einzelzimmer.
(*e*) Wann kommt Mr Hodgkins in die Schweiz?

5 Complete these sentences by using the separable verbs correctly.

Examples
Mein Zug (ankommen) um elf Uhr.
Mein Zug *kommt* um elf Uhr *an*.

(*a*) Frau Scharf (ankommen) am Montag.
(*b*) Wir (abholen) sie vom Bahnhof.
(*c*) Die Tagung (stattfinden) in Leipzig.
(*d*) Wann (abfahren) der Zug?
(*e*) (Weiterfahren) Sie mit der Bahn?

6 How would you say the following in German?

(*a*) We're flying to New York on Thursday.
(*b*) I'm travelling to Innsbruck by train on 3rd March.
(*c*) She's flying from Munich on 5th April.
(*d*) I'll be in Düsseldorf at 8.30.
(*e*) The conference is in Frankfurt on 20th June.
(*f*) He'll meet you from the station at 10 o'clock.
(*g*) The train is in Passau at 7.30.
(*h*) They're travelling to Linz next Monday by train.

Kapitel 3

Unterwegs

An der Auskunft

 Michael Newby flies from Manchester to Düsseldorf. On arrival at the airport he asks the way to the station so that he can catch a train to Düsseldorf main station.

Newby	Entschuldigen Sie, bitte. Ich will vom Flughafen zum Hauptbahnhof. Wo fährt die S-Bahn ab?
Angestellte	Dort drüben ist die Rolltreppe zur S-Bahn.
Newby	Danke schön.
Angestellte	Bitte schön.
	(*An der S-Bahn-Station*)
Newby	Wann fährt denn der nächste Zug zum Hauptbahnhof?
Beamter	Um elf Uhr dreiundzwanzig von Gleis eins. Er kommt um elf Uhr fünfunddreißig am Hauptbahnhof an.
Newby	Was kostet das?
Beamter	Eine Mark achtzig. Die Fahrkarte bekommen Sie vom Automaten dort drüben.
Newby	Vielen Dank.
Beamter	Bitte schön.

Practice

1 Asking the way

You have just landed at Düsseldorf airport. You need to get from the airport to Düsseldorf main station. You do not know where the station is, so you enquire at the information desk. What do you say in German?

Sie	(Say 'excuse me' and ask where the trains to the main station run from.)
Angestellte	Dort drüben ist die Rolltreppe zur S-Bahn.

Sie	(Thank the person for this information.)
Angestellte	Bitte schön.
	(*You take the escalator to the station, then find an official who gives you further instructions.*)
Sie	(Ask when the next train goes to the main station.)
Beamter	Um dreizehn Uhr zwanzig von Gleis eins. Er kommt um dreizehn Uhr dreiunddreißig an.
Sie	(Ask how much it costs.)
Beamter	Zwei Mark sechzig. Die Fahrkarte bekommen Sie dort drüben.
Sie	(Thank the clerk.)
Beamter	Bitte schön.

Information

Für die U-Bahn (*underground train*) und die S-Bahn (*local train*) kaufen Sie Ihre Fahrkarte normalerweise vom Automaten. Dann müssen Sie die Fahrkarte entwerten, bevor Sie in die Bahn einsteigen. Der Entwerter stempelt das Datum und die Uhrzeit auf die Fahrkarte.

Eine S-Bahn

Am Fahrkartenschalter

While travelling through Germany, a holidaymaker decides to visit Rothenburg. This is part of his conversation at Münich main station.

Reisende	Einmal nach Rothenburg, bitte.
Beamter	Einfach oder hin und zurück?
Reisende	Hin und zurück.
Beamter	Erster oder zweiter Klasse?
Reisende	Zweiter Klasse.
Beamter	Zweiundsiebzig Mark, bitte.
Reisende	Können Sie wechseln? Ich habe nur einen Fünfhundertmarkschein.

Practice

1 Answer these questions about the conversation on page 33.

(*a*) Kauft der Reisende eine oder zwei Fahrkarten?
(*b*) Fährt er erster oder zweiter Klasse?
(*c*) Was kostet seine Fahrkarte?
(*d*) Warum muß der Beamte wechseln?
(*e*) Wieviel Geld bekommt der Reisende zurück?

The 24-hour clock

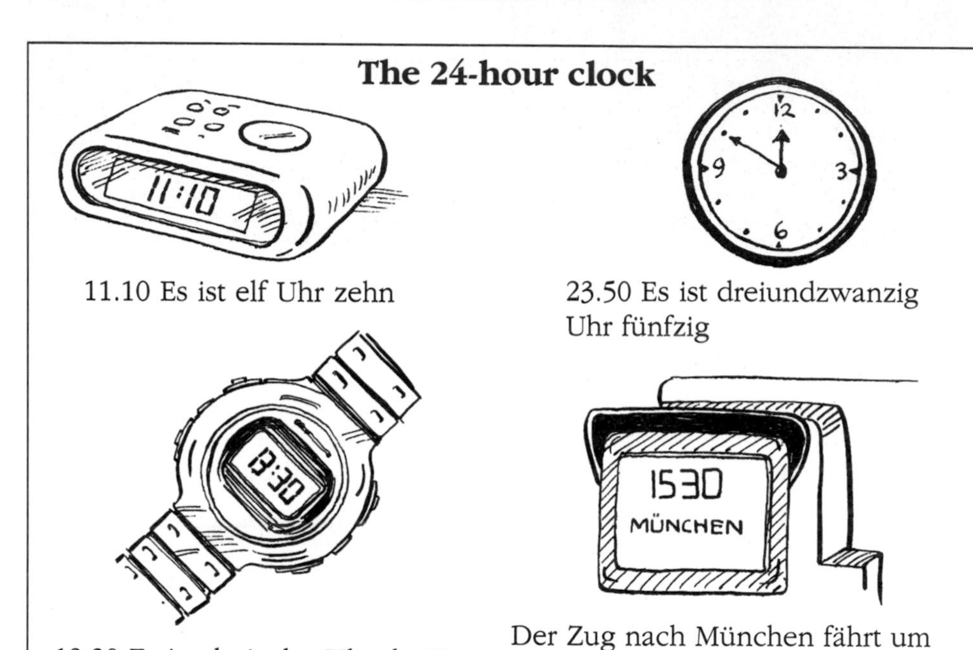

11.10 Es ist elf Uhr zehn

23.50 Es ist dreiundzwanzig Uhr fünfzig

13.30 Es ist dreizehn Uhr dreißig

Der Zug nach München fährt um 15.30

2 Express the following numbers in German:

(*a*) 17	(*f*) 35
(*b*) 25	(*g*) 27
(*c*) 96	(*h*) 74
(*d*) 88	(*i*) 51
(*e*) 49	(*j*) 63

3 Dictation

Listen to the cassette and write down the telephone numbers as they are dictated to you.

4 Asking for information

Get together with a partner, and using the following table make up conversations along the lines of the example below.

Richtung	Abfahrt	Gleis	Ankunft
München	07.30	2	10.20
Hannover	09.45	3	13.10
Lübeck	11.24	6	16.56
Ludwigshafen	18.12	4	21.35
Bonn	15.39	1	22.16

Example

- • Wann fährt der nächste Zug nach München, bitte?
- ▪ Um sieben Uhr dreißig von Gleis zwei.
- • Und wann kommt er in München an?
- ▪ Um zehn Uhr zwanzig.

5 Buying train tickets

Use the following table to make up conversations along the lines of the example below.

Richtung	Preis	Fahrt	Wieviele	Klasse
Köln	DM5,—	→	2	2
Hauptbahnhof	DM20,—	→	2	1
Nürnberg	DM34,26	⇄	1	1
Mannheim	DM69,35	⇄	3	2
Hamburg	DM17,50	→	1	2

- • Zweimal nach Köln. Was kostet es bitte?
- ▪ Einfach oder hin und zurück?
- • Einfach.

- ■ Erster oder zweiter Klasse?
- ● Zweiter Klasse.
- ■ Zehn Mark bitte.

Hauptbahnhof, Frankfurt

Am Bahnhof

Liz Young, a translator working in Germany, goes to the information desk at Frankfurt main station to enquire about trains to Aachen.

Übersetzerin	Wann fährt der nächste Zug nach Aachen?
Angestellter	Um elf Uhr siebenundvierzig.
Übersetzerin	Fährt der Zug direkt nach Aachen?
Angestellter	Nein, Sie müssen in Köln umsteigen.
Übersetzerin	Wann kommt der Zug in Köln an?
Angestellter	Um vierzehn Uhr. Um vierzehn Uhr acht fahren Sie dann von Köln nach Aachen weiter.
Übersetzerin	Und wann bin ich in Aachen?
Angestellter	Um fünfzehn Uhr drei.
Übersetzerin	Von welchem Gleis fährt der Zug nach Köln?
Angestellter	Von Gleis zwei.
Übersetzerin	Ich danke Ihnen für die Auskunft.
Angestellter	Gern geschehen.

Practice

1 Buying a ticket

You are going to a business conference in Berlin and you need to get a train ticket from Frankfurt to Berlin. What do you say in German?

Sie (Ask when the next train to Berlin leaves.)
Angestellter Um neun Uhr dreiundzwanzig.
Sie (Ask if it is a direct train.)
Angestellter Nein, Sie müssen in Hannover umsteigen.
Sie (Ask when the train arrives in Hannover.)
Angestellter Um zwölf Uhr achtunddreißig. Um dreizehn Uhr vier fahren Sie dann von Hannover nach Berlin weiter.
Sie (Ask when you will get to Berlin.)
Angestellter Um siebzehn Uhr vierundzwanzig.
Sie (Ask which platform the Hannover train leaves from.)
Angestellter Von Gleis drei.
Sie (Say thank you for the information.)
Angestellter Nichts zu danken.
(*You then make your way to the ticket counter.*)
Sie (Ask for one ticket to Berlin.)
Beamter Einfach oder hin und zurück?
Sie (Ask for a second-class return ticket.)
Beamter Zweihundert Mark, bitte.

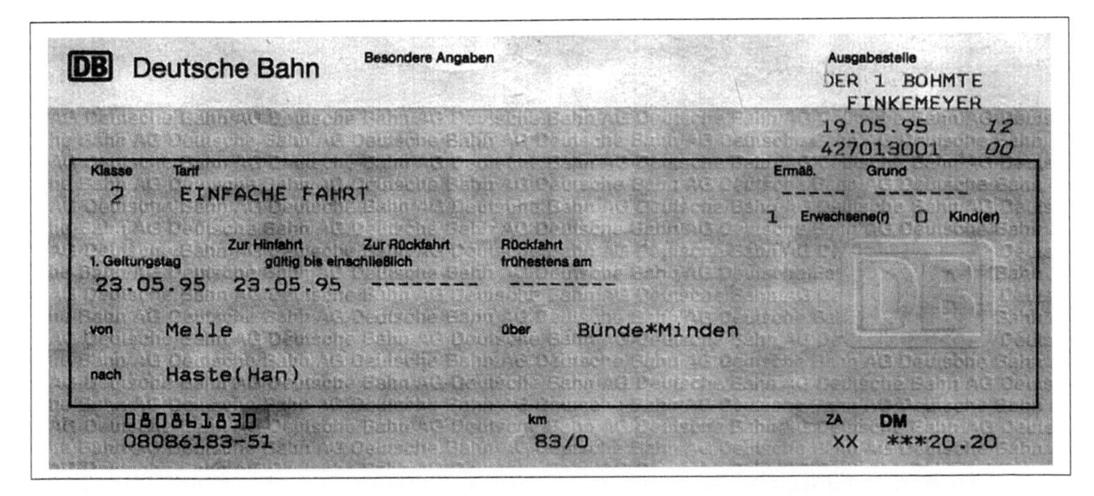
DB Deutsche Bahn
Besondere Angaben
Ausgabestelle
DER 1 BOHMTE
FINKEMEYER
19.05.95 12
427013001 00
Klasse 2
Tarif EINFACHE FAHRT
Ermäß. -----
Grund -------
1 Erwachsene(r) 0 Kind(er)
1. Geltungstag 23.05.95
Zur Hinfahrt gültig bis einschließlich 23.05.95
Zur Rückfahrt --------
Rückfahrt frühestens am --------
von Melle
über Bünde*Minden
nach Haste(Han)
080861830
08086183-51
km 83/0
ZA XX
DM ***20.20

Eine einfache Fahrkarte

2 Listening comprehension

Listen to the four dialogues on cassette and then complete the table below. The first line has been filled in for you.

Gespräch	Zielort	Abfahrt	Gleis	Umsteigen	Ankunft in Zielort
1	Frankfurt	8.30	4	Stuttgart	11.45
2					
3					
4					

Information

Der Fahrausweisautomat - Bedienungsanleitung

1 Wählen

Für Reisen bis 60 Kilometer benutzen Sie den Automaten. Die Zielbahnhöfe stehen alphabetisch auf einer Liste. Wählen Sie zuerst Ihr Ziel. Neben dem Ziel ist eine Tastatur. Drücken Sie dann die Taste von Ihrem Zielbahnhof.

2 Zahlen

Der Fahrpreis erscheint oberhalb der Tastenreihe. Unterhalb des Fahrpreises ist der Münzeinwurf. Werfen Sie das Geld dort ein (also zahlen).

3 Nehmen

Der Automat funktioniert schnell und einfach. Innerhalb von zwei Sekunden erhalten Sie dann Ihren Fahrausweis.

3

A visitor to Germany uses a ticket machine for the first time. Read the following account, then re-tell it in the third person.

Ich bin in Deutschland und will eine Fahrkarte von Düsseldorf nach Mönchengladbach lösen. Ich muß den Automaten benutzen, aber es ist nicht einfach, und ein Beamter muß mir helfen. Ich drücke die Taste fur Mönchengladbach. Dann werfe ich den Fahrpreis ein und erhalte den Fahrausweis. Ich entwerte den Fahrausweis, bevor ich in die Bahn einsteige.

4 At the station in Frankfurt you are approached by someone who has forgotten his glasses and asks you to decipher the timetable. Answer his questions:

(*a*) Ich fahre um 07.47 nach Düsseldorf. Kann ich direkt fahren, oder muß ich umsteigen?
(*b*) Ist das ein D-Zug?
(*c*) Wann komme ich in Düsseldorf an?

Make up similar conversations using the example and the timetable.

DB

Fahrplanauszug

Winter

Frankfurt(M) → Düsseldorf 264 Km

Verkehrszeiten	ab	Zug	an	Service	Umsteigen in	an	ab	Zug
Sa, So- u Feiertage	0.42	Ⓢ	5.30		Mainz	1.19	2.30	D218
					Köln	4.32	4.56	E5001
werktags außer Sa, nicht 24., 31.XII.	0.42	Ⓢ	5.35		Mainz	1.19	2.30	D218
					Köln	4.32	5.03	E5003
Mo bis Sa, nicht 25.XII. bis 3.I., 2. bis 4.IV., 23.V.	0.42	Ⓢ	5.59		Mainz	1.19	2.30	D218
					Köln	4.32	5.35	IC633
	0.42	Ⓢ	7.44		Mainz	1.19	2.30	D218
					Köln	4.32	5.00	N3101
					Hagen	6.36	6.48	E3172
	4.39	D824	8.05	🍸				
	6.49	IC631	9.34					
	7.26	D222	10.15	🍸				
	7.47	IC668	10.28		Köln	10.00	10.04	IC518
Mo bis Sa, nicht 25.XII. bis 3.I., 2. bis 4.IV., 23.V.	7.49	IC639	10.34					
	8.47	IC666	11.28		Köln	11.00	11.04	IC500
	8.49	EC31	11.34					
	9.14	D2020	12.34		Kobl	10.56	11.03	IC616
					Köln	11.54	12.10	IC608
	9.14	D2020	13.03					
Mo bis Sa, auch 17.IV., nicht 25.XII. bis 3.I., 2. bis 4.IV., 23.V.	9.47	IC526	12.28					
Mo bis Sa, nicht 25.XII bis 3.I., 2. bis 4.IV., 23.V.	9.49	IC608	12.34					
	10.47	IC664	13.28		Köln	13.00	13.04	IC516
Mo bis Sa, nicht 25.XII. bis 3.I., 2. bis 4.IV., 23.V.	10.49	IC606	13.34					
Mo bis Sa, nicht 25.XII. bis 3.I., 2. bis 4.IV., 23.V.	11.47	IC524	14.28					
	11.49	IC531	14.34					
	12.47	IC628	15.28		Köln	15.00	15.04	EC8
	12.49	IC602	15.34					
	13.47	EC26	16.28					
	13.49	IC600	16.34					
	14.47	IC522	17.28					

5 Listening comprehension

You are waiting for a colleague near the enquiry point at Hannover's main station and can hear some of the enquiries that are being dealt with. What can you understand? Note down the travel information that is given using the following headings: Destination, Departure time, Arrival time, Change trains (where?), Type of ticket, Price of ticket.

6 You work for a German company. Your employer has picked up this leaflet and has asked you to explore the possibility of obtaining a disk. In particular she asks you the following questions. Give her the answers.

(*a*) Gefällt Ihnen diese Idee? Warum?
(*b*) Wieviele Bahnhöfe und Züge sind auf der Diskette und im elektronischen Kursbuch?
(*c*) Enthält die Diskette die Fahrpreise?
(*d*) Kann man Fahrscheine buchen und Plätze reservieren?
(*e*) Wo ist das Bestell Center?

Elektronische Fahrplanauskunft auf PC

Ihre Reiseplanung mit den Deutschen Bahnen machen Sie jederzeit einfach und schnell auf Ihrem PC. Mit den drei Info-Systemen Ihrer Wahl.

Elektronische Städteverbindungen Deutschland auf Diskette:

- ca. 7000 Bahnhöfe
- ca. 48 000 Züge
- mit Zuggattung, Zugnummer, Umsteigezeiten, den wichtigsten Auslandsverbindungen etc.
- Fahrpreise 1. und 2. Klasse und Entfernungen (zusätzliches Diskettenpaket gegen gesonderte Berechnung)

2 Disketten (3½"). Für DOS-PCs (auch Laptop oder Notebook) mit mind. 80 386 CPU.
Empfohlen: 2 MB RAM. Benötigt 4 MB auf der Festplatte.
WINDOWS-Version (ab WINDOWS 3.1) mindestens 4 MB RAM.

Elektronisches Kursbuch auf CD-ROM:

- ca. 10 000 Bahnhöfe
- ca. 60 000 Züge
- Fahrpreise 1. und 2. Klasse und Entfernungen
- mit den Kursbuch-Daten.

Für DOS-PCs mit mind. 80 386 CPU und 12 cm CD-ROM-Laufwerk.
Empfohlen: 4 MB RAM.
Speicherplatz 12 MB.
WINDOWS-Version (ab WINDOWS 3.1) mindestens 6 MB RAM erforderlich.

Elektronisches Reise-Centrum mit Datex-J (Btx). Nutzen Sie Datex-J, und genießen Sie sofort diese Vorteile:

- Zugriff auf alle Zugverbindungen, Zeiten und Fahrpreise (1. und 2. Klasse).
- Online mit der "Elektronischen Verkehrsauskunft" (EVA) der Bahn.
- Buchung von Fahrscheinen, Platzreservierung.
- Information und Buchung von Serviceleistungen wie z.B. KurierGepäck, Rail & Road (Mietwagen).

Außerdem können Sie auf rund 3000 weitere Informations-Angebote elektronisch zugreifen.

Weitere Informationen erhalten Sie von:
Deutsche Bahn AG
Bestell Center
Elektronische Medien
Postfach 1157
53821 Troisdorf
Telefon 0 22 41/94 77 77
Telefax 0 22 41/94 77 99

Summary

Useful phrases

1 Enquiring about train times	Wann fährt der nächste Zug nach/zum/zur . . . ? Wann kommt der Zug in/an . . . an?
2 Asking if you have to change	Muß ich umsteigen? Fährt der Zug direkt nach . . . ?
3 Enquiring about platforms	Von welchem Gleis fährt der Zug nach . . . ?
4 Enquiring about cost	Was kostet das?
5 Buying tickets	Einmal/zweimal/dreimal nach . . . Einmal einfach Einmal hin und zurück Erster/zweiter Klasse
6 Asking for change	Können Sie bitte wechseln?
7 Saying you are welcome	Bitte schön Gern geschehen Nichts zu danken

Language forms

1 The accusative case

(a) The direct object

The accusative is used to show the element in a sentence called the direct object, i.e. the person or thing that receives the action of a particular verb. The masculine words for 'the' and 'a' are affected if they accompany a direct object. (The feminine, neuter and plural words are not affected.)

The masculine words change in the following way:

der becomes ***den***
ein becomes ***einen***

Examples

Ich sehe ***den*** *Zug.*
I see the train.

Er kauft ***einen*** *Fahrschein.*
He's buying a ticket.

(b) Accusative prepositions

This change also occurs with certain prepositions. These are words that show links or connections. Prepositions that bring about accusative spelling forms are:

für (for)
durch (through)
gegen / *wider* } (against)
ohne (without)
um (around)

Examples

Die Sekretärin reserviert ein Hotelzimmer für ***den*** *Geschaftsführer.*
The secretary is reserving a hotel room for the managing director.

Die Verkaufsleiterin fährt nie ohne ***einen*** *Stadtplan nach London.*
The sales manager never travels to London without a street map.

2 The dative case

(a) The indirect object

The dative is used to show the element in a sentence called the indirect object, i.e. the person or thing to which something goes.

All words for 'the' and 'a' are affected if they accompany an indirect object. The following changes of spelling occur:

(i) The

der and *das*	become ***dem***
die (feminine singular)	becomes ***der***
die (plural for all genders)	becomes ***den***

All nouns that accompany the dative plural *den* end with an *n.*

(ii) A

ein (masculine and neuter)	becomes ***einem***
eine (feminine)	becomes ***einer***

Examples

Wir schreiben ***dem*** *Einkaufsleiter einen Brief.*
We are writing a letter to the senior buyer.

Ich sende ***der*** *Geschäftsleiterin ein Paket.*
I'm sending a parcel to the managing director.

(b) Verbs taking the dative

The following verbs bring about dative forms of 'the' and 'a'. They all contain the idea of something going to someone. The two example sentences in (a) (ii) show this.

empfehlen	(to recommend)
geben	(to give)
sagen	(to say)
schicken/senden	(to send)
schreiben	(to write)
wünschen	(to wish – something to someone)

Three other verbs that also take the dative, but not directly with the idea of something being imparted to someone, are:

danken	(to thank)
gefallen	(to please)
helfen	(to help).

However, the implicit meaning of each of these verbs is 'to give thanks to', 'to be pleasing to', 'to be helpful to'. The 'to' signifies an indirect object, hence the dative use of these verbs.

(c) Dative prepositions

Dative forms of 'the' and 'a' also occur with certain prepositions. Some common dative prepositions are:

aus (out of)	*nach* (after, to)
bei (at, by)	*seit* (since)
gegenüber (opposite)	*von* (from)
mit (with)	*zu* (to)

Examples

aus ***dem/einem*** *Bahnhof* (m)
out of the/a station

gegenüber ***der/einer*** *Kirche* (f)
opposite the/a church

nach ***dem/einem*** *Treffen* (n)
after the/a meeting

Note *Von* and *dem* are often shortened to *vom*; *zu* and *dem* to *zum*.

3 Possessive adjectives

These are words showing whose something is.

singular	**plural**
mein (my)	*unser* (our)
dein (your – with *du*)	*euer* (your – with *ihr*)
Ihr (your – with *Sie*)	*Ihr* (your – with *Sie*)
sein (his, its, one's)	*ihr* (their)
ihr (her, its, one's)	

After prepositions, possessive adjectives change in the same way as 'a' (see 2 (a) (ii)).

Examples

*Ich will ein Zimmer für unser**en** Verkaufsleiter reservieren.*
I want to reserve a room for our sales manager.

*Die Sekretärin reserviert ein Zimmer für ihr**e** Geschäftsführerin.*
The secretary is reserving a room for her managing director.

4 Modal verbs

These are verbs that express the degree of pressure or freedom a person experiences when doing something. They include the ideas of possibility, willingness and compulsion. In English they include such verbs as 'ought', 'should', 'must', 'can', 'may' and 'want'.

Three common modal verbs in German are:

können (can, be able)	*müssen* (must, have to)	*wollen* (want)
ich kann	ich muß	ich will
du kannst	du mußt	du willst
Sie können	Sie müssen	Sie wollen
er / sie } kann	er / sie } muß	er / sie } will
wir können	wir müssen	wir wollen
ihr könnt	ihr müßt	ihr wollt
Sie können	Sie müssen	Sie wollen
sie können	sie müssen	sie wollen

Examples

*Ich **kann** leider nicht gehen.*
I unfortunately can't go.

*Wir **müssen** nach Wien fliegen.*
We have to fly to Vienna.

*Sie **wollen** mit der Bahn fahren.*
They want to travel by train.

Notice how the verb linked with the modal verb stands at the end of the sentence.

Additional exercises

1 Complete the sentences on page 45 by inserting the correct form of 'the' in the accusative case.

(*a*) Sie erhalten ______ Fahrschein innerhalb von zwei Sekunden.
(*b*) Nehmen Sie ______ Rolltreppe dort drüben.
(*c*) Werfen Sie ______ Geld dort ein.
(*d*) Ich benutze schnell ______ Automaten.
(*e*) Können Sie ______ Geld wechseln?

2 Complete the following sentences by inserting the correct form of 'a' in the accusative case.

(*a*) Sie bekommen ______ Fahrkarte vom Automaten.
(*b*) Ich habe nur ______ Fünfhundertmarkschein.
(*c*) Kaufst du ______ Buch?
(*d*) Nein, ich kaufe ______ Kassette.
(*e*) Suchen Sie ______ Fahrplan?

3 Complete the sentences with an appropriate accusative preposition from the following list: *für, durch, gegen, ohne, um.*

(*a*) Das Buch ist ______ meinen Mann.
(*b*) ______ Geld kann ich nicht fahren!
(*c*) Die Vertreter sitzen ______ den Tisch und verhandeln.
(*d*) Sie müssen ______ die Eingangshalle (*foyer*) gehen.
(*e*) Ich schwimme ______ den Strom *(current).*

4 Change the word for 'the' where appropriate to match the verb or preposition with which it stands.

(*a*) Ich empfehle (die) Geschäftsleiterin ein Hotel in Essen.
(*b*) Wir senden (der) Lagerverwalter (*warehouse manager*) ein Paket.
(*c*) Sie wünscht (das) Personal einen guten Aufenthalt.
(*d*) Er sagt (die) Sekretärin, er kann nicht kommen.
(*e*) Er dankt (der) Ingenieur für das Buch.
(*f*) Der Bahnhof steht gegenüber (die) Firma.
(*g*) Wir essen nach (das) Treffen (*meeting*).
(*h*) Hans fährt immer mit (die) Bahn.
(*i*) Seit (der) Aufenthalt in Deutschland spreche ich besser Deutsch.
(*j*) Sie kommt jetzt aus (das) Hotel.

5 Add the correct ending to the possessive adjectives shown.

(*a*) Ich will ein Zimmer mit Bad für mein___ Geschäftsführerin buchen.
(*b*) Das Paket ist für Ihr___ Lagerverwalter.
(*c*) Der Brief ist von ihr___ Mann.
(*d*) Ein Park steht gegenüber unser___ Firma.
(*e*) Fahrt ihr mit eur___ Kind nach Chikago?

6 Extend the following sentences by including the appropriate form of the modal verb shown.

Example
Ich schreibe heute der Firma Rockwool. (müssen)
Ich *muß* heute der Firma Rockwool *schreiben*.

(*a*) Wir fliegen im Mai zu einer Tagung nach Dresden. (müssen)
(*b*) Der Dolmetscher arbeitet in Paris. (können)
(*c*) Sie reserviert ein Zimmer mit Dusche. (wollen)
(*d*) Mr Turner besucht die Firma Sasshofer. (müssen)
(*e*) Wann kommen Herr und Frau Detlav nach Glagow? (wollen)
(*f*) Fahren Sie nächsten Monat nach Köln zur Messe? (können)
(*g*) Fahre ich direkt nach Mannheim? (können)
(*h*) Schreibst du dem Direktor einen Brief? (wollen)
(*i*) Ich steige in Frankfurt um. (müssen)
(*j*) Wann kommst du nach Ulm? (können)

Kapitel 1–3

Zusätzliche Aufgaben

1 A colleague (or friend) has asked you to phone Germany to ask for details of a forthcoming trade fair. While on the phone you have to give your colleague's name and work address. Spell these out.

2 **Pair-work**

(*a*) You are interviewing a student who has applied to your company for some holiday work. You need to obtain some personal information on their background. Ask the applicant the following questions:

(i) Wie ist Ihr Name?
(ii) Ihre Staatsangehörigkeit?
(iii) Woher kommen Sie?
(iv) Ihre Adresse bitte.
(v) Haben Sie Familie?
(vi) Ihr Geburtsdatum?
(vii) Wann können Sie anfangen?

When you have completed asking the questions, report back to ensure you have understood properly. Then write a short memo to your boss outlining the details you have obtained.

(*b*) You are attending an interview conducted in German. Answer the interviewer's questions above.

3 You are due to go on a German exchange and decide to write a letter of introduction to your exchange partner. As well as introducing yourself, ask your partner some questions about him/herself. (Do not write the whole letter, just the relevant section.)

4 You are attending a conference in Germany. While waiting for it to start you strike up a conversation with other delegates. Give them some background information on yourself, e.g. your work, your family, your linguistic abilities.

5 Herr Schuster has a busy morning ahead of him. Listen to his secretary giving him an outline of the day, and note down what will be happening, and when, using the following headings: Time, Appointment.

6 You have left your answerphone on. Note down the names and telephone numbers of the callers.

7 **Pair-work**

(*a*) You are expecting some German-speaking visitors to your company/home and receive a call from one of them, asking how they can reach your company/home from the UK airport using public transport. Give appropriate instructions.

(*b*) Take the part of a German person planning to visit the UK. Ask your host how to reach your destination using public transport from the airport.

Useful phrases: *ein Taxi, einen Bus, einen Zug nehmen; mit dem Bus, Zug, der Bahn fahren; umsteigen; die Fahrkarte.*

8 Find two German addresses (your teacher will help if necessary). Dictate these and spell them out to a partner, then check if they have been understood.

9 You are doing work experience in Germany. A fax comes from England. Note down the contents for your boss in German.

> John Adamson and Dave Gregson will be flying from Manchester to Munich on 14 June. They will arrive in Munich at 10.20 and then travel on to Kempten by train. They should arrive in Kempten at about 12.30. John Adamson will be staying for three days (leaving again on 17 June). Dave Gregson will be staying until 16 June, then continuing to Dresden.

10 You and some colleagues are due to attend a conference in Germany. Spell out their names in German to the organiser.

11 While in Germany you decide to visit Bonn. You phone the tourist office and listen to the following text on the answerphone. You have to listen to it more than once to get all the facts down. Fill in the gaps in the text.

Bonn liegt am _______. Bonn ist als _______ sehr wichtig. Von Interesse in Bonn sind _______ _______, _______ _______ und das Rathaus; auch interessant sind das _______ und die _______ (_______ _______). Bonn ist mit dem _______, _______ _______ _______, _______ _______ _______ (über _______ _______) und sogar mit dem Dampfer _______ _______ _______ gut erreichbar.

12 Besides speaking German, it is important to have some background information on Germany and its language. Read the text on page 50, then complete the sentences after the text.

Die Bundesrepublik Deutschland und der deutsche Sprachraum

Deutschland liegt mitten in Europa und hat 16 Länder. Man spricht Deutsch in der Bundesrepublik, in Österreich und in der Schweiz. Das sind drei Nachbarländer. Die Hauptstädte dieser Länder sind Berlin, Wien und Bern.

Deutschland ist Mitglied der Europäischen Union (EU) und treibt großen Handel mit den anderen EU-Ländern: Belgien, Dänemark, Finnland, Frankreich, Griechenland, Großbritannien, Holland, Irland, Italien, Luxemburg, Österreich, Portugal, Schweden und Spanien. Deutschland sucht jetzt neue Handelspartner in Osteuropa sowie im Westen.

(*a*) Die Hauptstadt der Bundesrepublik heißt _________.
(*b*) In Österreich spricht man _________.
(*c*) Bern ist in _________.
(*d*) Die EU hat _________ Mitglieder.
(*e*) Deutschland treibt Handel mit dem _________ und sucht neue Handelspartner im _________.

Kapitel 4

Unterkunft in Deutschland

Am Empfang

On arrival at the Hotel Coenen Michael Newby deals with the registration formalities at the reception desk.

Empfangsdame	Guten Tag, mein Herr.
Newby	Guten Tag. Ich habe ein Zimmer reserviert.
Empfangsdame	Ihr Name bitte?
Newby	Ich heiße Michael Newby.
Empfangsdame	Ach ja, Sie sind auf Geschäftsreise von der Firma Anglia Chemicals, nicht wahr?
Newby	Ja, stimmt. Ich bin Geschäftsführer der Firma Anglia Chemicals.
Empfangsdame	Bitte füllen Sie diese Seite des Anmeldeformulars aus, Herr Newby.
Newby	Selbstverständlich. Also, Tag meiner Ankunft . . . der vierte Oktober.
Empfangsdame	So, Zimmer Nummer neun – Einzelzimmer mit Bad im ersten Stock. Hier ist Ihr Schlüssel. Es ist sehr schön. Einen Fahrstuhl haben wir auch. Er ist gleich um die Ecke. Wir bringen Ihr Gepäck nach oben, wenn Sie wollen.
Newby	Danke, das geht schon.

Practice

1 Answer these questions about Mr Newby's arrival at the hotel.

(*a*) After giving his name, what is Newby asked to do?
(*b*) Where is his room situated?
(*c*) What does the receptionist point him to?
(*d*) Where will he find this?
(*e*) What does he decline?

2 Registering at a hotel

You have just arrived at the reception desk of a hotel in Frankfurt. What do you say in German?

Empfangsdame Guten Tag, mein Herr/gnädige Frau.
Sie (Greet the receptionist and say you have reserved a single room with a bath.)
Empfangsdame Ihr Name, bitte?
Sie (Give your name.)
Empfangsdame Ach ja, Sie kommen aus England, nicht wahr?
Sie (Say that yes, you do.)
Empfangsdame Bitte füllen Sie dieses Anmeldeformular aus, Herr/Frau . . .
Sie (Say yes, of course you will. Ask what number your room is.)
Empfangsdame Also, Zimmer Nummer dreiundvierzig im dritten Stock.
Sie (Ask where the lift is.)
Empfangsdame Er ist da drüben, sehen Sie? Wir bringen Ihr Gepäck nach oben, wenn Sie wollen.
Sie (Say thank you, but you can manage.)

3 Listening comprehension

Listen to the passage about the visitor to the Arabella Hotel in Duisburg, then fill in the registration form on his behalf.

Anmeldeformular

Name ____________

Vorname__________

Staatsangehörigkeit

Straße _____________

Wohnort ____________

Paß-Nr ___________

Ankunft ________________ Abreise _______________

Zimmer-Nr__________

Firma__________

Unterschrift ________________

Im Gasthof Lehen

Herr König and his family are on a touring holiday in the Austrian Tyrol. They stop at the *Gasthof Lehen* which features in the list of local hotels (*Zimmernachweis*). They would like to spend three nights there.

Herr König	Guten Tag. Haben Sie noch Zimmer frei?
Inhaber	Für wieviele Personen?
Herr König	Für zwei Erwachsene und zwei Kinder. Ich möchte ein Doppelzimmer und zwei Einzelzimmer für drei Nächte.
Inhaber	Ja, das geht. Wir haben ein schönes Doppelzimmer und auch zwei Einzelzimmer.
Herr König	Haben Sie Zimmer mit Bad?

Inhaber	Nein, Zimmer mit Bad haben wir nicht, nur mit Dusche. Auch mit Fernsehen und Balkon, wenn Sie wollen. Alle Zimmer sind schön.
Herr König	Gut. Ihr Gasthof hat ja eine herrliche Aussicht auf die Berge. Die ist wirklich sehr schön. Ich finde es hier sehr angenehm. (*He then discusses with the owner whether they require full or half board, when meals are served, and the hotel's charges.*)
Inhaber	Möchten Sie Voll- oder Halbpension?
Herr König	Lieber Halbpension. Tagsüber möchten wir die Sehenswürdigkeiten der Umgebung besichtigen. Wann gibt es Frühstück und Abendessen?
Inhaber	Frühstuck ab sieben Uhr. Abendessen gibt es um halb sieben.
Herr König	Was kostet die Halbpension?
Inhaber	Für die Erwachsenen dreihundertvierzig Schilling, für die Kinder ist es billiger, zweihundertzehn Schilling pro Nacht.
Herr König	Können wir die Zimmer sehen?
Inhaber	Ja, gern. Kommen Sie bitte mit . . .
Herr König	Die Zimmer sind prima. Die nehmen wir, also das Doppelzimmer, das große Einzelzimmer hinten und das kleine Zimmer vorne.

Practice

1 Complete the phrases in column A with an appropriate phrase from column B, according to the information in the dialogue:

Column A	*Column B*
Man kann	die Familie nicht.
Die Zimmer haben	zwei Einzelzimmer.
Für ein Kind kostet	wenn man will.
Für die Kinder gibt es	die Berge sehen.
Der Vater und die Mutter möchten	ein Zimmer mit Halbpension 210 Schilling.
Fernsehen und Balkon kann man auch haben,	ein Doppelziminer.
Vollpension möchte	Frühstück um 07.00 bekommen.
Vom Gasthof kann man	Dusche.

2 Use the symbols below to complete the dialogues.

Personen	Zimmer	Mit Bad oder Dusche?	Nächte
(*a*) 		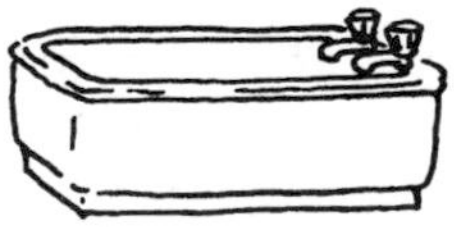	4
(*b*) 			5
(*c*) 	 		2

(*a*) *Empfangsdame* Guten Tag, gnädige Frau.
Dame
Empfangsdame Ein Einzelzimmer? Ja. Für wieviele Nächte bitte?
Dame
Empfangsdame Mit Bad oder Dusche?
Dame
Empfangsdame Also, Nummer sechzehn ist noch frei.
Dame

(*b*) *Empfangsdame* Guten Tag, bitte schön?
Herr
Empfangsdame Ja. Möchten Sie ein Doppelzimmer?
Herr
Empfangsdame Für wieviele Nächte?
Herr
Empfangsdame Möchten Sie ein Zimmer mit Bad oder Dusche?
Herr

(*c*) *Empfangsdame* Guten Abend.
Herr
Empfangsdame Ja, für wieviele Personen?
Herr
Empfangsdame Also, ein Doppelzimmer und...?
Herr
Empfangsdame Und möchten Sie auch Bad oder Dusche?
Herr
Empfangsdame Für wieviele Nächte bitte?
Herr

3 What would you say if you wanted to:

(*a*) ask if there are any rooms free
(*b*) reserve a double room for two nights
(*c*) ask when breakfast is
(*d*) ask for a single room with a shower.

4 You work at a tourist office. A German client is making preliminary enquiries about a hotel before booking a room. Complete the gaps with the appropriate pronoun.

Example Ist das Zimmer noch frei?	Ja, es ist noch frei.
Wie ist das Hotel?	____ ist klein, sehr ruhig und liegt am Stadtrand.
Hat das Hotel einen Parkplatz?	Ja, und ____ hat auch eine Garage.
Was kostet die Garage?	____ kostet DM 10 pro Nacht.
Hat man eine gute Aussicht vom Hotel?	Ja, ______ ist ganz wunderbar.
Hat das Hotel einen Garten?	Ja, ______ ist sehr schön und auch sonnig.

5 On your desk you find the following note from your head of department.

Please phone Hotel Kaiserhof, Munich, and book a single room with a shower for Ken Williams (the sales manager) for three nights. He will be flying to Germany on 20 March.

Get together with a partner and make up a suitable conversation, one taking the part of yourself, the other of the receptionist at the Hotel Kaiserhof.

6 You are working at a Holiday Inn hotel. Here are some typical questions asked by the guests. Use the information below and on page 58 to answer their questions.

(*a*) Kann ich im Hotel Briefmarken kaufen?
(*b*) Wann ist das Schwimmbad geöffnet?
(*c*) Wie heißt das Restaurant?
(*d*) Gibt es einen Friseur im Hotel?
(*e*) Wieviele Konferenzräume hat das Hotel?
(*f*) Kann man mit Kreditkarten bezahlen?
(*g*) Wo kann man Post abgeben?
(*h*) Wo erhält man Tageszeitungen?

Hotelinformation

Abreisezeit 13:00 Uhr. Spätere Abreisezeit nach Vereinbarung mit der Rezeption.

Bank/Geldwechsel An der Rezeption. Die aktuellen Wechselkurse werden täglich in der Empfangshalle angezeigt. Devisen werden bis zu einem Betrag von DM 300, – eingetauscht.

Briefmarken Erhältlich an der Rezeption.

Fitness Ein Saunagang, Schwimmen im Innen- und Außen-Pool oder einige entspannende Minuten unter dem Solarium lassen Sie Abstand von dem Streß des Tages gewinnen.
Öffnungszeiten:
Montag–Freitag 7:00–22:30 Uhr
Samstag/Sonntag 8:00–21:00 Uhr
Feiertag

Fotokopien Kontaktieren Sie bitte die Rezeption.

Frühstück Frühstück vom reichhaltigen Buffet bekommen Sie zwischen 6:30 Uhr und 10:30 Uhr im Restaurant "Le Cygne".

Friseur Unseren Empfangsmitarbeiter vereinbaren gerne einen Termin für Sie bei einem Friseur im Ort.

Konferenzräume 6 Konferenzräume – Totalkapazität für 250 Personen. Für weitere Information kontaktieren Sie bitte die Bankettabteilung.

Kreditkarten Wir akzeptieren folgende Kreditkarten: American Express, Diners Club, Eurocard/Access/Mastercard, JCB, En Route, Visa

Post Der Briefkasten befindet sich neben dem Hoteleingang. Leerung täglich einmal außer sonntags.

Restaurant Unser Restaurant "Le Cygne" bietet Ihnen frische, leichte, deutsche Küche und internationale Gerichte an.
Geöffnet:
Montag – Freitag von 6:30 Uhr bis 15:00 Uhr/ und 18:30 Uhr bis 23:00 Uhr
Samstag von 6:30 Uhr bis 11:00 Uhr
Sonntags/Feiertags von 6:30 Uhr bis 15:00 Uhr

Telefax/Telex Telegramme	Bitte geben Sie Ihre Nachrichten an der Rezeption ab. Gern übermitteln wir Ihre Nachrichten.
Weckdienst	Geben Sie Ihre Wünsche an der Rezeption bekannt.
Zeitungen	Tageszeitungen und Magazine erhalten Sie an der Rezeption.

Look at the text below and find the German word for:

(*i*) Pull through
(*j*) Give back
(*k*) Pull
(*l*) Push.

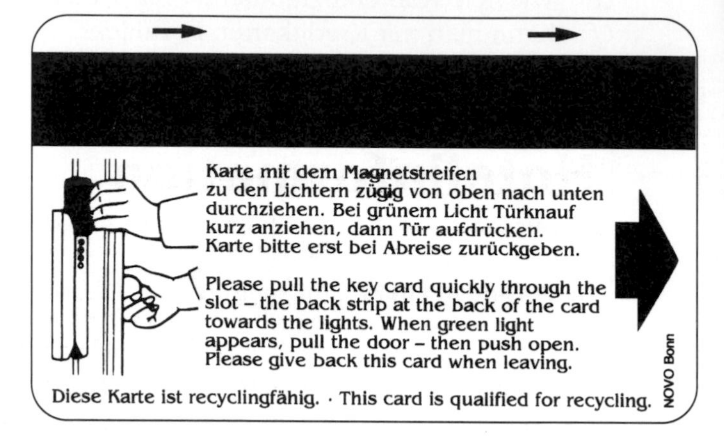

7a Listening comprehension

Mr Walker is phoning a German hotel from the UK to enquire about accommodation for a business trip to Germany. Listen to the cassette.

b Here is the fax sent by the German hotel. Are all the facts correct, or are there some points which Mr Walker will have to clarify? Make a note of them.

Betr: Reservierung für die Firma Smithdown

Wir danken Ihnen für Ihre Anfrage und möchten folgendes anbieten:
2 Doppelzimmer
3 Einzelzimmer
Vom 11. bis zum 16. Juni
Konferenzzimmer-Reservierung: am 15. Juni. Es ist leider nur vormittags frei, also von 9.00 -13.00 Uhr
Zimmerpreise: Einzelzimmer DM98,- bis DM118,-; Doppelzimmer DM155,- bis 185,-
Frühstück: ab 7.00 Uhr
Warme Küche: von 11.30 bis 22.00 Uhr
Restaurant: 18 bis 22.30 Uhr
Wir bitten höflichst um Ihre Antwort so bald wie möglich

8 Your company plans to hold a residential conference in South Germany for 30 guests in order to promote a new product. You have been entrusted with the task of finding a suitable hotel at which to stage the conference. After much inquiry and consultation you draw up a shortlist of the three shown on this page.

Hotel Restaurant Adler
Heiligenbergerstraße 20
7798 Pfullendorf
OBERER LINZGAU
Telefon: 07552/8054
Besitzer: Willi Nusser

48 Betten
alle Zimmer mit Bad/Dusche, WC,
Telefon, teilweise Radio und TV
Übernachtung mit Frühstück pro Person
Einzelzimmer von DM 60.– bis DM 65.–
Doppelzimmer von DM 115.– bis DM 125.–,
Frühstücksbüfett,
warme Küche von 11.30 Uhr bis 14.00 Uhr und 18.00 bis 22.00 Uhr
Parkplätze, Garagen
4 Gasträume für 15 bis 90 Personen
Bauernstube, Konferenzräume
kein Ruhetag

Hotel Central
an der Freiheitshalle
Kulmbacher Straße
8670 Hof
OBERFRANKEN
Tel.: 09281/6884 · Telex: hocen 643932
Besitzer: H. Eckert

100 Betten
alle Zimmer mit Dusche bzw. Bad/WC
Telefon, Minibar, Radio und TV
Übernachtung mit Frühstücksbüfett EZ DM 89.–,
DZ DM 139.–, Suiten EZ DM 190.–, DZ DM 250.–,
zwei Restaurants:
"Hofer Stuben" warme Küche von 11.30 bis 14.00 Uhr u. von 18.00 bis 22.00 Uhr, Montag Ruhetag;
"Kastaniengarten" warme Küche von 18.00 bis 23.00 Uhr,
im Verbund mit der Freiheitshalle
Räumlichkeiten bis 800 Personen;
Ideal für Konferenzen, Tagungen und Kongresse
Whirlpool, Dampfsauna, finnische Sauna und med. Massage, Parkplätze vorhanden

Gasthof - Hotel "Krone"
Hahnenkammstr. 37
und
Hotel "Krone am Park"
Hellersweg 1
8755 Alzenau - Wasserlos
Telefon: 06023/6024-6026
Besitzer: Adolf Reising

Stammhaus - Gasthof - Hotel "Krone"
37 Betten, mit Dusche, WC, Telefon, Frühstücksbüfett
Übernachtungspreis pro Person im Einzelzimmer von DM 45.– b. DM 48.–, Doppelz. von DM 54.– b. DM 88.–
warme Küche von 11.30 Uhr bis 14.00 Uhr
18.00 Uhr bis 22.00 Uhr
Eigene Metzgerei. Tagungsraum für ca. 20 - 50 Personen
Unser neues Haus "Krone am Park"
50 Betten, Dusche, WC, Telefon, Frühstücksbüfett + TV.
Übernachtungspreis pro Person im Einzelzimmer von DM 73.– bis DM 85.–, Doppelzimmer DM 120.–,
Suite DM 148.–; Garagen, Parkplätze;
Freizeitangebot: Fitneßraum, Sauna, Solarium, Kegelbahn, Tennisplatz, Liegewiese,
Tagungsraum für ca. 20 - 50 Personen.

The final choice must satisfy the following conditions:

(*a*) Evening meal must be available until 22.00.
(*b*) All rooms must have a bath or shower.
(*c*) All rooms must have a radio, TV and a telephone.
(*d*) There must be parking facilities.
(*e*) The hotel must offer a range of recreational facilities.

Which of the three do you decide on?

9 Mr Johnson is to travel to Bavaria on business to discuss the purchase of some machinery. He receives the following letter from the company he will be visiting, confirming his accommodation.

Maschinenfabrik Schmidt GmbH
Klosterstr. 5
8081 Althegnenberg

Managing Director
J J Instruments plc
Unit 10
Pennine Trading Estate
GB-Manchester M25 6LX

20. Mai 1996

Sehr geehrter Herr Johnson,

wir danken Ihnen für Ihr Schreiben vom 5.5.96 und möchten folgendes bestätigen.

Sie kommen am dritten Juli nach Deutschland und bleiben bis zum achten. Sie werden uns vom vierten bis zum siebten hier in der Fabrik besuchen. Kommen Sie mit dem Wagen oder mit der Bahn, oder fliegen Sie? Das Hotel Zum Goldenen Stern und das Hotel Sonne haben im Juli noch Zimmer frei. Das Hotel Sonne ist teurer aber besser. Wir können Ihnen dieses Hotel sehr empfehlen. Der Inhaber, Herr Lindemann, und seine Frau sind sehr freundlich. (Sie sprechen fast kein Englisch, aber das macht ja nichts. Sie können jetzt gut Deutsch.) Das Essen ist gut, die Zimmer sind ruhig und haben Dusche und Toilette. Parkplätze hat das Hotel auch. Ein Einzelzimmer ist also vorläufig reserviert.

Ich fahre nächste Woche in Urlaub, aber mein Kollege, Herr Braun, und meine Sekretärin, Frau Schreiber, sind hier im Büro.

In den nächsten paar Tagen werden wir Ihnen weitere Informationen über unsere Instrumente, Preise, Verkaufsbedingungen usw. zuschicken.

Mit freundlichen Grüßen

Jeismann

Karl-Heinz Jeismann
Geschäftsführer

(*a*) Translate the letter into English.
(*b*) Send a fax on behalf of Mr Johnson to Herr Jeismann at Maschinenfabrik Schmidt which says the following:
  (i) thank him for his letter
  (ii) Mr Johnson will be bringing his wife so please reserve a double room
  (iii) Mr and Mrs Johnson will be staying until 10th July and travelling by car so please reserve a parking place.

10 A colleague at work wants to rent a flat in Switzerland during the summer. He has asked you to read the following advertisement which he found in a Swiss accommodation leaflet, and also to answer some questions for him.

> In der Wohnung: ein Schlafzimmer, zwei Kinderzimmer, Eßzimmer, Wohnzimmer, Küche, Badezimmer, Balkon mit wunderbarer Aussicht auf Berge und See, Fahrstuhl im Haus, Parkplätze, Garten (leider keine Tiere). Zehn Minuten mit dem Auto/Bus von Stadtmitte und Bahnhof.
> In der Stadt: modernes Schwimmbad, bunte Parks, römisches Museum, großer Zoo, alter Dom.
> Für nähere Informationen telefonieren oder schreiben Sie an:
> Schneider-Appartements, Bachstr. 4. Zürich. Tel: 01/202 39 47,
> Fax: 01/202 3876

Now answer your colleague's questions:
(*a*) What are the views like?
(*b*) I am not taking the car. Can we reach the town centre easily?
(*c*) Is there a lift?
(*d*) Is there a railway station there?
(*e*) What are the main tourist attractions?
(*f*) How do I find out more information?

11 Listening comprehension

While travelling through Austria a couple stop at a tourist information office (*Verkehrsverein*) to enquire about accommodation. Listen to tbe cassette, then answer the questions that follow.
(*a*) In what kind of location do the couple want accommodation?
(*b*) How is the *Parkhotel* described?
(*c*) How do prices at the *Gasthof Huber* compare with those of the *Parkhotel*?
(*d*) What is situated behind the *Gasthof*?

Summary

Useful phrases

1	Saying you have reserved a room	Ich habe ein Zimmer reserviert
2	Saying that something is correct	Ja, (das/es) stimmt
3	Saying of 'course'	Selbstverständlich Natürlich
4	Saying you can manage	Danke, das geht schon
5	Asking if rooms are available	Haben Sie noch Zimmer frei?
6	Asking for particular rooms and facilities	Ich möchte ein/zwei Einzelzimmer/ Doppelzimmer mit Bad/Dusche/ Balkon/Fernsehen/Telefon
7	Asking about meal times	Wann gibt es Frühstück und Abendessen?
8	Asking about prices	Was kostet Halbpension?
9	Asking to see rooms	Können wir die Zimmer sehen?
10	Saying you like the rooms	Die Zimmer sind sehr schön
11	Saying you will take the rooms	Die nehmen wir
12	Asking someone to recommend you something	Können Sie uns einen/eine/ein . . . empfehlen?
13	Saying you prefer something	Lieber ein(e) . . .
14	Saying something is acceptable	Das geht

Language forms

1 The future tense

There are two ways of expressing the future in German:

(a) Use the ordinary present tense

Examples

Er ***fliegt*** *morgen nach Brüssel.*
He will be flying to Brussels tomorrow.

Der Zug ***ist*** *um elf Uhr in Zürich.*
The train will be in Zurich at 11 o'clock.

(b) Use the verb *werden* plus the infinitive of the verb

werden

ich werde (I will/shall)	*wir werden* (we will/shall)
du wirst (you will/shall)	*ihr werdet* (you will/shall)
Sie werden (you will/shall)	*Sie werden* (you will/shall)
er/sie wird (he/she will/shall)	*sie werden* (they will/shall)

The infinitive stands at the end of the sentence.

Examples

Ich ***werde*** *ein Hotelzimmer für Mr Newby* ***reservieren***.
I will reserve a hotel room for Mr Newby.

Wir ***werden*** *im April nach Leipzig zur Messe* ***fahren***.
We shall be travelling to the trade fair in Leipzig in April.

2 The imperative

When speaking to someone with whom you are not on familiar terms, you form the imperative by putting *Sie* after the infinitive of the verb. In the case of separable verbs, the *Sie* goes after the core part of the verb, the separable prefix goes to the end.

Examples

Zeigen Sie *mir bitte das Zimmer.*
Show me the room please.

Bitte ***füllen*** *Sie dieses Formular* ***aus***.
Please fill in this form.

3 Adjective agreement after 'a'

After *ein/eine/ein* and their related forms the adjective will have the following endings:

	Masculine	*Feminine*	*Neuter*
Nominative	ein gut*er* Chef	eine gut*e* Chefin	ein billig*es* Zimmer
	(a good boss)	(a good boss)	(a cheap room)
Accusative	einen gut*en* Chef	eine gut*e* Chefin	ein billig*es* Zimmer
Dative	einem gut*en* Chef	einer gut*en* Chefin	einem billig*en* Zimmer

(*a*) Adjectives following *mein, dein, sein, ihr* etc. in the singular have exactly the same endings as after *ein* etc.

Examples

*Mein neu****er*** *Chef heißt Bauer.*
My new boss is called Bauer.

*Hier ist ein Brief von ihrem englisch**en** Vertreter.*
Here's a letter from their English representative.

(*b*) Adjectives following *mein, dein, sein, ihr,* etc. in the plural end with *en.*

Example

*Die Geschäftsleiterin schreibt unseren amerikanisch**en** Kollegen.*
The managing director is writing to our American colleagues.

4 Saying 'this' and 'these'

The words for 'this' and 'these' in German are subject to the same changes of form as *der/die/das.*

	Masculine	*Feminine*	*Neuter*	*Plural*
Nominative	dieser	diese	dieses	diese
Accusative	diesen	diese	dieses	diese
Dative	diesem	dieser	diesem	diesen

5 How to say 'it'

The word for 'it' in German differs according to the gender of the thing referred to.

Examples

***Der Fahrstuhl** ist um die Ecke.* The lift is round the corner.	***Er** ist um die Ecke.* It is round the corner.
***Die Aussicht** ist schön.* The view is beautiful.	***Sie** ist schön.* It is beautiful.
***Das Zimmer** ist groß.* The room is big.	***Es** ist groß.* It is big.

6 Formation of the comparative

The comparative is formed by adding *er* to the adjective or adverb.

Examples

billig (cheap) ⟶ *billig**er*** (cheaper)
schnell (quickly) ⟶ *schnell**er*** (more quickly)

If a word has one syllable, an umlaut is added to the a, o or u unless one is already there.

Examples

alt (old) ⟶ *ält**er*** (older)
groß (big) ⟶ *größ**er*** (bigger)
früh (early) ⟶ *früh**er*** (earlier)

Some comparatives do not follow this pattern. They have their own particular forms.

Examples
gut (good) ⟶ *besser* (better)
hoch (high) ⟶ *höher* (higher)
viel (much) ⟶ *mehr* (more)

Additional exercises

1 Use *werden* to form the future of the following sentences.

(*a*) Ich fahre zur Tagung nach Bonn.
(*b*) Mein Chef schreibt einem Kollegen in London.
(*c*) Wir nehmen das Doppelzimmer im Rheinhotel.
(*d*) Die Konferenz findet in Berlin statt.
(*e*) Arbeiten Sie in Kanada?
(*f*) Du wohnst in Dresden, nicht wahr?
(*g*) Die Sekretärin ruft Mr Clark.
(*h*) Studiert ihr in Tübingen?
(*i*) Ich hole Frau Berger vom Bahnhof ab.
(*j*) Gerhard und ich besuchen die Firma Klett.

2 How would you give the following instructions in German?

(*a*) Please reserve a single room in the Hotel Coenen.
(*b*) Write to John Evans.
(*c*) Phone the sales manager.
(*d*) Thank Arnold Graf for his letter.
(*e*) Visit Anglia Chemicals on Monday.
(*f*) Fly to Frankfurt on Thursday.
(*g*) Change trains in Frankfurt.
(*h*) Collect Frau Gruber from the station.
(*i*) Show me the room, please.
(*j*) Please fill in the form.

3 Complete the adjectives with the correct ending.

(*a*) Dort drüben ist meine neu______ Chefin.
(*b*) Erich ist ein gut______ Lagerverwalter.
(*c*) Unsere englisch ____ Kollegen kommen am Montag.
(*d*) Das ist ein schön ____ Zimmer.
(*e*) Seine deutsch ____ Sekretärin heißt Elke.
(*f*) Der Gasthof hat eine herrlich ____ Aussicht.
(*g*) Ich suche ein billig ____ Hotel.

(*h*) Unser Hotel hat einen sonnig ____ Garten.
(*i*) Er arbeitet bei einer groß ____ Firma.
(*j*) Wir wohnen in einer modern ____ Stadt.

4 Replace the words for 'the' with a suitable word for 'this' or 'these'.

(*a*) **Der** Bahnhof ist sehr modern.
(*b*) **Die** Kollegen sind aus Japan.
(*c*) **Das** Zimmer hat eine herrliche Aussicht.
(*d*) Ich möchte **den** alten Dom besichtigen.
(*e*) Wir fahren mit **dem** Bus in die Stadtmitte.
(*f*) Bitte füllen Sie **das** Formular aus.
(*g*) **Die** Zimmer nehmen wir.

5 Replace the words in bold with the correct German word for 'it'.

(*a*) **Das Zimmer** ist reserviert.
(*b*) **Die Tagung** findet nächste Woche statt.
(*c*) **Der Zug** ist um neun Uhr in Erfurt.
(*d*) **Die Firma** ist in Regensburg.
(*e*) **Das Hotel** ist billig aber bequem.
(*f*) **Der Bus** fährt in die Stadtmitte.

6 Are the following statements true or false?

(*a*) Bonn ist groß, aber Köln ist größer.
(*b*) Das Matterhorn ist hoch, aber Snowdon ist höher.
(*c*) Der Bus fährt schnell, aber der Zug fährt schneller.
(*d*) Ein Mercedes kostet viel, aber ein Rolls Royce kostet mehr.
(*e*) Ein Fünfhundertmarkschein ist gut, aber ein Hundertmarkschein ist besser.
(*f*) Sechs Uhr ist früh, aber sieben Uhr ist früher.
(*g*) Bier ist billig, aber Whisky ist billiger.
(*h*) Duisburg ist schön, aber Heidelberg ist schöner.
(*i*) Die Universität Heidelberg ist alt, aber die Universität Oxford ist älter.
(*j*) Eine Jugendherberge (*youth hostel*) ist angenehm, aber ein Luxushotel ist angenehmer.

Kapitel 5

Essen und Trinken

Im Hotel Coenen

Herbert Walter, Lotte Meyer and Ewald Weidmann arrive at the *Hotel Coenen* to take Michael Newby to one of their factories and then out to lunch.

Walter	Guten Morgen, Herr Newby. Wie geht es Ihnen?
Newby	Gut danke. Ich war gestern abend sehr müde, aber jetzt geht es mir besser. Ich habe sehr gut geschlafen.
Walter	Sie kennen schon meine Kollegin Frau Meyer und meinen Kollegen Herrn Weidmann?
Newby	Ja, wir haben uns in Altrincham kennengelernt. Tag, Frau Meyer. Tag, Herr Weidmann. Es freut mich sehr, Sie wiederzusehen.
Meyer	Gleichfalls, Herr Newby. Haben Sie eine gute Reise gehabt?
Newby	Ziemlich gut, danke.
Weidmann	Sind Sie zum ersten Mal in Mönchengladbach?
Newby	Ja.
Walter	Wir können Ihnen später die Sehenswürdigkeiten der Stadt zeigen, wenn Sie Lust haben.
Newby	Ja, das möchte ich gerne. Ich habe so viel von Mönchengladbach gehört. Bekannte von mir sind oft auf Geschäftsreise hier gewesen.

Practice

1 Complete the phrases in column A with an appropriate phrase from column B, according to the information in the dialogue.

Column A	*Column B*
Es freut Michael Newby,	sehr gut geschlafen.
Michael Newby hat	nicht mehr müde.
Michael Newby ist	Herrn Weidmann und Frau Meyer wiederzusehen.
Michael Newby kennt schon	zum ersten Mal in Mönchengladbach.
Heute ist Michael Newby	Frau Meyer und Herrn Weidmann.

2 Meeting people

You are being taken out to lunch by your German host on the first day of a business trip to Hamburg. You are collected at your hotel in Hamburg. What do you say in German?

Gastgeber	Guten Morgen, Herr/Frau . . . Wie geht es Ihnen?
Sie	(Say you had a good sleep last night. You were very tired but now you are better.)
Gastgeber	Sie kennen meinen Kollegen, Herrn Desch?
Sie	(Say yes, you met at a conference in Munich. Say you are pleased to meet Herr Desch again.)
Desch	Gleichfalls, Herr/Frau . . . Haben Sie eine gute Reise gehabt?
Sie	(Say thank you, you have had quite a good one.)
Gastgeber	Sind Sie zum ersten Mal in Hamburg, Herr/Frau . . . ?
Sie	(Say yes.)
Gastgeber	Wir zeigen Ihnen später die Sehenswürdigkeiten, wenn Sie wollen.
Sie	(Say you would like that, you have heard so much about Hamburg.)

3 You are visiting a company in Gladbeck and wish to stay at the *Hotel Schultenhof*. You have a few queries. Answer them by consulting the brochure on the following page.

(*a*) Sie möchten ein Zimmer mit Bad. Geht das?
(*b*) Wo können Sie parken?
(*c*) Am Dienstag abend wollen Sie mit Kollegen im Restaurant essen. Geht das?
(*d*) Wann ist das Restaurant nicht geöffnet?

Hotel-Restaurant-Café

mit dezenter Unterhaltungsmusik

Unser Hotel ist durchgehend (warme Küche) geöffnet von 11.30 bis 1.00 Uhr nachts.

– Kein Ruhetag -

Wir sind ein Spezialitäten-Restaurant (Wild, Fisch und Balkan-Grill). Internationale und bürgerliche Küche. Ausreichender Parkplatz am Hause. Hotelzimmer mit Dusche, WC und Telefon. (Gäste-Garagen und Hofparkplatz). 2 Bundeskegelbahnen im Hause. Wir erwarten Sie – und danken für Ihren Besuch.

Familie Šime Jović

Restaurant mit gemütlichen Sitznischen

Im Restaurant

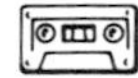

Some time later Walter, Meyer, Weidmann and Newby arrive at the restaurant of the Hotel Schultenhof. Here is part of their conversation.

Walter Guten Tag, wir haben einen Tisch für vier Personen reserviert.
Kellner Ja. Bitte schön, meine Herrschaften. Dort in der Ecke.
Walter Können Sie mir bitte die Speise- und Getränkekarte bringen? Wir möchten bestellen.

Kellner	Ja, sofort . . .
Walter	(*Später*) Haben Sie schon gewählt? . . . Herr Ober.
Kellner	Bitte sehr, was darf es sein?
Newby	Ich möchte bitte Wiener Schnitzel mit Röstkartoffeln, Gemüse und Salat.
Kellner	Möchten Sie eine Vorspeise?
Newby	Ja, vielleicht doch. Bringen Sie mir einen kleinen Salat.
Kellner	Und zu trinken?
Newby	Eine Flasche Bier, bitte, König Pilsener. Und als Nachtisch bekomme ich einen Pfannkuchen mit Zitrone. Das schmeckt mir immer so gut.
Meyer	Ich möchte gern eine Ochsenschwanzsuppe, und als Hauptgericht rheinischen Sauerbraten mit Kartoffeln und Rotkohl. Das esse ich sehr gern. Als Nachspeise bekomme ich Apfelkompott.
Kellner	Und was trinken Sie?
Meyer	Ein Glas Weißwein.

Practice

1 Ordering food and drink

You are in a restaurant in Germany with a colleague. You order your meal. What do you say in German?

Sie	(Ask if they have a table for two.)
Kellner	Jawohl, mein Herr/gnädige Frau. Dort in der Ecke.
Sie	(Ask for the menu and wine list.)
Kellner	Ich bringe sie sofort . . .
Sie	(Tell the waiter you have made your choice.)
Kellner	Bitte sehr, was darf es sein?

Sie	(Say you would like oxtail soup for starters, followed by Wiener Schnitzel with roast potatoes, vegetables and salad.)
Kellner	Etwas zu trinken dazu?
Sie	(Say you would like a glass of red wine.)
Kellner	Möchten Sie eine Nachspeise?
Sie	(Say yes, you would like a sundae and a cup of coffee.)

2 Study this menu, then get together with other students and make up conversations similar to the one in exercise 1.

Hotel zum Adler

Speisekarte

Vorspeisen
Französische Zwiebelsuppe
Ochsenschwanzsuppe

Hauptgerichte
Süßsaure Matjes
mit Salzkartoffeln und
Tomaten

Heilbutt mit
Kartoffelpüree und Salat

Wiener Schnitzel
mit Pommes frites, Champignons und Erbsen

Pfeffersteak (sehr scharf)
mit Reis und Karotten

Nachspeisen
Obstsalat
Birne Hélène
Gemischtes Eis
Haselnußcreme

3 Study this dialogue between a waiter and a couple in a café.

Kellner Bitte sehr, was darf es sein?
Sie Ich möchte eine Tasse Kaffee bitte.
Er Eine Tasse Zitronentee für mich bitte.
Kellner Sonst noch etwas?
Sie Ich möchte auch ein Stück Apfelstrudel.
Er Und ich bekomme ein Vanille-Eis bitte.
Er (*Später*) Darf ich bitte die Rechnung haben?
Kellner Also, ein Kaffee, das kostet DM 3,50, ein Tee DM 3,50, ein Stück Apfelstrudel DM 4,00 und ein Eis DM 3,10. Alles zusammen macht das vierzehn Mark und zehn Pfennig.
Er Also, bitte schön.
Kellner Ich danke Ihnen.

Now make up similar conversations in small groups, using words from the list of prices below.

Preistafel

Warme Getränke

Tasse Kaffee	2,80
Tasse Tee mit Zitrone oder Milch	2,80
Tasse Espresso	2,90
Tasse Kakao	2,90

Torten und Kuchen

Erdbeertorte mit Sahne	4,00
Apfelstrudel	3,50
Schokoladenkuchen	3,00
Käsekuchen	3,00

Eisspezialitäten

Vanille, Erdbeer, Schokolade	4,00
Gemischtes Eis mit Sahne	5,00
Eis-Kaffee	5,00
Schwarzwaldbecher	6,50

4 Listening comprehension

Some colleagues are making their choice of food before settling down to a working breakfast. What is each of them ordering?

	Coffee	Tea	Egg	Roll	Toast	Marmalade	Juice	Yoghurt	Ham	Cheese
Schröder										
Richter										
Friedrich										
Weber										
Taylor										
Schneider										

5

While working in Germany you go to the *Enka Restaurant* one day for your lunch. Tell your colleagues back at work about the restaurant and your meal. The following words might be useful:

- wählen, die Speisekarte bringen, die Getränkekarte, Weißwein, Rotwein, bekommen, trinken, schmecken
- als Vorspeise/Hauptgericht/Nachspeise, die Rechnung, kosten

Remember to use the perfect tense.

Speiseplan

ENKA ENKA ENKA ENKA
Enka
Kasino

vom	9 – 13 November
MONTAG	Geflügelcremesuppe Gefüllte Wirslngroulade mit magerer Fleischfüllung Würfelkartoffeln Eichblatt-Radieschensalat Dessert
DIENSTAG	Suppe Wiener Schnitzel mit Pommes frites Farmer Salat Dessert
MITTWOCH	Suppe Geschnitzeltes Schweinefleisch in Rahmsauce m. Champignons und Tomaten, Gabelspaghetti Kopf- u. Selleriesalat Dessert
DONNERSTAG	Grüne Erbsensuppe mit geräucherter Bockwurst Brötchen Schokoladencreme mit Birne
FREITAG	Selleriecremesuppe Bayrischer Leberkäse mit Spiegelei, Röstkartoffeln Chinakohl- u. Wachsbrechbohnensalat Dessert

6 Writing/sustained speaking

Sie haben gerade mit Kollegen gegessen. Hier ist Ihre Rechnung.

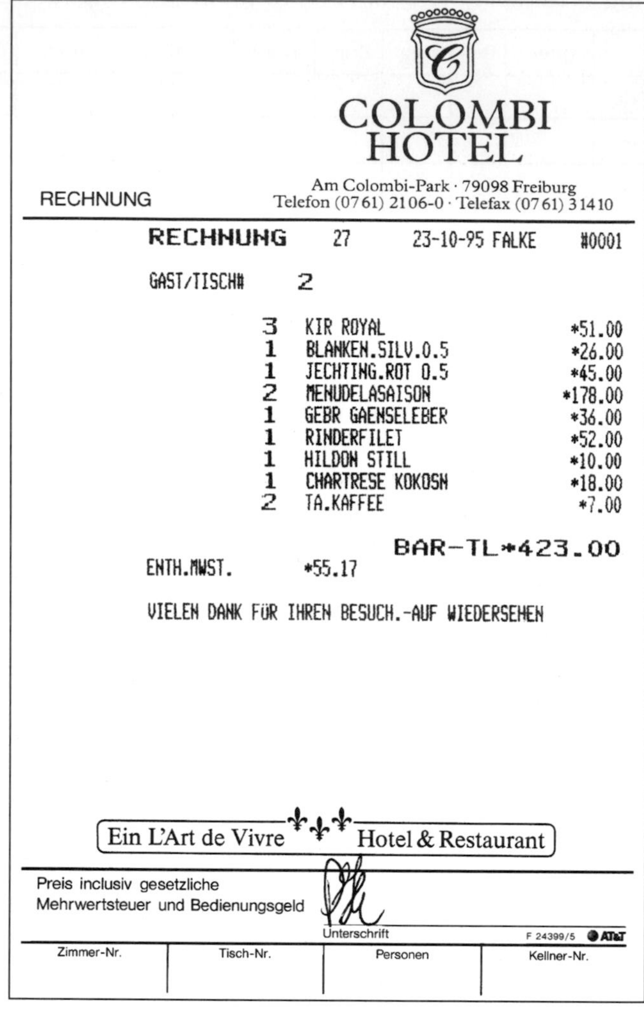
COLOMBI HOTEL

RECHNUNG

Am Colombi-Park · 79098 Freiburg
Telefon (07 61) 21 06-0 · Telefax (07 61) 3 14 10

RECHNUNG 27 23-10-95 FALKE #0001

GAST/TISCH# 2

3	KIR ROYAL	*51.00
1	BLANKEN.SILV.0.5	*26.00
1	JECHTING.ROT 0.5	*45.00
2	MENUDELASAISON	*178.00
1	GEBR GAENSELEBER	*36.00
1	RINDERFILET	*52.00
1	HILDON STILL	*10.00
1	CHARTRESE KOKOSN	*18.00
2	TA.KAFFEE	*7.00

BAR-TL*423.00

ENTH.MWST. *55.17

VIELEN DANK FÜR IHREN BESUCH.-AUF WIEDERSEHEN

Ein L'Art de Vivre Hotel & Restaurant

Preis inclusiv gesetzliche Mehrwertsteuer und Bedienungsgeld

Unterschrift

F 24399/5 AT&T

Zimmer-Nr.	Tisch-Nr.	Personen	Kellner-Nr.

(*a*) Wie heißt der Restaurant?
(*b*) Welche Nummer hat Ihr Tisch?
(*c*) Sie haben Gänseleber gegessen. Was hat sie gekostet?
(*d*) Ihre Kollegin hat Rinderfilet gegessen. Was hat es gekostet?
(*e*) Wieviel Wein haben Sie bestellt?
(*f*) Wieviele Kollegen haben Kaffee getrunken?
(*g*) Was ist der Gesamtbetrag?
(*h*) Was enthält der Gesamtbetrag?
(*i*) Wie hoch ist die Mehrwertsteuer?
(*j*) Verstehen Sie den Satz „Vielen Dank für Ihren Besuch"?

7 Employees at the tourist office in Munich often have to answer tourists' questions on restaurants. Pair up each query with the correct answer.

(*a*) Wo kann man etwas typisch Bayerisches essen?	Von der eigenen Metzgerei
(*b*) Sind alle diese Restaurants jeden Tag geöffnet?	Komödianten Stadl, Pamukkale Restaurant
(*c*) Wo muß man reservieren?	Komödianten Stadl
(*d*) In welchem Restaurant kann man auch kegeln?	Pamukkale Restaurant
(*e*) Wo kauft das Restaurant Haxnbauer das Fleisch für seine Gäste?	Haxnbauer
(*f*) Wo gibt es Live-Musik?	Pamukkale Restaurant

Spezialist für Seafood aus aller Welt

Nähe Maximilianstr.
täglich ab 18 Uhr
Montag Ruhetag

80539 München
Stollbergstraße 11
Tel.: 0 89/29 87 87
Fax 0 89/22 31 66

PAMUKKALE
★★★★★★★★
RESTAURANT
Türkische Spezialitäten · Pils-Pub - Kegelbahnen - Biergarten
täglich 11.30-01 Uhr · Di. Ruhetag! · bis 23.30 Uhr warme Küche
jeden Fr. u. Sa. Live-Musik u. Bauchtanz · ausreichend Parkplätze
Kreuzhofstraße 10 – 81476 München · Telefon 0 89 /

KomödiantenStadl

Wenn Sie gute Küche lieben (bayerisch od. international), gute Drinks und Live-Musik, dann ist hier der richtige Platz für Sie. In unserer original bayerischen Atmosphäre können Sie typische Münchner Lebensart genießen. Immer ein Erlebnis für Besucher ebenso wie für Münchner. Unsere Spezialität: Gerichte vom »heißen Stein«.
Von 19.00 Uhr bis 3.00 Uhr morgens geöffnet.

Bräuhausstr. 8 · Tel. 29 74 03 · direkt hinterm Hofbräuhaus

...weltbekannt und sehenswert
Haxnbauer
München
GRILLRESTAURANT · HAXNBRATEREI · PARTYSERVICE
Viele Schmankerl, köstliche Grillspezialitäten vom Spieß und Rost. Immer frische Apfelkücherl. Bier vom Faß. Gepflegten Wein. Eigene Metzgerei. Gemütliche schöne alte Stuben. Nebenzimmer und Festsaal. Bitte reservieren Sie rechtzeitig.
Tel.: 22 19 22 / 29 53 09 Münzstr.8 und Sparkassenstr.

8 You have been sent by your company to gain work experience in their German office. This morning your boss left you this list of tasks to be done in his absence.

Flughafen-Reisebüro anrufen und Flugkarte bestellen.
Meine Marketing-Zeitschrift kaufen.
Hotelzimmer in Bremen für nächsten Dienstag reservieren.
Mit dem Restaurant Schloßhof sprechen und Tisch für zwei Leute für 13.00 reservieren.
Export-Formulare ausfüllen.
Brief an die Firma Mann GmbH tippen.
Zum Bahnhof fahren und Hans Schoening um 11.45 abholen.

You have had a busy morning. On your boss's return give him a quick resume of your activities.
Example Ich *habe* das Flughafen-Reisebüro *angerufen.* Dann habe ich . . .

9 Read the following sentences:

In meiner Freizeit gehe ich gern ins Kino, und ich höre auch gern Musik. Ich treibe sehr gern Sport. Im Winter spiele ich Fußball, aber im Sommer gehe ich lieber schwimmen.

Now write similar sentences saying what your hobbies are. Use the words *gern* and *lieber* and some of these words and phrases:

- in die Oper/ins Theater/in die Stadt/auf die Jagd/zur Disko gehen
- ins Ausland/nach Schottland fahren
- zu Hause bleiben, fernsehen, Radio hören, basteln
- Tischtennis/Golf spielen, trampen, zelten, das Auto reparieren

10 Reading

A friend asks you for some information on the Piazza Romana. Answer her questions.

Die PIAZZA ROMANA ist von 12.00 – 15.00 Uhr und von 18.00 – 24.00 Uhr geöffnet. Lassen Sie sich über die Telefon Nr. 7 rechtzeitig einen Tisch reservieren. Ob Sie elegant oder leger kommen – Sie sind uns immer liebe Gäste.

Französisches Flair (im Sommer auch auf der Straße) offeriert *Die Brasserie*. Aber natürlich auch alles, was genußvoll satt macht: Fisch und Fleisch vom Grill, zahlreiche verschiedene Delikatessen und Leckerbissen von unserem Gourmet-Buffet (die leckeren Desserts nicht gezählt), Weine und Champagner offen. Bedienen Sie sich oder lassen Sie sich bedienen. Wir richten uns ganz nach Ihren Wünschen.

Die Brasserie ist durchgehend von 12.00 bis 01.00 Uhr nachts geöffnet. Ab 07.00 Uhr finden Sie in unserer Brasserie unser berühmtes Frühstücksbuffet. Damit fängt der Tag wahrhaftig elysisch an.

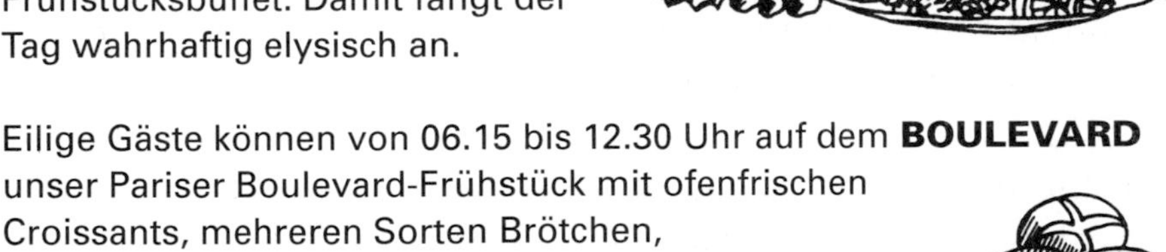

Eilige Gäste können von 06.15 bis 12.30 Uhr auf dem **BOULEVARD** unser Pariser Boulevard-Frühstück mit ofenfrischen Croissants, mehreren Sorten Brötchen, frischgepreßtem Orangensaft und duftendem Kaffee einnehmen.

(*a*) Wann kann man in der Piazza Romana essen?
(*b*) Wo kann man im Sommer sitzen, wenn man in der Brasserie ißt?
(*c*) Was kann man dort trinken?
(*d*) Kann man dort um Mitternacht essen?
(*e*) Um wieviel Uhr kann man auf dem Boulevard frühstücken?
(*f*) Was kann man dort essen? Und trinken?

11 Listening comprehension

During the course of their meal Michael Newby and his colleagues talk about the restaurant and different cuisine. Listen to their conversation and then answer these questions in English.

(*a*) What does Newby say about the restaurant and the food? Give as much information as possible.
(*b*) Why is Newby so familiar with German cuisine?
(*c*) What was significant about his first trip to Linz?
(*d*) Why does Walter prefer German to English food?
(*e*) For what does Weidmann have a weakness?

12 Reading comprehension

Das Essen

Die drei Mahlzeiten in Deutschland sind das Frühstück, das Mittagessen und das Abendessen. Zum Frühstück ißt man normalerweise Brötchen, Brot oder Toast mit Butter, Marmelade oder Honig. Viele Leute essen auch ein gekochtes Ei. Zu trinken bekommt man Tee oder Kaffee. Oft nimmt man ein zweites Frühstück zur Arbeit mit, wenn man sehr früh zu Hause gefrühstückt hat.

Für viele Leute ist das Mittagessen die Hauptmahlzeit. Dann ißt man entweder zu Hause oder in einem Restaurant, wenn man in der Stadt arbeitet. Das Mittagessen besteht aus einer Suppe, danach Fleisch und Gemüse und oft, aber nicht immer, aus einem Nachtisch, zum Beispiel Eis, Pudding oder Obst.

Mittags hört man sehr oft im Büro den Ausdruck 'Mahlzeit'. Das sagt man zu seinen Kollegen und Kolleginnen, wenn man essen geht, und wenn man zurückkommt.

Nachmittags trinkt man oft Tee oder Kaffee, aber auch Mineralwasser, manchmal auch mit Kuchen.

Das Abendessen ist etwas einfacher. Man ißt zum Beispiel Brot mit Schinken, Käse, Wurst, Salat oder Tomaten. Abends trinken viele Deutsche ein Glas Wein oder Bier.

Using the information in the text you have just read, write a short summary in German on the following topics:

(*a*) Essen im Büro
(*b*) Essen zu Hause
(*c*) Trinken.

Summary

Useful phrases

1	Saying how you feel	Ich bin sehr müde Es geht mir jetzt besser
2	Asking if someone is known	Sie kennen schon Herrn/Frau . . .?
3	Saying you have already met	Wir haben uns in . . . kennengelernt
4	Saying you are pleased to see someone again	Es freut mich sehr, Sie wiederzusehen
5	Saying something would be nice	Das möchte ich gerne
6	Saying you have heard a lot about a place	Ich habe viel von . . . gehört
7	Saying you have a table reserved for four	Ich habe einen Tisch für vier Personen reserviert
8	Asking for the menu and wine list	Können Sie mir bitte die Speise- und Getränkekarte bringen?
9	Asking what somebody would like	Was darf es sein?
10	Ordering food and drink	Ich möchte bitte Wiener Schnitzel mit Röstkartoffeln, Gemüse und Salat Bringen Sie mir einen kleinen Salat Ich bekomme einen Pfannkuchen Ich möchte gern eine Ochsenschwanzsuppe Ein Glas Weißwein/eine Flasche Bier, bitte
11	Asking if someone likes the food	Wie schmeckt Ihnen das Essen? Schmeckt es Ihnen?
12	Saying you like the food	Das Essen schmeckt prima

13 Asking for the bill

Die Rechnung, bitte!
Darf ich bitte die Rechnung haben?
Zahlen, bitte!

Language forms

1 The perfect tense

This tense expresses what has happened in the past. It is formed by using the present tense of *haben* or *sein* with the past participle of a particular verb.

The past participle of regular (weak) verbs is formed by replacing the *en* of the infinitive with a *t* and placing *ge* at the beginning.

Examples
hören (to hear) → ***ge**hör**t*** (heard)
kaufen (to buy) → ***ge**kauf**t*** (bought)

Irregular (strong) verbs have their own individual past participles.

Examples

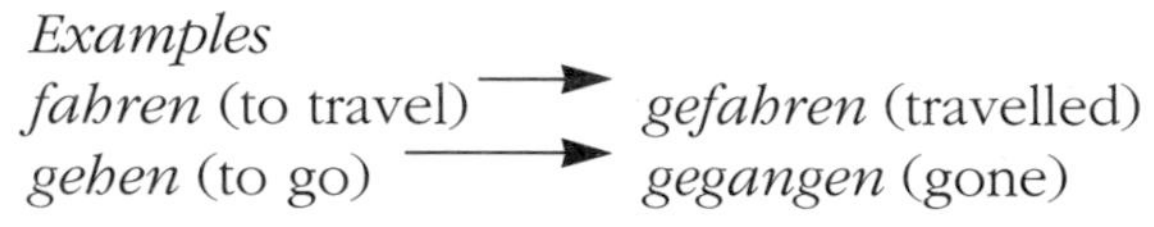

fahren (to travel) → *gefahren* (travelled)
gehen (to go) → *gegangen* (gone)

(a) Verbs with *haben*

Verbs that do not suggest movement or a change of state (see (b) below) form the perfect tense with *haben*. They follow the pattern of *hören*.

hören (to hear)

ich habe gehört (I have heard)	*wir haben gehört* (we have heard)
du hast gehört (you have heard)	*ihr habt gehört* (you have heard)
Sie haben gehört (you have heard)	*Sie haben gehört* (you have heard)
er/sie/es hat gehört (he/she/it has heard)	*sie haben gehört* (they have heard)

Examples

*Ich **habe** so viel von Mönchengladbach **gehört**.*
I have heard so much about Mönchengladbach.

*Wir **haben** Radio **gehört**.*
We have been listening to the radio.
(Literally: We have heard the radio.)

(b) Verbs with *sein*

Sein is used to form the perfect tense of verbs that suggest movement from one place to another (e.g. *gehen* – to go, *kommen* – to come) or a change of state (e.g. *aufwachen* – to wake up, *werden* – to become).

These verbs follow the pattern of *fahren* below, although they will not necessarily form their past participle in exactly the same way.

fahren (to travel)

ich bin gefahren (I have travelled)	*wir sind gefahren* (we have travelled)
du bist gefahren (you have travelled)	*ihr seid gefahren* (you have travelled)
Sie sind gefahren (you have travelled)	*Sie sind gefahren* (you have travelled)
er/sie/es ist gefahren (he/she/it has travelled)	*sie sind gefahren* (they have travelled)

Examples

Der Einkaufsleiter ***ist*** *gestern nach Stuttgart* ***gefahren***.
The sales manager travelled to Stuttgart yesterday.

(*Note* In English the auxiliary verb 'have' can be omitted from the past tense, as in the example here. In German the auxiliary verbs *haben* and *sein* cannot be omitted.)

Die Vertreterin ***ist*** *schon* ***gegangen***.
The representative has already gone.

(c) The perfect tense of separable verbs.

With separable verbs the past participle follows the prefix.

Examples

ausfüllen (to fill in) → *aus**gefüllt*** (filled in)
ankommen (to arrive) → *an**gekommen*** (arrived)

Ich ***habe*** *das Formular* ***ausgefüllt***.
I have filled in the form.

Der Zug ***ist*** *schon* ***angekommen***.
The train has already arrived.

With *compound verbs,* only the second verb has a past participle. The first verb remains in the infinitive.

Example

kennenlernen → kennen**gelernt**

Ich ***habe*** *den Personalchef in Freiburg* ***kennengelernt***.
I got to know the personnel manager in Freiburg.

(d) Verbs beginning with *be/emp/ent/er/ge/ver/zer* or ending with *ieren*

The past participles of these verbs do not have *ge* at the beginning.

Examples

empfehlen (to recommend) → *empfohlen* (recommended)
passieren (to happen) → *passiert* (happened)

Ich habe dem Einkaufsleiter das Hotel Imperial empfohlen.
I recommended the Hotel Imperial to the senior buyer.

Was ist passiert?
What has happened?

2 Personal pronouns

Nominative	*Accusative*	*Dative*
ich	mich	mir
du	dich	dir
Sie	Sie	Ihnen
er	ihn	ihm
sie	sie	ihr
es	es	ihm
man (*one*)	einen	einem
wir	uns	uns
ihr	euch	euch
Sie	Sie	Ihnen
sie	sie	ihnen

(a) Accusative pronouns

These are used when they are the object of a verb, or if they follow an accusative preposition.

Examples

Ich hole ***ihn*** *vom Flughafen ab.*
I'll fetch him from the airport.

Dieser Brief ist für ***dich*** *.*
This letter is for you.

(b) Dative pronouns

These are used when they are the indirect object of a verb, or if they are used with dative verbs or dative prepositions.

Examples

Ich schreibe ***ihr*** *einen Brief.*
I'll write her a letter.

Wir fliegen mit ***ihm*** *nach New York.*
We're flying with him to New York.

The following expressions also take the dative:

Wie geht es ***Ihnen?*** *Es geht* ***mir*** *gut, danke.*
How are you? I'm well, thanks
(Literally: How goes it to/for you? It's going well to/for me, thanks.)

Schmeckt es ***Ihnen?*** *Es schmeckt* ***mir*** *gut.*
Do you like the food? I like it.
(Literally: Does it taste good to you? It tastes good to me.)

3 Word order in subordinate clauses

As we have already seen in Chapter 2, the verb is the second element in a sentence (i.e. main clause).

However, in a subordinate clause the verb must go to the end of the clause. Subordinate clauses can easily be recognised because they begin with linking words which include:

als (when)	*seit* (since)
daß (that)	*weil* (because)
ob (whether)	*wenn* (if, whenever)

obgleich
obwohl } (although)

Examples

Wir können Ihnen später die Sehenswürdigkeiten zeigen, ***wenn*** *Sie Lust* ***haben***.
We can show you the sights later if you wish. (Literally: if you have the desire.)

Ich habe ihn in Tübingen kennengelernt, ***als*** *ich dort Student* ***war***.
I got to know him in Tubingen when I was a student there.

4 Gern/lieber

(a) gern

This means 'gladly', 'willingly', 'with pleasure'. When used with a verb, it indicates that someone *likes* doing something.

Examples

Ich esse gern Wiener Schnitzel.
I like to eat Viennese veal cutlet.

Wir gehen gern ins Theater.
We like going to the threatre.

(b) lieber

This is the comparative of *gern* and means 'more gladly', 'more willingly', 'with greater pleasure'. It is used to express preference.

Examples

Ich esse gern Wiener Schnitzel, aber ich esse lieber Fisch.
I like to eat Viennese veal cutlet but I prefer fish.

Wir gehen gern ins Theater, aber wir gehen lieber ins Kino.
We like going to the theatre but we prefer going to the cinema.

Additional exercises

1 Answer these questions with a full sentence in the perfect tense, using *haben*. Assume that the answer is always 'yes'.

(*a*) Haben Sie eine gute Reise gehabt?
(*b*) Hast du Mrs Richards die Sehenswürdigkeiten gezeigt?
(*c*) Hat er gut geschlafen?
(*d*) Hat sie Herrn Desch auf der Tagung in München kennengelernt?
(*e*) Haben wir einen Tisch reserviert?

2 Answer these questions with a full sentence in the perfect tense, using *sein*. Assume that the answer is always 'yes', and add the information in brackets.

(*a*) Ist der Zug angekommen? (It arrived at 11 o'clock)
(*b*) Ist Frau Kern schon gegangen? (She went on Friday)
(*c*) Wann ist der Bus abgefahren? (It left at 9.30)
(*d*) Sind Sie zum ersten Mal in Essen? (I've often been here on business)
(*e*) Wann sind die Kollegen aus England gekommen? (They came yesterday)

3 Replace the nouns in brackets with an accusative pronoun.

(*a*) Bitte holen Sie (Dr. Leitner) vom Flughafen ab.
(*b*) Dieser Brief ist für (Frau Grün).
(*c*) Haben Sie ein Zimmer für (meinen Mann und mich) reserviert?
(*d*) Hast du (die Kollegen aus Kanada) gesehen?
(*e*) Ich fahre nicht ohne (den Dolmetscher).

4 Replace the nouns in brackets with a dative pronoun.

(*a*) Zeigen Sie (Frau Springer) die Sehenswürdigkeiten.
(*b*) Schreiben Sie (dem Einkaufsleiter) einen Brief.
(*c*) Die Firma hat (dem Einkaufsleiter und mir) ein Hotel empfohlen.
(*d*) Guten Tag, Dr. Fried. Wie geht es (Dr. Fried)?
Danke, es geht (Dr. Fried) gut.
(*e*) Der Dolmetscher fährt mit (dem Betriebsleiter und der Einkaufsleiterin).

5 Link the two clauses with the word in brackets.

(*a*) Ich reserviere ein Zimmer im Hotel Reinhard.
(weil) Es ist ein gutes Hotel.
(*b*) Wir gehen nicht ins Kino.
(weil) Wir haben keine Lust.
(*c*) Sie hat ihn in Wien kennengelernt.
(als) Er war auf einer Tagung dort.
(*d*) Herr Newby hat mich gefragt.
(ob) Ich fliege am Montag nach Hamburg.
(*e*) Sie können mir die Sehenswürdigkeiten zeigen.
(wenn) Ich komme im August nach Wien.

6 Say you like the first thing mentioned, but you prefer the second.

Example Ich gehe ins Kino. Ich gehe ins Theater.
Ich gehe gern ins Kino, aber ich gehe lieber ins Theater.

(*a*) Ich trinke Tee. Ich trinke Kaffee.
(*b*) Ich esse Apfelstrudel. Ich esse Erdbeertorte.
(*c*) Ich schreibe Briefe. Ich telefoniere.
(*d*) Ich fahre mit der Bahn. Ich fliege.
(*e*) Ich spreche Englisch. Ich spreche Deutsch.

Kapitel 6

Einkaufen

Auf der Straße

Charles Stewart, a computer programmer on business in Düsseldorf, begins to look for presents for his family. He asks the way to the *Königsallee* and enquires about shops.

Programmierer	Entschuldigen Sie bitte. Ich suche die Königsallee.
Passant	Ach, die Kö ist gar nicht so weit. Gehen Sie hier geradeaus bis zur Kreuzung, dann nehmen Sie die erste Straße links, die Steinstraße. Sie führt direkt zur Kö.

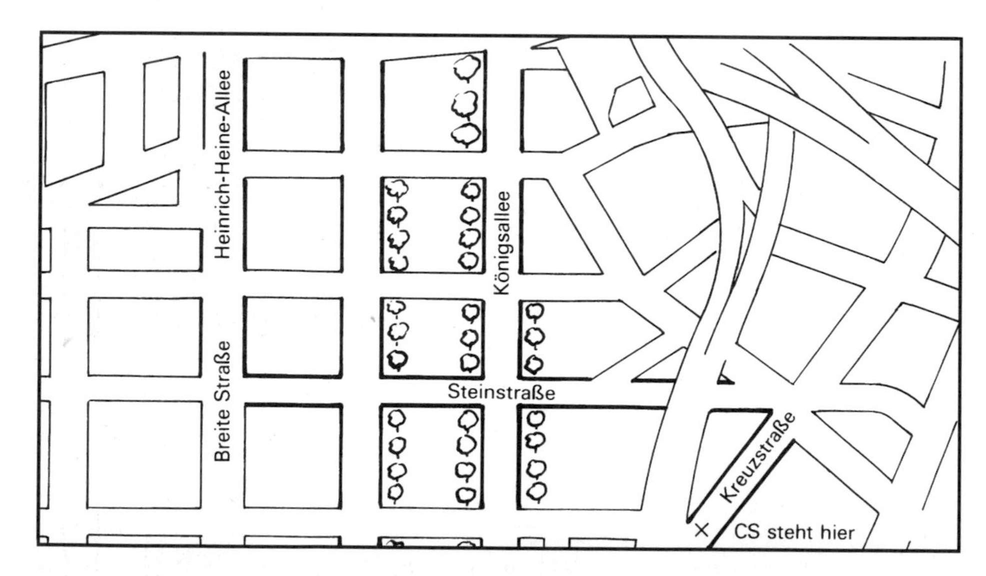

Programmierer	Herzlichen Dank. Können Sie mir auch ein Geschäft in der Königsallee empfehlen, wo ich Geschenke für meine Familie in England kaufen kann?
Passant	Was für Geschenke wollen Sie denn?

Programmierer Na ja, Parfüm, T-Shirts, Bücher . . . Ich weiß nicht genau.

Passant Also, bei Habitus finden Sie bestimmt das Richtige. Dann gibt's noch Benetton und das Modehaus Heinemann, wenn Sie Bekleidung suchen. Parfüm kriegen Sie in der Parfümerie Douglas. Auf der Kö gibt's sehr viele Geschäfte. Es gibt da fast alles.

Programmierer Aber die Preise . . .

Passant Das stimmt. Wenn Sie etwas billiger einkaufen wollen, dann müssen Sie in ein Kaufhaus oder in die Altstadt gehen.

Programmierer Die Altstadt, wie komme ich am besten dahin?

Passant Gehen Sie die Steinstraße entlang, bis Sie zur Kö kommen. Dann gehen Sie immer noch geradeaus bis zur Breite Straße. Dort geht es rechts weiter. Gehen Sie die Breite Straße hinunter bis in die Heinrich-Heine-Allee. Die Altstadt liegt dann auf der linken Seite.

Programmierer Ich danke für Ihre Hilfe.

Passant Nichts zu danken. Gern geschehen. Auf Wiedersehen.

Die Königsallee

Practice

1 Asking the way

You want to buy some presents for your family before travelling home from a congress in Innsbruck. You stop someone in the street to ask the way. What do you say in German?

Sie	(Say 'excuse me', you want to buy presents for your family in England. Ask if they can recommend a suitable shop.)
Passant	Was für Geschenke wollen Sie denn eigentlich?
Sie	(Say you do not yet know exactly, possibly books, perfume or T-shirts.)
Passant	Also, in den kleinen Gassen in der Altstadt finden Sie viele Geschenkartikel in den Andenkengeschäften.
Sie	(Say you know, but they are rather expensive.)
Passant	Dann müssen Sie zur Maria-Theresien-Straße gehen. Dort finden Sie Warenhäuser. Die verkaufen fast alles.
Sie	(Ask what is the best way to get there.)
Passant	Also, gehen Sie hier die Universitätsstraße entlang bis zum Burggraben. Gehen Sie dann links bis zur Kreuzung. Rechts sehen Sie den Verkehrsverein und links die Maria-Theresien-Straße.
Sie	(Thank the passer-by for their help.)
Passant	Nichts zu danken.

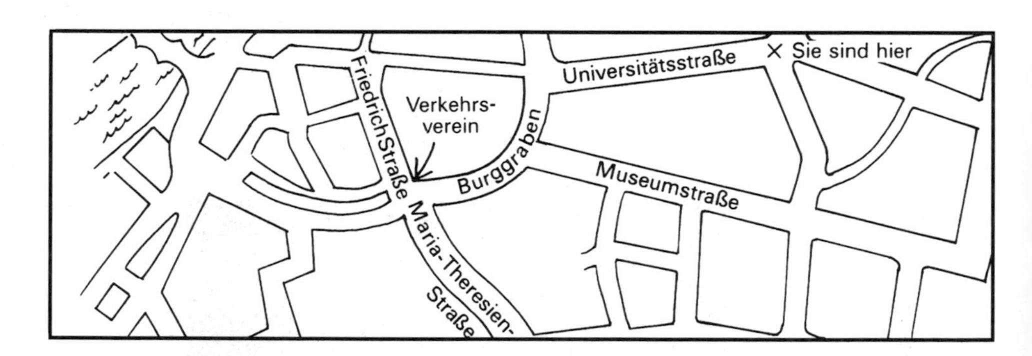

Information
Normalerweise sind deutsche Geschäfte und Postämter montags bis freitags zwischen 08.00 oder 09.00 und 18.30 offen. Samstags müssen alle Geschäfte um 14.00 schließen, aber am ersten Samstag im Monat dürfen sie bis 18.00 offen bleiben (sogenannter 'langer Samstag').

2 You are visiting Germany. While in the tourist office you hear the following conversations. With the help of the map complete the gaps with a suitable word or phrase.

Berliner Straße
Dortmunder Weg
Münchener Straße
Hochstraße
Hamburger Straße
× Sie sind hier

(*a*) Ich suche die Hochstraße. Wie komme ich am besten dahin?
Gehen Sie hier geradeaus, dann nehmen Sie die erste Straße ______________.

(*b*) Ich suche die Berliner Straße. Wie komme ich am besten dahin?
Gehen Sie hier ____________ bis zur ____________ . Dort gehen Sie nach ____________ und dann nehmen Sie die ____________.

(*c*) Wie komme ich am besten zur Münchener Straße, bitte?
Gehen Sie ____________ bis zur ____________, dann gehen Sie die Hamburger Straße ______________ . Die Münchener Straße ist ______________ rechts.

(*d*) Now answer the following question:
Wie komme ich am besten zum Dortmunder Weg?

Verkehrsamt, Reitnau

3 While visiting Germany an English businessman wishes to buy a few presents for his family and colleagues. Look at the advertisements below, then say what a German colleague might reply to his queries.

Example Für meine Frau will ich eine Halskette kaufen.
Dann gehen Sie am besten zum Schmuckfachgeschäft Mössing.

(*a*) Für meine Frau will ich eine Flasche Parfüm kaufen.
(*b*) Für meine Sekretärin will ich ein Buch kaufen.
(*c*) Wo kann ich für meinen Chef eine Flasche Weißwein kaufen?
(*d*) Für meine Tochter möchte ich ein schönes Geschenk kaufen.
(*e*) Für meinen Sohn möchte ich eine Uhr kaufen.
(*f*) Für meine Kamera muß ich einen Film kaufen.

Im Warenhaus

Bob Nicholson, a British sales representative, is in a German department store buying presents for his family at the end of a business trip. Read the conversation and then answer the questions that follow.

Verkäufer	Guten Tag. Was darf es sein?
Vertreter	Wo bekomme ich Parfüm?
Verkäufer	Das bekommen Sie in der Parfümerie im zweiten Stock.
Vertreter	Danke. Wo ist die Rolltreppe?
Verkäufer	Da vorne, sehen Sie?
Vertreter	Ach ja. Und in welchem Stock finde ich T-Shirts?
Verkäufer	Die gibt's hier im Erdgeschoß.
	(*Einige Minuten später*)
Verkäuferin	Kann ich Ihnen helfen?
Vertreter	Danke. Ich weiß nicht, ob mein Sohn lieber ein T-Shirt oder Spielzeug möchte.
Verkäuferin	Wie alt ist denn Ihr Sohn?
Vertreter	Er wird dieses Jahr sechs Jahre alt.
Verkäuferin	Vielleicht interessiert ihn ein T-Shirt mit Micky Maus-Motiv?
Vertreter	Das gibt's auch in Deutschland! Das gefällt ihm ganz bestimmt. Also, ich nehme eins. Welche Farben haben Sie denn?
Verkäuferin	Wir haben blau, gelb, schwarz und braun.
Vertreter	Ja gut, ein blaues bitte.
Verkäuferin	Welche Größe hat Ihr Sohn?
Vertreter	Ach, das ist schwer. Ungefähr sechsundzwanzig *inches*. Ich habe hier eine Umrechnungstabelle. Mal sehen . . . Also, das sind ungefähr 65 Zentimeter.
Verkäuferin	Das hier wird ihrem Sohn sicher passen.
Vertreter	Was kostet es bitte?
Verkäuferin	Siebzehn Mark neunzig.
Vertreter	Bitte schön. Und für meine Tochter will ich eine Kassette kaufen. Wo ist die Musikabteilung, bitte?
Verkäuferin	Die finden Sie im dritten Stock.
Vertreter	Vielen Dank.

Practice

1 Answer the following questions:

(*a*) Wo im Warenhaus kann man Parfüm kaufen? Und T-Shirts?
(*b*) Was weiß der Vertreter nicht?
(*c*) Wie alt ist der Sohn des Vertreters im Moment?
(*d*) Welches Motiv gefällt seinem Sohn?
(*e*) Was kostet das T-Shirt?
(*f*) Welche deutsche Größe trägt der Sohn?
(*g*) Warum geht der Vertreter zum dritten Stock?

2 Buying presents

You are in a German department store buying a T-shirt and a toy (*das Spielzeug*). What do you say in German?

Verkäuferin	Was darf es sein?
Sie	(Say you want to buy a T-shirt for your daughter.)
Verkäuferin	Wie alt ist Ihre Tochter denn?
Sie	(Say she will be thirteen this year.)
Verkäuferin	Vielleicht gefällt ihr dieses T-Shirt mit Lufthansa-Motiv. Das ist etwas typisch Deutsches. Wir haben es in verschiedenen Farben . . . rot, schwarz, weiß, gelb und blau.
Sie	(Say you like the red T-shirt.)
Verkäuferin	Welche Größe, bitte?
Sie	(Say you would like 81 centimetres and ask what it costs.)
Verkäuferin	18 Mark.
Sie	(Ask where you can buy a toy for your son.)
Verkäuferin	Im zweiten Stock.
Sie	(Thank the assistant and say goodbye.)
Verkäuferin	Auf Wiedersehen.

3 Study this plan of a German department store (*Kaufhaus*) and then answer the following questions.

Erdgeschoß

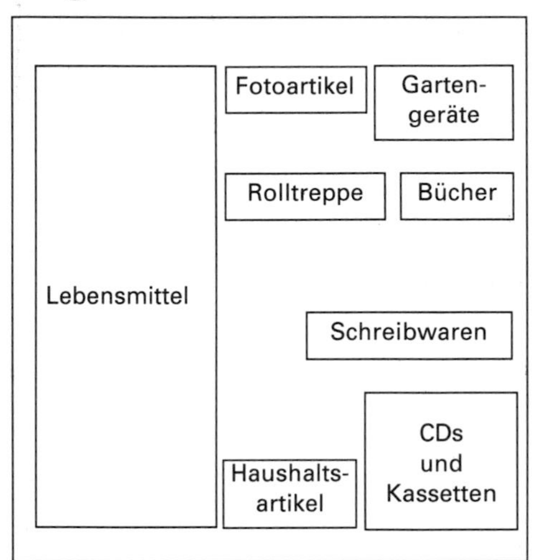

Erster Stock

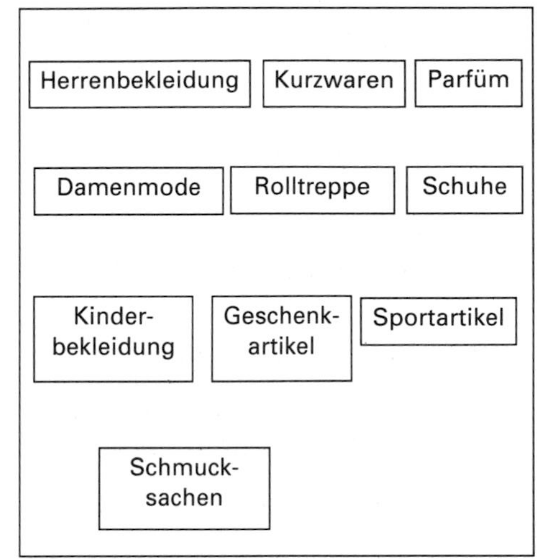

Zweiter Stock

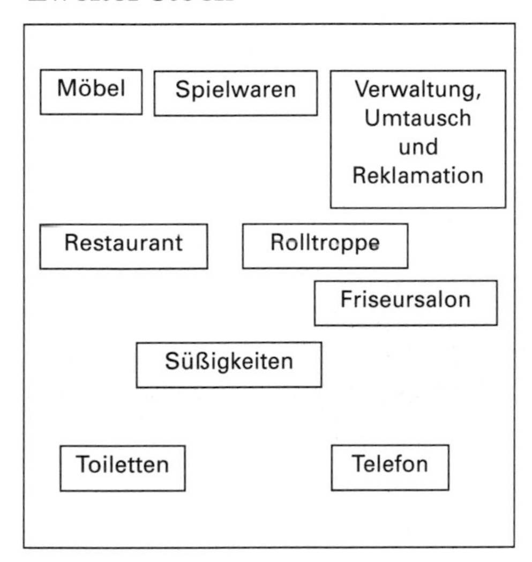

(*a*) In welchem Stock ist die Parfümerie?
(*b*) In welchem Stock sind CDs und Kassetten?
(*c*) Wo ist das Restaurant?
(*d*) Wo kann man telefonieren?
(*e*) In welchem Stock kann man einen Film kaufen?
(*f*) Wo ist die Schreibwarenabteilung?
(*g*) Wo findet man Lebensmittel?
(*h*) In welchem Stock ist die Musikabteilung?

4 Listening comprehension

Some colleagues have been on a shopping trip in the lunch break and are comparing notes on their return to the office. What has everyone done and how much did they pay?

5

You are helping a colleague choose a new camera and you see this advert. You tell your friend about it. Answer her questions.

(*a*) Haben diese beiden Kameras Autofocus?
(*b*) Haben beide Kameras automatischen Filmtransport (vorwärts/rückwarts)?
(*c*) Muß man für diese Kameras ein Blitzlicht kaufen?
(*d*) Gibt es eine Tasche dazu?

Minolta RIVA Zoom Pico, kompakte KB-Sucherkamera mit Autofocus, Motor-Zoom-Objektiv 38 - 60 mm, Belichtungsautomatik, DX-Codierung, motor. Filmtransport vorwärts/rückwärts, eingeb. Blitz

269,–

Braun trend Zoom 105, vollautomatische KB-Sucherkamera, elektronischer Verschluß mit Mehrfachbelichtungsmöglichkeit, Infrarot-Autofocus-System, LCD-Display, motor. Filmtransport vorwärts/rückwärts, eingeb. Blitz, inkl. Tasche und Lithiumbatterie

349,–

6 Im Lebensmittelgeschäft

Read the following dialogue, then using the adverts below and other vocabulary you have learnt make up similar dialogues with a partner.

- Guten Tag. Was darf es sein?
- ▪ Ich möchte ein Kilo Pfirsiche bitte.
- Zwei Mark siebenundsiebzig bitte. Sonst noch etwas?
- ▪ Ja, zehn Eier bitte. Was macht das?
- Eine Mark neunundneunzig und eine Mark neunundzwanzig. Das macht drei Mark achtundzwanzig.
- ▪ Bitte schön.
- Danke.

Remember also the following phrases:

- Ich danke für Ihre Hilfe.
- Nichts zu danken.
- Kann ich Ihnen helfen?
- Vielen Dank.
- Sie wünschen?
- Wieviel möchten Sie?

Pillsbury Knack & Back
6 Country-Brötchen oder 4 Baguette Brötchen je 300 g, 6 Buttermilch-Brötchen, Original franz. Croissants oder Pizzateig je 250 g oder Hörnchen 200 g
je Dose

Bauer Butterkäse
sahnig mild, weichschnittig
45% Fett i. Tr.
100 g
-.99

riesig einkaufen

Exquisa Käsekuchensnack
70-g-Packung
real,- Preis
0,98

Livio Pflanzenöl
1-Liter-Dose
real,- spezial
2,98

Uncle Bens Fix
für Fleischpfannen
versch. Sorten
je 320/340/350-g-Glas
2.99

Ital. Pfirsiche
HKL.I
1 kg
2.77

Holl. / Span. Tomaten
HKL.I
1 kg
1.79

Iglo 15 Fischstäbchen
tiefgefroren
450-g-Packung
2.99

Zott Starfrucht Joghurt
3,8% Fett oder
Leicht
1,5% Fett
versch. Sorten
je 200-g-Becher
-.79

7 Answer the following questions:

Example Gefällt Ihnen dieses Parfüm?  Ja, es gefällt mir gut.

(*a*) Gefällt Ihnen diese Kassette? 

(*b*) Paßt mir dieses T-Shirt? 

(*c*) Gefällt Ihnen dieses Zimmer? 

(*d*) Passen Ihnen diese Schuhe? 

(*e*) Wie geht es ihm? 

(*f*) Schmeckt Ihnen der Wein? 

8 How do you say in German:

(*a*) I am looking for a food shop.
(*b*) I don't know exactly.
(*c*) Thank you for your help.
(*d*) My daughter will be seven years old this year.

9 Listening comprehension

While waiting for a business colleague at the reception desk of a large German hotel you can hear the receptionist dealing with the queries of other guests. Listen to her instructions to each of the visitors, then using the map on page 97 establish the destination of each one and complete the table below. *Gast A* has been done for you.

	Destination	
Person	**Number (1–6)**	**Place**
Gast A	1	Tourist information office
Gast B		
Gast C		
Gast D		
Gast E		

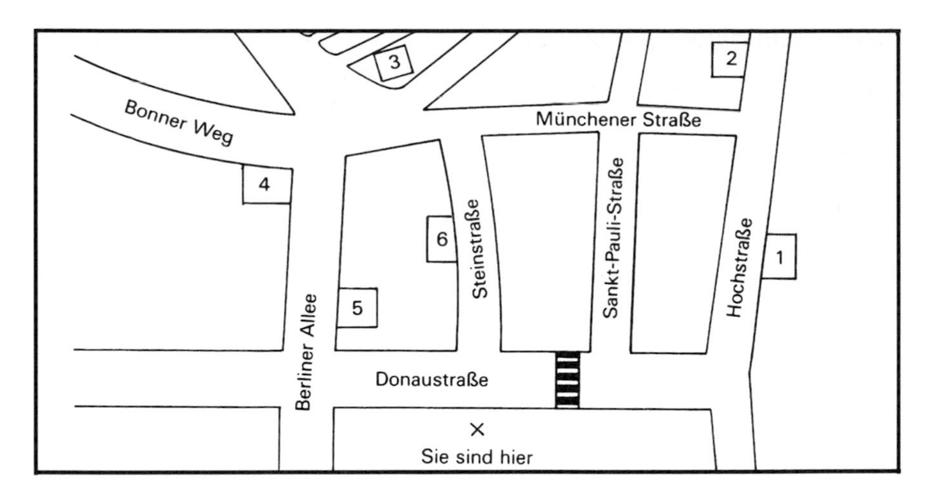

Summary

Useful phrases

1 Asking the way to somewhere	Ich suche die Königsallee Wo ist die . . . ? Wie komme ich am besten zur Münchener Straße? Wie komme ich am besten dahin?
2 Saying you don't exactly know	Ich weiß nicht genau
3 Asking about prices	Ist das nicht sehr teuer?
4 Thanking someone for his/her help	Ich danke für Ihre Hilfe
5 Asking on what floor something can be found	In welchem Stock finde ich . . . ?
6 Saying you are only looking	Ich schau nur Ich schau mich nur um
7 Asking where a particular product is sold	Wo kann ich bitte Parfüm kaufen?
8 Asking if you can help	Kann ich Ihnen helfen?

Language forms

1 The verb *wissen*

Wissen is a commonly used irregular verb. It means 'to know' in the sense of knowing facts, but not in the sense of knowing people or places. The latter meaning is communicated by the verb *kennen*, which is regular in the present tense. *Wissen* is conjugated as follows:

wissen (to know)

ich weiß	wir wissen
du weißt	ihr wißt
Sie wissen	Sie wissen
er / sie / es } weiß	sie wissen

2 *Werden* without accompanying verb

(a) Meaning 'will/shall be'

We have already met *werden* as an auxiliary verb used to form the future tense (Chapter 4). When used this way it means 'will' or 'shall'. When used on its own it can have the meaning 'will be' or 'shall be'.

Examples

Die Firma ***wird*** *dieses Jahr hundert Jahre alt.*
The firm will be 100 years old this year.

Sie ***wird*** *bald Mutter.*
She will soon be a mother.

(b) Meaning 'to get' or 'to become'

On its own, *werden* can also mean 'to get' or 'to become'.

Example

Es ***wird*** *dunkel.*
It's getting dark.

3 Demonstrative pronouns

These are the words for 'the' used as an emphatic way of saying 'he/him', 'she/her', 'it' and 'they/them'. They match the gender of the noun to which they refer.

Examples

Wo ist ***der Geschäftsführer****, bitte?* ***Der*** *ist im Moment nicht hier.*
Where is the managing director, please? He's not here at the moment.

Der Automat *funktioniert nicht. Ist* ***der*** *kaputt?*
The machine doesn't work. Is it broken?

Die Gegend *gefällt mir.* ***Die*** *ist wirklich schön.*
I like the area. It's really beautiful.

Wo ist ***mein Gepäck****, bitte?* ***Das*** *steht in der Eingangshalle.*
Where is my luggage, please? It's in the foyer.

Die Zimmer *sind prima.* ***Die*** *nehmen wir.*
The rooms are excellent. We'll take them.

4 Indefinite pronouns

These mean 'one' in the following senses:

I like those sweaters. I'll take *one.*
Only *one* of the candidates can get the job.

It has the following forms:

	Masculine	*Feminine*	*Neuter*
Nominative	einer	eine	eins
Accusative	einen	eine	eins
Dative	einem	einer	einem

Examples

Die Kandidaten sind alle gut, aber nur ***einer*** *bekommt die Stelle.*
The candidates are all good but only one will get the job.

Ich kaufe ***eine*** *von diesen Zeitschriften.*
I'll buy one of these magazines.

Diese T-Shirts gefallen mir. Ich nehme ***eins.***
I like these T-shirts. I'll take one.

5 Interrogative adjectives

These mean 'which' or 'what' as shown in the following examples:
I don't know *which* company will get the contract.
What size does your son wear?

In German the words for 'which' or 'what' are formed in the same way as 'the'.

	Masculine	*Feminine*	*Neuter*	*Plural*
Nominative	welcher	welche	welches	welche
Accusative	welchen	welche	welches	welche
Dative	welchem	welcher	welchem	welchen

Examples

In ***welchem*** *Stock finde ich T-Shirts?*
On what floor will I find T-shirts?

Welche *Größe trägt Ihr Sohn?*
What size does your son wear?

Welches *Hotel empfehlen Sie?*
Which hotel do you recommend?

6 Numerals 100+

100 – hundert
101 – hunderteins
102 – hundertzwei
103 – hundertvier
usw. (etc.)

200 – zweihundert
201 – zweihunderteins
202 – zweihundertzwei
203 – zweihundertdrei
usw.

300 – dreihundert
400 – vierhundert
usw.

1000 – tausend (This is used in the same way as *hundert* above)
2399 – zweitausenddreihundertneunundneunzig

Additional exercises

1 *Wissen* or *kennen?* Which of these verbs would you use if you had to say the following in German?

(*a*) She knows Spain quite well.
(*b*) You know it makes sense!
(*c*) Do you know Frau Schneider?
(*d*) He thinks he knows everything!
(*e*) I don't know Munich at all.

2 Are the following statements true or false?

(*a*) In England wird es im Sommer um 16 Uhr dunkel.
(*b*) Die Preise werden höher, wenn Produkte knapp (*short*) werden.
(*c*) Im Jahr 1997 wird Hongkong chinesisches Territorium.
(*d*) Nach acht Uhr wird es neun Uhr.

3 Replace the word or words in brackets by the correct form of the demonstrative pronoun (*der, die, das* etc.).

(*a*) (Die Geschäftsleiterin) ist im Moment nicht hier.
(*b*) (Das Parfüm) gefällt mir.
(*c*) Sie findet (ihn) nicht freundlich.
(*d*) (Die Schuhe) passen ihm nicht.
(*e*) (Die Kassetten) finden Sie im dritten Stock.

(*f*) Von (Robert) hört man nichts.
(*g*) Für (meinen Sohn) möchte ich eine Uhr kaufen.

4 Complete the gaps with the appropriate word for 'one'.

(*a*) Ich kaufe ______ von diesen Uhren.
(*b*) Die Pullover gefallen mir. Ich nehme ______.
(*c*) ______ von den Vertretern kommt aus Liechtenstein.
(*d*) ■ Ich suche ein Hotel.
• Sie finden ______ um die Ecke.
(*e*) Du fährst nicht gern mit dem Luftkissenboot (*hovercraft – neuter*), oder?
Das stimmt. Aber im Sommer fahre ich mit ______.

5 Add the appropriate endings to the word for 'which' in the following sentences.

(*a*) Welch ____ Hotel empfehlen Sie?
(*b*) Welch ____ Mann ist der Lagerverwalter?
(*c*) Welch ____ Bücher lesen Sie?
(*d*) Welch ____ Wein trinken Sie?
(*e*) Welch ____ Firma besuchen Sie?
(*f*) Von welch ____ Haltestelle fährt der Bus ab?
(*g*) Mit welch ____ Zug fahre ich nach Ulm?

6 How do you write the following numbers in German?

(*a*) 220 (*c*) 310 (*e*) 561 (*g*) 677 (*i*) 1423
(*b*) 172 (*d*) 978 (*f*) 436 (*h*) 789 (*j*) 7593

Kapitel 4–6

Zusätzliche Aufgaben

1 Role-play

(*a*) You have invited a German-speaking person to the company where you work. When your visitor arrives, welcome him/her, ask if this is their first visit to this country, and ask what method of transport they used.

(*b*) Take the part of a German visitor to a UK company. Answer your host's questions, saying that you often come to England, you flew to London, then got the train and a taxi.

2 Here is an extract from the brochure of the Grange Hotel which you know quite well. A German business contact has been recommended to stay there and asks you a few questions on its facilities. Answer his questions in German.

Useful vocabulary: *auf dem Land, fünf Kilometer von . . . entfernt, der Farbfernseher, der Radiowecker, der Fön, die Selbstbedienung, der Parkplatz, die Autobahn.*

> Set in rural surroundings, the Grange Hotel provides extensive on-site car parking and is conveniently situated for the motorway network (about eight kilometres away) and is only five kilometres from the city centre. Whether you are looking for a place to hold business meetings, spend an enjoyable weekend or celebrate a special occasion, you will always find a warm welcome here.
>
> All 45 rooms are en-suite, with telephone, colour TV, radio alarm, hairdryer and hospitality tray. We have a choice of snack self-service restaurant facilities (open 6.00–21.30) or you can eat at your leisure in the Beaujolais restaurant (open 7.00–10.00 for breakfast and 18.30–22.30 for evening meals). Our French chef naturally specialises in French cuisine, but we also offer an excellent English menu.
>
> The four purpose-built meeting rooms can accommodate up to 60 guests for board meetings, training courses and social functions.
>
> Prices: Single room: £60.00, Double/twin room £70.00

(*a*) Wieviele Zimmer hat das Hotel?
(*b*) Ist das Hotel mit dem Auto gut zu erreichen?
(*c*) Kann man dort gut parken?
(*d*) In England sehe ich gern fern. Ist das möglich?
(*e*) Wie ist das Essen dort?
(*f*) Um wieviel Uhr kann man frühstücken?
(*g*) Wieviele Konferenzzimmer hat das Hotel und für wieviele Leute?
(*h*) Was kostet das Hotel pro Übernachtung?
(*i*) Ist das Hotel in der Stadtmitte?
(*j*) Wie sind die Zimmer?

3 You are describing some British dishes to German visitors who are in the UK for the first time. They ask about Yorkshire pudding and fish and chips.
Useful phrases: *Das schmeckt wunderbar, das ist typisch englisch/schottisch, das Mehl, die Milch, das Ei, der Fisch, die Pommes frites, der Eierteig.*

4 You are due to go to Germany and need to book accommodation for three colleagues and yourself.

(*a*) Send a fax to the Hotel Stern asking for whatever rooms you require from 17–20 October.
(*b*) Later in the day the following fax arrives back from the hotel:

Ihre Faxreservierung: 17–20 Oktober
Leider sind wir an den Tagen geschlossen – wegen notwendiger Reparaturen. Am 27.10 läuft alles wie normal. Möchten Sie eine Reservierung ab 27. machen?
Mit freundlichen Grüßen
Klein
Hotel Stern

(*c*) Send a fax in reply. Thank them for their fax, state that you have to be in Germany on 17 October and ask if they can recommend another hotel.

5 A colleague is thinking of going on holiday to Germany and asks you to tell her about the contents of an information sheet she has found. Summarise the text for her.

Unterkunft in Deutschland
Deutschland bietet eine Unterkunft für jeden Geschmack. Geschäftsleute, Familien und Studenten können alle eine geeignete Unterkunft finden. In fast allen Städten gibt es Hotels, Appartements, Ferienwohnungen, Privatzimmer, Campingplätze und auch Jugendherbergen.

Die großen Luxushotels bieten oft sehr viel, zum Beispiel, mehrere Restaurants, Konferenz- oder Tagungsräume, Garagen, eigenes Schwimmbad, Sauna und Fitneßräume. Hier kann man bequem und mit allem Komfort wohnen beziehungsweise arbeiten. Es gibt auch billigere Hotels und Gasthöfe. Man kann Halb- oder Vollpension nehmen oder in einem Hotel garni wohnen.

6 On your holidays you have visited a restaurant which was highly recommended by a German colleague. Send your colleague a postcard giving details of what you ate, and your impressions of the restaurant.

7 (*a*) One of your colleagues at the German company where you are working is leaving, and you go shopping to buy her a present. You see a few possibilities shown in the adverts below. What do the adverts say about the items?

(*b*) **Pair-work**

(i) You look for other presents and you ask a shop assistant for ideas. Ask also about quality, guarantee and price.

(ii) Take the part of a shop assistant and offer advice to the customer.

Useful phrases: *eine Vase, eine Lampe, eine Uhr, eine Garantie, guter Qualität, garantiert für ein Jahr, eine gute Auswahl, welche Farbe möchten Sie?*

8 You are shopping in a German department store. The store has various special offers which are announced from time to time over the tannoy. Make a note of what goods are being announced, their prices and how long the offers will last, under the following headings: Goods on offer, Price, Valid until.

9 While waiting in a queue at a German supermarket you notice that some people are spending a lot of money. How much do they spend?

10 You are near Limbach on business and find some publicity material about the district. Read the following extract from it, then translate it into English for the colleague with whom you are travelling.

> Limbach ist ein kleines Dorf im Odenwald mit 2200 Einwohnern. Es liegt im südlichen Odenwald. Wegen der guten Luft ist es ein Luftkurort. Zu allen Zeiten, im Sommer wie im Winter, im Frühling wie im Herbst, kommen deshalb viele Leute von Mannheim und Frankfurt, um dort in der guten Luft Spaziergänge zu machen.
> Limbach selbst liegt in einem Tal. Von weitem sichtbar ist die schöne Kirche mitten im Dorf. Obgleich Limbach in einem Tal liegt, ist es dennoch 500 Meter über dem Meeresspiegel. Auf den Höhen ringsum sind Wälder und Felder. Es gibt deshalb viele Bauernhöfe. Limbach besitzt auch zwei Fabriken. Limbach hat auch einen Arzt, einen Zahnarzt und eine Apotheke. Brot und Brötchen und Kuchen kann man in den zwei Bäckereien kaufen, und Fleisch in den zwei Metzgereien. Es gibt auch zwei Lebensmittelgeschäfte, sowie eine Gärtnerei, wo man Obst und Gemüse kaufen kann, und eine Gaststätte natürlich. Zeitungen und Zeitschriften findet man im Schreibwarengeschäft. Für die Schönheit sorgen zwei Friseure.

11 **Pair-work**

You are temporarily working in a hotel. Your colleague is reading out new bookings to you. Make a note of them in a booking sheet with the following headings: Name, Zimmer, Datum, Beherbergung.

12 You are taking part in a German holiday house-exchange system. Write a description of your house for the brochure.

Useful vocabulary: *das Einfamilienhaus, das Reihenhaus, der Bungalow, das Apartment, unten, oben, in der Stadtmitte, in einem Vorort, auf dem Land.*

13 You have a lot to do at work and need some help from your colleague. Using the imperative form (see page 63), get your colleague to:

(*a*) Phone the managing director with your travel plans
(*b*) Get you a flight from Hamburg to Bremen for next Monday
(*c*) Send a fax (which you give to your colleague) to the bank
(*d*) Reserve the conference room for tomorrow at 13.00
(*e*) Buy your newspaper
(*f*) Fill in the travel forms
(*g*) Make a cup of coffee
(*h*) Write a letter to Bennen GmbH to confirm you will be coming on 5 September.

Kapitel 7

Krankheit und Unfall

Beim Arzt

While on a visit to a German factory, a British engineer, John Faulkner, feels unwell. He phones a doctor's surgery, and then goes to see the doctor.

Ingenieur Guten Tag. Ich möchte einen Termin für heute.
Stimme Moment bitte. Ich sehe mal nach . . . Können Sie um elf Uhr zwanzig kommen?
Ingenieur Ja, das geht.
Stimme Wie ist Ihr Name, bitte?
Ingenieur Ich heiße Faulkner.
Stimme Wie schreibt man das?
Ingenieur F-A-U-L-K-N-E-R. Ich bin Engländer.
Stimme Haben Sie einen Krankenschein?
Ingenieur Ich habe einen internationalen Krankenschein.
Stimme Bringen Sie den bitte mit.
(*Beim Arzt*)
Arzt Was fehlt Ihnen denn?
Ingenieur Ich habe Kopfschmerzen und Magenweh.
Arzt Wie lange haben Sie diese Schmerzen schon?
Ingenieur Seit gestern abend. Ich habe gar nicht geschlafen.
Arzt Machen Sie bitte den Mund auf . . . Hm, Ihr Hals ist rot und Sie haben auch Fieber . . . Sie haben eine Grippe. Sie müssen sofort ins Bett.

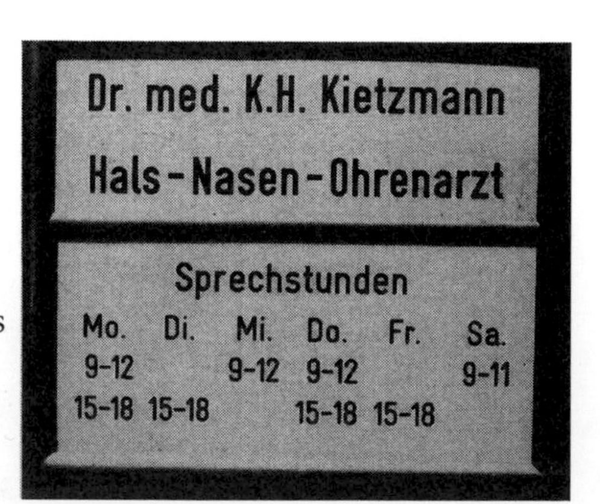

Ingenieur	Ach, wie ärgerlich!
Arzt	Ich gebe Ihnen ein Rezept. Eine Apotheke finden Sie gleich um die Ecke.
Ingenieur	Also, danke, Herr Doktor. Soll ich gleich bezahlen, oder schicken Sie mir die Rechnung?
Arzt	Die Sprechstundenhilfe erledigt das alles.
Ingenieur	Danke. Auf Wiedersehen.
Arzt	Auf Wiedersehen. Gute Besserung!

Practice

1 Answer the following questions on the engineer's visit to the doctor.

(*a*) What time is the engineer's appointment?
(*b*) What is he asked to do after giving his name?
(*c*) What documentation is he asked to bring with him?
(*d*) What pains does he complain of to the doctor?
(*e*) Since when has he had these pains?
(*f*) What sort of night did he have?
(*g*) What is the doctor's diagnosis?
(*h*) What does he tell the engineer to do?
(*i*) What is the engineer's reaction?
(*j*) Where is the nearest chemist?
(*k*) Who deals with the question of the doctor's payment?

2 Making an appointment

The morning after arriving in Vienna to attend an international conference, you feel quite unwell. You decide to see a doctor. You phone the surgery to arrange an appointment. What do you say in German?

Sie	(Say you would like an appointment for today.)
Stimme	Moment mal, bitte . . . Können Sie um elf Uhr dreißig kommen?
Sie	(Say that is fine.)
Stimme	Wie ist Ihr Name, bitte?
Sie	(Say your name is . . . You are English.)
Stimme	Buchstabieren Sie das bitte.
Sie	(Spell out your name.)
Stimme	Haben Sie eine Krankenversicherung?
Sie	(Say you have a medical insurance record card [E111].)
Stimme	Bringen Sie den bitte mit.

3 Study the following conversation and phrases, then in pairs make up similar conversations.

- ● Wie geht es Ihnen?
- ■ Nicht gut.
- ● Was fehlt Ihnen?
- ■ Ich habe Halsschmerzen.
- ● Wie lange haben Sie diese Schmerzen schon?
- ■ Seit Montag.
- ● Am besten gehen Sie zur Apotheke/zum Arzt.
- ■ Ja, das mache ich.
- ● Also, gute Besserung.
- ■ Danke.

<table>
<tr><td rowspan="3">Mein</td><td colspan="2">Kopf
Mund
Hals
Rücken
Herz
Finger</td><td rowspan="5">tut</td><td rowspan="6">weh.</td></tr>
<tr><td>linker
rechter</td><td>Arm
Fuß</td></tr>
<tr><td>linkes
rechtes</td><td>Bein
Ohr
Auge</td></tr>
<tr><td rowspan="2">Meine</td><td>linke</td><td>Hand</td></tr>
<tr><td colspan="2">Nase</td></tr>
<tr><td>Meine</td><td>Arme
Füße
Beine
Ohren
Augen</td><td colspan="2">tun</td></tr>
</table>

Ich habe	Kopfschmerzen. Magenschmerzen. Zahnschmerzen. einen Schnupfen/eine Erkältung. Halsschmerzen. Husten. Durchfall. Ohrenschmerzen.

Information
Wenn ein Arbeitnehmer in der Bundesrepublik krank ist, muß er am dritten Tag zum Arzt (oder zur Ärztin) gehen. Wenn er wirklich nicht arbeiten kann, bekommt er vom Arzt eine Arbeitsunfähigkeitsbescheinigung (*sick note*). Diese Bescheinigung muß der Arbeitnehmer dann seinem Arbeitgeber geben. Der Arbeitgeber muß den Lohn für sechs Wochen weiterzahlen, wenn der Arbeitnehmer so lange krank bleibt.

In der Apotheke

John Faulkner goes to the chemist to collect his medicine.

Apothekerin Guten Morgen. Kann ich Ihnen helfen?
Ingenieur Guten Morgen. Ich war gerade beim Arzt. Ich habe hier ein Rezept, bitte sehr.
Apothekerin Danke . . . Also, Sie bekommen Tabletten.
Ingenieur Wie oft muß ich die einnehmen?
Apothekerin Drei Tabletten pro Tag.
Ingenieur Muß ich die vor oder nach dem Essen einnehmen?
Apothekerin Nehmen Sie immer vor dem Essen *eine* Tablette mit etwas Wasser ein.
Ingenieur Und wie lange muß ich die einnehmen?
Apothekerin Bis sie alle aufgebraucht sind. Und wenn die Schmerzen nicht nachlassen, informieren Sie den Arzt sofort.
Ingenieur Also gut, ich danke Ihnen.
Apothekerin Nichts zu danken. Ich wünsche Ihnen gute Besserung.

Practice

1 At the chemist

After seeing the doctor in Germany, you go to the chemist with a prescription. What do you say in German?

Apotheker Guten Morgen. Kann ich Ihnen helfen?
Sie (Good morning. I have just been to the doctor. I have a prescription. Here it is.)
Apotheker Danke . . . Also, Sie bekommen Tabletten.
Sie (How often do I have to take them?)
Apotheker Drei Tabletten täglich.
Sie (Before or after meals?)
Apotheker Immer vor dem Essen, mit etwas Wasser.
Sie (How long do I have to take them?),
Apotheker Bis sie alle aufgebraucht sind. Und wenn es Ihnen nicht besser geht, gehen Sie sofort wieder zum Arzt.
Sie (Thank you. How much do the tablets cost?)
Apotheker Acht Mark zehn.

2 Everyone at your place of work in Germany seems to be ill. Match each of the symptoms to one of the advertisements below and on the opposite page.

(*a*) Mein Kopf tut weh, und ich bin erkältet.
(*b*) Mein Magen tut weh, und ich muß die ganze Zeit zur Toilette laufen.
(*c*) Meine Nase ist verstopft. Ich kann kaum atmen.
(*d*) Ich bin ganz nervös und kann nicht schlafen.
(*e*) Mein Hals tut weh.
(*f*) Ich huste Tag und Nacht.
(*g*) Ich habe eine Augenentzündung.

Schnupfenspray in die Nase sprühen, und dann ist die Nase nicht mehr verstopft. Es hilft schnell und wirkt für Stunden. Am Tag und bei Nacht.

Bei Kopfschmerzen, Zahnschmerzen, Grippe usw. nehmen Sie 2–3 Tabletten.

Durchfall?

Dieses besonders gute Mittel bringt Ihnen rasche Besserung. Besonders gut bei Reise- und Sommerdurchfällen

Schmidt-Medikamente

Unsere Hustentropfen befreien Sie schnell von Hustenreiz. Mit oder ohne Wasser einnehmen.

frubienzym® HALSSCHMERZ TABLETTEN

Hopfen-Tabletten

Nur 2 Tabletten bringen Ihnen gesunden Schlaf und ruhige Nerven.

3 Listening comprehension

While waiting for your prescription at the chemist you overhear some other customers' conversations. What can you understand? Take notes under the following headings: Ailment and duration, Type of medication, How often to be taken, Other instructions.

4 (*a*) Notfälle

Study the following dialogue about a factory accident.

- Hallo, können Sie mir bitte helfen? In der Fabrik ist ein Unfall passiert.
- ■ Was ist denn geschehen?
- Frau Lohmann ist die Treppe heruntergefallen.
- ■ Ist sie verletzt?
- Ja, ihre Beine und ihr Rücken tun sehr weh.
- ■ Rufen Sie schnell einen Krankenwagen.

(*b*) While you are working in Germany your colleague, Herr Norwak, suddenly becomes very ill. He has stomach-ache and a headache. You report this to your boss, Herr Kröger. Complete the following conversation.

Sie	Herr Kröger,________________________________
Herr Kröger	Was fehlt ihm denn?
Sie	____
Herr Kröger	Ist er sehr krank?
Sie	____
Herr Kröger	Rufen Sie schnell einen Krankenwagen.

5 Get together with a partner and work out a dialogue based on the following situations.

(*a*) While walking to work you witness a traffic accident. You rush into the nearest office to call the police. Give the office worker in charge the location of the accident and tell him that at least one person is injured. He or she should therefore call an ambulance as well.

(*b*) Someone rushes into your office in Germany to report a traffic accident and to ask you to call the police. Ask where the accident is and whether you should call an ambulance. Say that you will do it straight away.

6 Listening comprehension

On arriving at work one morning you listen to your boss's telephone answering machine and find a message from an Austrian company. After listening to the message write a memo for your boss (Mr Hall) giving the gist of the phone call.

After consulting with Mr Hall send a fax in reply. In this you should:

(*a*) say you hope Dr Benning gets better.

(*b*) say the first dates mentioned by Frau Wagner are not suitable as Mr Hall will not be in the office next week, but the second alternative would be suitable.

(*c*) ask Frau Wagner to let you know Dr Benning's plans. You can then book a hotel room and tell other colleagues about the appointment.

7 While working at a doctor's surgery you find this quiz in a magazine. See how many questions you can correctly answer.

Was wissen Sie über gesunde Ernährung?

Richtige Ernährung hilft uns, gesund und leistungsfähig zu bleiben. Was wissen Sie darüber? Unser Quiz verrät es Ihnen. Nur eine Antwort ist richtig.

1. Unser Tisch ist reichlich gedeckt – wir leben wie im Schlaraffenland. Doch beim Essen wird vieles falsch gemacht. Welches sind die häufigsten Fehler?
(a) wir essen zu viel, zu fett, zu süß
(b) wir essen zu wenig Bananen
(c) wir trinken zu wenig Saft

2. Zuviel Fett kann nicht nur dick, sondern langfristig auch krank machen. Welches der folgenden Lebensmittel enthält am meisten davon?
(a) Vollmilchschokolade
(b) Leberwurst
(c) Erdnüsse

3. Vollkornprodukte, Obst und Gemüse sind besonders ballaststoffreich. Was bewirken Ballaststoffe?
(a) sie kräftigen die Muskeln
(b) sie förden die Verdauung
(c) sie machen dick

4. Zuviel Kochsalz begünstigt die Entstehung von Bluthochdruck. In welchem der folgenden Lebensmittel ist am meisten Kochsalz versteckt?
(a) Reis
(b) Salami
(c) Apfel

5. Falscher Umgang mit rohen Eiern ist die häufigste Ursache für eine Salmonellenvergiftung. Wo werden rohe Eier am besten aufbewahrt?
(a) im Kühlschrank
(b) im Küchenschrank
(c) auf der Fensterbank

Auflösung auf der nächtsten Seite.

From a quiz published in *GesundheitsMagazin* (16.01.95)

Auflösung

1. (a) Unsere Eßgewohnheiten widersprechen zu oft dem wirklichen Bedarf unseres Körpers. Wir essen zuviel, zu fett, zu süß und zu salzig, und wir trinken zuviel Alkohol. Gemüse und Rohkost hingegen bleiben oft auf der Strecke.

2. (c) 100 Gramm Vollmilchschokolade enthalten 30 Gramm „verstecktes" Fett, 100 Gramm Leberwurst im Durchschnitt 41 Gramm und Erdnüsse 48 Gramm. Da Fett die meisten Kalorien hat, schlagen Erdnüsse also besonders zu Buche.

3. (b) Die pflanzlichen Quell- und Füllstoffe regen die Darmbewegung an und sorgen für eine regelmäßige Darmentleerung. Ernährungswissenschaftler empfehlen deshalb 30 Gramm Ballaststoffe täglich.

4. (b) Pökelwaren enthalten besonders viel „verstecktes" Salz. Äpfel und Reis hingegen sind so kochsalzarm, daß sie sich prima für eine Bluthochdruck-Diät eignen.

5. (a) Um eine Salmonelleninfektion zu vermeiden, sollten Sie Eier immer im Kühlschrank aufbewahren und möglichst frisch verwenden. Bei Zimmertemperatur können sich Salmonellen explosionsartig vermehren und Eier in „Zeitbomben" verwandeln.

Summary

Useful phrases

1	Making an appointment	Ich möchte einen Termin für heute
2	Asking someone to spell their name	Wie schreibt man das? Buchstabieren Sie das bitte
3	Asking what is wrong with someone	Was fehlt Ihnen? Was ist mit Ihnen los? Welche Beschwerden haben Sie?
4	Saying what is wrong with you	Ich habe Kopf-, Magen-, Ohrenschmerzen/weh Ich habe Durchfall/Fieber/ Husten/Schnupfen/eine Grippe
5	Expressing annoyance	Ach, wie ärgerlich!
6	Wishing someone a speedy recovery	Gute Besserung!
7	Asking how often to take tablets	Wie oft muß ich die Tabletten einnehmen?
8	Asking if tablets should be taken before or after meals	Muß ich die Tabletten vor oder nach dem Essen einnehmen?

9 Asking how long tablets should be taken — Bis wann muß ich die Tabletten einnehmen?

10 Asking what has happened — Was ist geschehen?

Language forms

1 The modal verbs *dürfen*, *mögen*, *sollen*

dürfen (may, to be allowed)	*mögen* (to like)	*sollen* (ought, should)
ich darf	ich mag	ich soll
du darst	du magst	du sollst
Sie dürfen	Sie mögen	Sie sollen
er / sie / es } darf	er / sie / es } mag	er / sie / es } soll
wir dürfen	wir mögen	wir sollen
ihr dürft	ihr mögt	ihr sollt
Sie dürfen	Sie mögen	Sie sollen
sie dürfen	sie mögen	sie sollen

Examples

Darf *ich hier rauchen?*
May I smoke here?/Am I allowed to smoke here?

Mögen *Sie die Musik von Beethoven?*
Do you like Beethoven's music?

Soll *ich gleich bezahlen, oder schicken Sie mir die Rechnung?*
Should I pay now, or will you send me the bill?

Note A very commonly used form of *mögen* is *ich möchte, du möchtest* etc. meaning 'I would like, you would like' etc.

2 *Schon* and *seit*

The word *schon* and *seit* are used to indicate for how long something has been going on. Literally *schon* means 'already' and *seit* means 'since'. They can be used interchangeably, as the example below shows.

Example

How long have you had the pains?

This can be expressed in two ways:

(a) *Wie lange haben Sie die Schmerzen schon?*
(Literally: How long have you the pains already?)

(*b*) *Seit wann haben Sie die Schmerzen?*
(Literally: Since when have you the pains?)

Notice that the present tense is used in German with *schon* and *seit* whereas the past tense is used in English. Notice too that a plural noun with *seit* will end with an *n* or *en*.

Example

*Seit zwei Jahr**en*** For two years

3 Subordinate clause before main clause

We have already seen in Chapter 5 that the verb in a subordinate clause stands at the end of the clause. This is the case regardless of whether the subordinate clause precedes or follows the main clause. However, it makes a difference to the position of the verb in the main clause if it follows or precedes a subordinate clause.

(*a*) If the main clause *precedes* the subordinate clause, the verb in the main clause is the second element. The clauses are separated by a comma in written German.

Example

*Die Firma **geht** bankrott, wenn das Projekt nicht gelingt.*
The firm will go bankrupt if the project doesn't succeed.

(*b*) If the main clause follows the subordinate clause, the verb in the main clause stands at the beginning of the clause. The clauses are separated by a comma in writing. We then have the formula *verb-comma-verb.*

Example

*Obleich er krank **ist**, **geht** er heute zur Arbeit.*
Although he's ill, he's going to work today.

Additional exercises

1 While travelling in Germany you are unwell and have to visit the doctor. In the waiting-room you hear the following conversations among the other patients. Complete the gaps as appropriate using the correct forms of *können, dürfen, mögen, müssen, sollen* or *wollen.*

Ich ______ heute Herrn Dr. Braun sprechen. Ich habe seit Montag Magenschmerzen und ______ nichts essen oder trinken. Ich ______ nur schlafen.

Ich habe eine Grippe. Ich habe Kopfschmerzen, und meine Arme und Beine tun weh. Ich ______ morgen nach Österreich fliegen. Wenn es mir aber nicht besser geht, ______ ich nicht fahren. Ich ______ aber fahren, weil ich meine Freunde besuchen ______.

Mein Hals tut weh. Ich ______ Schmerztabletten nehmen, aber ich ______ täglich nur drei nehmen. Ich ______ nicht arbeiten, weil ich nicht sprechen ______.

2 Ludwig Erzberger is feeling too ill to go to work as he has just got flu. Extend each of the statements below with a modal verb indicating how he should approach the particular action mentioned.

Example
Er geht ins Bett.
Er *soll* ins Bett gehen.

Er geht schwimmen.
Er *darf nicht* schwimmen gehen.

(*a*) Er ruft die Firma an.
(*b*) Er geht zum Arzt.
(*c*) Er geht zur Arbeit.
(*d*) Er nimmt Schmerztabletten.
(*e*) Er geht ins Kino.
(*f*) Er schläft.
(*g*) Er trinkt Wasser.

3 Answer the following questions with full sentences using *schon* or *seit* as appropriate with the information given in brackets.

Examples
• Wie lange sind Sie schon in London? (drei Jahre)
■ Ich bin schon drei Jahre in London.

• Seit wann sind Sie in London?
■ Ich bin seit drei Jahren in London.

(*a*) Wie lange arbeiten Sie schon bei Siemens? (zehn Jahre)
(*b*) Wie lange sind Sie schon Betriebsleiter? (sechs Jahre)
(*c*) Seit wann hat Ihre Firma einen Zweigbetrieb in Frankreich? (1972)
(*d*) Wie lange fahren Sie schon Auto? (zwanzig Jahre)
(*e*) Seit wann lernen Sie Deutsch. (mein Urlaub in Wien)
(*f*) Wie lange sind Sie schon unterwegs? (zwölf Stunden)
(*g*) Seit wann sind Sie verheiratet? (April)
(*h*) Seit wann haben Sie Schmerzen? (gestern)
(*i*) Seit wann hat Ihre Kollegin diese Krankheit? (die Ferien)

Kapitel 8

Geld, Bank und Post

Auf der Bank

Charles Roberts, an export manager, arrives in Germany on business. As he has had no time to obtain foreign currency in England, he goes straight to a bank on his arrival.

Angestellter Guten Tag. Kann ich Ihnen helfen?
Exportleiter Kann ich hier Reiseschecks einlösen?
Angestellter Ja, das können Sie schon. Darf ich Ihren Paß sehen?
Exportleiter Selbstverständlich. Bitte schön.
Angestellter Danke schön. Also, wieviel Geld möchten Sie?
Exportleiter Ich möchte für zweihundert Pfund D-Mark.
Angestellter Haben Sie nur Reiseschecks oder auch Bargeld?
Exportleiter Ich habe kein Bargeld, nur Reiseschecks. Wie steht der Kurs im Moment?
Angestellter Für ein Pfund bekommen Sie DM 2,18.
Exportleiter Vor einem Jahr habe ich viel mehr bekommen.

Angestellter	So, unterschreiben Sie hier, bitte. Das Geld bekommen Sie drüben an der Kasse.
Exportleiter	Geben Sie mir bitte sechs Fünfzigmarkscheine, acht Zehnmarkscheine und etwas Kleingeld. Vielen Dank. Auf Wiedersehen.

Information

Können Sie bitte wechseln?

Können Sie bitte diesen Zehnmarkschein in zwei Fünfmarkscheine wechseln?

Wenn Sie Geld wechseln wollen, gehen Sie zum Geldwechsel in der Bank.

Deutsches Kleingeld

Practice

1 Cashing cheques

You are in a bank in Germany. What do you say in German?

Angestellter	Guten Tag. Kann ich Ihnen helfen?
Sie	(Ask if you can cash Eurocheques here.)
Angestellter	Ja, das können wir schon machen. Darf ich Ihren Paß sehen?
Sie	(Say yes, of course. Here it is.)
Angestellter	Danke schön . . . Also, wieviel Geld möchten Sie?
Sie	(Say you want German currency for £100. Ask what the exchange rate is at the moment.)
Angestellter	DM 2,14 für ein Pfund. Wie möchten Sie das Geld?

Sie (Say you would like three fifty-mark notes and some change.)

Angestellter Wenn Sie hier unterschreiben . . . So, danke. Gehen Sie jetzt bitte zur Kasse.

Sie (Say thank you very much. Goodbye.)

2 You are travelling abroad to Germany, Switzerland and Austria. In each country you have to go to the bank to exhange currency. Make up suitable dialogues with a partner, using the following table as a guide.

Land	Bargeld	Reiseschecks	Kurs	Scheine	Kleingeld
Deutschland		£100	DM 2,18/£	3 × 50, – DM 5 × 10, – DM	✓
Deutschland	£55		DM 2,18/£	3 × 20, – DM 1 × 50, – DM	✓
Schweiz		£90	sfr 1.79/£	15 × 10, – sfr	✓
Österreich	£25	£130	öS 15.41/£	20 × 100 öS 4 × 50 öS	✓

3 You write to various banks requesting information about Eurocheque cards. The *Sparkasse Freiburg* sends you their booklet. One of your colleagues would also like to get a Eurocheque card. Read the extract from the booklet on the facing page and answer her questions.

(*a*) Kann man Geld außerhalb der Schalteröffnungszeiten abheben?
(*b*) Kann man die Karte nur an seiner eigenen Bank benutzen?
(*c*) Wann kann man den Kontostand abfragen?
(*d*) In wievielen Ländern kann man Bargeld bekommen?
(*e*) Bietet die ec-Automatenkarte andere Vorteile?

eurocheque-Automatenkarte und ec-Geldautomat

Wie kann ich jederzeit über mein Geld vom Girokonto verfügen?

Die kleine eurocheque-Automatenkarte bietet Ihnen große Vorteile

- als Bedienerschlüssel für Geldautomaten:
  - Barabhebung an den ec-Geldautomaten der Sparkasse Freiburg auch außerhalb der Schalteröffnungszeiten
  - Abfrage des Kontostandes an den ec-Geldautomaten der Sparkasse Freiburg während der Geschäftszeiten
  - Verfügungen an ec-Geldautomaten anderer Banken und Sparkassen
- bei Barabhebung am Schalter Ihrer Geschäftsstelle:
  - Legitimation bei Barauszahlungen
- bei der Begleichung Ihrer Rechnung (in Verbindung mit eurocheques):
  - Anerkanntes Zahlungsmittel in Kaufhäusern, Hotels, Gaststätten usw.
  - Bargeld in 40 Ländern

4 Get together with a partner and work out a dialogue based on the following situations:

(*a*) You work for an international company in Germany. Your boss, Mr MacDonald, the Export Manager, has to travel to Scotland tomorrow to attend a conference. He needs travellers' cheques for the following amounts: two for £125, four for £75 and also £50 in loose change. Ring the bank to order the cheques and say that you would like to collect them tomorrow at 11.00.

(*b*) You work at a German bank and receive a call from Computer International requesting travellers' cheques. Greet the caller and ask what he or she wants. After noting down the customer's requests, remind him or her to bring a passport or identity card to the bank.

Useful words and phrases:

- Guten Tag, Deutsche Bank, Schmidt
- Wie kann ich Ihnen helfen?
- zwei Reiseschecks zu £150
- 50 Pfund in Bargeld
- Morgen geht in Ordnung
- im Wert von
- der Reisepaß
- der Personalausweis

5 Listening comprehension

You are listening to a colleague reading out some Swiss stock market results. Make a note of the year's highest and lowest prices (*Höchstwert* and *Tiefswert*) for each of the following companies: Klein, Braun, Interschweiz, Grün, Raster, Schneider, Doepfner, Hauert, Wehrli and Eicher.

Auf dem Postamt

While in Germany, Bob Bowman, a fitter, goes to the post office. He wants to post some letters and a parcel.

Monteur	Guten Tag. Ich möchte ein Paket schicken.
Beamtin	Ins Inland oder ins Ausland?
Monteur	Nach Hamburg. Was kostet das denn?
Beamtin	Ich muß es zuerst wiegen. . . So, zwölf Mark fünfzig, bitte. Hier ist der Einlieferungsschein für Ihr Paket. Sonst noch etwas?
Monteur	Und diese Briefe möchte ich nach München schicken. Geben Sie mir bitte zwei Briefmarken zu einer Mark.

Beamtin	Ein Inlandsbrief kostet nicht so viel.
Monteur	Ach, ja, der kostet ja nur achtzig Pfennig.
Beamtin	Also, ein Paket zu zwölf Mark fünfzig und zwei Briefmarken zu achtzig, das macht vierzehn Mark zehn zusammen.
Monteur	(*Hands over money*) Bitte schön. Wo kann ich meine Briefe einwerfen?
Beamtin	Den Briefeinwurf finden Sie gegenüber Schalter fünf.
Monteur	Danke schön. Auf Wiedersehen.
Beamtin	Auf Wiedersehen.

Practice

1 At the post office

You are at a German post office. You want to send a parcel and some letters to England. What do you say in German?

Sie	(Say good morning, you would like two one-mark stamps. Say you want to send the letters to England.)
Beamter	Bitte schön. Sonst noch etwas?
Sie	(Say you would like to send a parcel.)

Beamter	Ins Inland oder ins Ausland?
Sie	(Say it is going abroad, you want to send it to London. Ask how much this will cost.)
Beamter	Ich muß es zuerst wiegen . . . So, dreißig Mark, bitte.
Sie	(Ask if you can have a certificate of posting.)
Beamter	Ja, selbstverständlich. Haben Sie noch einen Wunsch?
Sie	(Say no, that is all, thank you. Ask where you can post your letters.)
Beamter	Der Briefeinwurf ist gegenüber Schalter neun.
Sie	(Say thank you very much. Goodbye.)

2 Was sagt man im Postamt?

You are at the post office. Make up dialogues along the lines of the example below.

Example

Sie	Geben Sie mir bitte drei Briefmarken zu achtzig Pfennig und eine Briefmarke zu einer Mark.
Beamter	Drei zu achtzig und eine zu einer Mark, das macht drei Mark vierzig.

3 You work as a translator for a British engineering company. The calendars and rulers intended as gifts for your German customers and promised to your subsidiary company in Duisburg for mid-December have not arrived. You receive a fax urgently requesting them.

> Bitte schicken Sie 20 große Kalender und rostfreie Lineale sofort an uns ab. Wir müssen sie möglichst noch vor Weihnachten, unbedingt aber vor Jahresende an unsere Kunden liefern.
> Mit freundlichen Grüßen
> Schmidt

Send a fax in German, explaining that you sent a parcel off yesterday. They should let you know if the parcel does not arrive as you have a certiticate of posting.

4 What would you say if you wanted to:

(*a*) cash travellers' cheques
(*b*) ask about the exchange rate
(*c*) ask for two 80-Pfennig stamps
(*d*) post a letter
(*e*) ask for change.

5 You and a friend go to a German post office to post some letters and buy some stamps from an automatic dispenser. Your friend does not entirely understand the text on the two books of stamps. Answer her questions.

Die Post
der Partner für Ihr Hobby
Versandstellen für Postwertzeichen
Postfach 20 00, 1000 Berlin 12
Postfach 20 00, 6000 Frankfurt 1
Postfach 20 00, 8480 Weiden

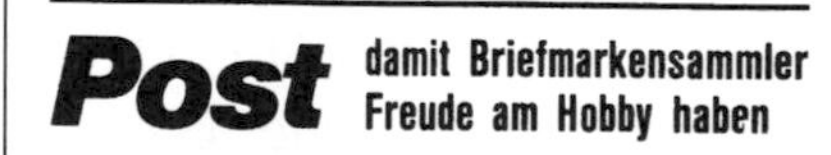

Selbstklebende Postwertzeichen

Abgabepreis 5 DM
2 Postwertzeichen zu 10 Pf
2 Postwertzeichen zu 60 Pf
2 Postwertzeichen zu 80 Pf
2 Postwertzeichen zu 100 Pf

(*a*) What does *selbstklebend* mean?
(*b*) What hobby does the left-hand book encourage?
(*c*) Why are there some addresses on the left-hand book?

6 Listening comprenension

You will hear a conversation between a British tourist and a clerk at a bureau de change. When you have listened to it, complete each sentence with the appropriate ending from the opposite column.

(*a*) Ich möchte englisches Geld . . .	sinkt ständig!
(*b*) Wie ist der Wechselkurs . . .	in D-Mark umwechseln.
(*c*) Vor zwei Jahren . . .	Ihren Paß sehen?
(*d*) Geben Sie mir D-Mark . . .	und etwas Kleingeld, bitte.

(*e*)	Ich will fünfzig Pfund . . .	für englisches Geld?
(*f*)	Darf ich . . .	war das noch DM 2,40.
(*g*)	Wollen Sie das Geld. ..	für hundert Pfund.
(*h*)	Ich möchte fünf Fünfzigmarkscheine und drei Zehnmarkscheine	in großen Scheinen?
(*i*)	Der Wechselkurs . . .	Reiseschecks einlösen.
(*j*)	Ach, das Pfund . . .	finden Sie auf der Quittung.

Summary

Useful phrases

1	Asking if you can cash travellers' cheques	Kann ich hier Reiseschecks einlösen?
2	Saying how much money you want to change	Ich möchte hundert Pfund wechseln Ich möchte englisches Geld in D-Mark umwechseln
3	Asking about the exchange rate	Wie steht der Kurs im Moment? Wie ist der Wechselkurs für englisches Geld?
4	Saying how you want the currency	Geben Sie mir bitte sechs Fünfzigmarkscheine, acht Zehnmarkscheine und etwas Kleingeld
5	Saying you want to send a parcel	Ich möchte ein Paket schicken
6	Asking for a certificate of posting	Kann ich einen Einlieferungsschein haben?
7	Asking for stamps	Geben Sie mir bitte zwei Briefmarken zu einer Mark/zu achtzig Pfennig
8	Agreeing with someone	Da haben Sie recht
9	Asking where you can post your letters	Wo kann ich meine Post einwerfen?

Language forms

1 The genitive case

The genitive case shows possession. In English it is often identified by the word 'of'.

Example The name of the company is Grundig.

The genitive case can be shown by an apostrophe followed by *s*.

Example The company's name is Grundig.

In German, the word for 'of' is absorbed into words such as the, a, my, your, his, this, etc. and shown by an ending on these words. The pattern is shown below.

(a) The genitive of 'the'

	Masculine	*Feminine*	*Neuter*	*Plural*
'of the'	des	der	des	der

Examples
Der Name ***der*** *Firma ist Grundig.* (feminine singular)
The name of the firm is Grundig.

Die Qualität ***der*** *Produkte ist erstklassig.* (plural)
The quality of the products is first class.

Note With masculine and neuter words an *s* (or sometimes *es*) is added to the word.

Examples
Der Sohn ***des*** *Betriebsleiter****s*** *ist Ingenieur.* (masculine singular)
The son of the managing director ist an engineer.

Der Inhaber ***des*** *Hotel****s*** *heißt Kettner.* (neuter singular)
The owner of the hotel is called Kettner.

Note In German it is usual to say 'the son of the managing director/the owner of the hotel' rather than 'the managing director's son/the hotel's owner', etc. Although the latter form exists, it would sound clumsy (other than perhaps for special effect as in poetry, for example) to say *Des Betriebleiters Sohn/Des Hotels Inhaber.*

However, the *s* of possession is usual with names, but note that there is no apostrophe in German.

Examples

Michaels Vater Michael's father

Gudruns Mann Gudrun's husband

Note that the word *Herr* adds an *n* in the genitive.

Example

Herrn Paternollis Visitenkarte.
Mr Paternolli's visiting card.

(b) The genitive of 'a'

	Masculine	*Feminine*	*Neuter*
'of a'	eines	einer	eines

This is used in exactly the same way as with 'the'.

Example

*Die Qualität **eines** Produkt**s** bestimmt den Preis.* (neuter)
The quality of a product determines the price.

Notice the *s* on the word *Produkt.*

(c) Genitive prepositions

The genitive is used with the following prepositions.

außerhalb	(outside [of])
innerhalb	(inside (of), within)
oberhalb	(on top of, above)
trotz	(in spite of)
während	(during)
wegen	(because of)

Examples

*Trotz **der** Rezession ist das Geschäft nicht schlecht.*
In spite of the recession business is not bad.

*Wegen **des** Wetter**s** bleiben wir zu Hause.*
Because of the weather we're staying at home.

2 Adjective agreement after 'the'

After the different forms of 'the', adjectives will have the following endings:

	Masculine	*Feminine*	*Neuter*	*Plural*
Nominative	e	e	e	en
Accusative	en	e	e	en
Genitive	en	en	en	en
Dative	en	en	en	en

These endings also apply after the German words for 'this', 'these', 'that', or 'those' (*dieser, jener* etc).

Examples

*Die neu**e** Verkaufsleiterin heißt Brigitte Bernhard.*

The new sales manager is called Brigitte Bernhard.

*Wegen des schlecht**en** Wetters gibt es heute keine Flüge.*
Because of the bad weather there are no flights today.

3 Adjective agreement with unaccompanied adjectives

Adjectives are not always preceded by 'a', 'the', 'this', etc. Sometimes they can stand alone, for example: red wine, cheap milk, rusty metal, high profits.
The endings on unaccompanied German adjectives are:

	Masculine	*Feminine*	*Neuter*	*Plural*
Nominative	er	e	es	e
Accusative	en	e	es	e
Genitive	en	er	en	er
Dative	em	er	em	en

Examples
*von zentral**er** Bedeutung* – of central importance
*deutsch**e** Weine* – German wines
*in regelmäßig**en** Abständen* – at regular intervals

4 How to say 'not a' or 'no'

In English we can say:
He has *not* got *a* passport *or* He has *no* passport.
In German a single word, *kein*, renders both the English versions.

The forms of *kein* are as follows (in the singular they are, in fact, the same as the forms of *ein*):

	Masculine	*Feminine*	*Neuter*	*Plural*
Nominative	kein	keine	kein	keine
Accusative	keinen	keine	kein	keine
Genitive	keines	keiner	keines	keiner
Dative	keinem	keiner	keinem	keinen

Examples

*Ich habe **kein** Auto.*
I have no car/I haven't got a car.

*Er hat **keinen** Paß.*
He has no passport/He hasn't got a passport.

*Haben Sie **keine** Zehnmarkscheine?*
Have you no ten mark notes?/Haven't you any ten mark notes?

Additional exercises

1 Complete the gaps in the following sentences with the correct form of 'the'.

(*a*) Ende ______ Monats fahren wir nach Wien.
(*b*) Wir möchten die Sehenswürdigkeiten ______ Stadt sehen.
(*c*) Das Restaurant ______ Hotels soll sehr gut sein.
(*d*) Ein Angestellter ______ Reisebüros hat ein Hotel empfohlen.
(*e*) Die Freundlichkeit ______ Österreicher ist weltbekannt.

2 Complete the gaps in the following sentences with the correct form of 'a'.

(*a*) Sie ist die Leiterin ______ Firma in Amerika.
(*b*) Die Marketingstrategie ______ Betriebs muß gut sein.
(*c*) Das Lernen ______ Fremdsprache ist für Geschäftsleute heute sehr wichtig.
(*d*) Er ist der Inhaber ______ Hotels in Dortmund.
(*e*) Die Kosten ______ Urlaubs in Hawaii sind mir zu hoch.

3 The following sentences have been broken. Match the correct halves by putting a number in the boxes. One has been done as an example.

a	b	c	d	e	f
iii					

(*a*) Trotz der Rezession
(*b*) Oberhalb des Eingangs
(*c*) Außerhalb der Stadt
(*d*) Während der Tagung
(*e*) Wegen des Wetters
(*f*) Innerhalb eines Jahres

i) kann man heute nicht fliegen.
ii) macht die Firma bankrott.
iii) ist das Geschäft gut.
iv) gibt es schöne Berge.
v) steht der Name des Hotels.
vi) arbeiten die Dolmetscher fleißig.

4 Change the adjectives in brackets to their correct form.

(*a*) Der (französisch) Wein schmeckt sehr gut.
(*b*) Am (folgend) Tag fliegen wir nach Paris.
(*c*) Bis Ende (nächst) Monats muß das Produkt fertig sein.
(*d*) Wann kommt die (japanisch) Kollegin an?
(*e*) Ich brauche einen (neu) Film.
(*f*) Wir haben die (schön) Berge gesehen.

5 How would you say the following in German?

(*a*) I would like English money.
(*b*) I need new shoes.
(*c*) I don't like black coffee.
(*d*) My wife buys French perfume.
(*e*) Do you have this T-shirt in different colours?

6 Turn the following sentences into their opposite using the appropriate forms of *kein*.

Example

Ich habe einen Paß.
Ich habe *keinen* Paß.

(*a*) Das ist ein gutes Hotel.
(*b*) Das Zimmer hat einen Balkon.
(*c*) Sie ist eine gute Betriebsleiterin.
(*d*) In Salzburg gibt es eine U-Bahn.
(*e*) Hier haben wir eine schöne Aussicht auf die Berge.
(*f*) Nach Hull fährt ein Luftkissenboot.
(*g*) Unsere Stadt hat eine große Buchhandlung.
(*h*) Wir brauchen neue Produkte.

Kapitel 9

Auto und Zoll

An der Zollgrenze

Steve Roberts is a lorry driver whose work frequently takes him through Germany to the Czech Republic. On this particular trip he is travelling to Prague to deliver some machinery. He stops at the German-Czech border.

Zollbeamter Guten Tag. Ihre Papiere bitte, Paß, Führerschein, grüne Versicherungskarte und Tachograph.
Fahrer Bitte schön.
Zollbeamter Alles in Ordnung. Wohin fahren Sie?
Fahrer Nach Prag. Ich liefere Maschinen.
Zollbeamter Wie weit sind Sie heute schon gefahren?
Fahrer Von Kassel, also ungefähr 50 Kilometer. Ich bin vorgestern mit dem Nachtschiff nach Rotterdam gekommen, dann gestern von Rotterdam nach Kassel gefahren.
Zollbeamter Was liefern Sie?
Fahrer Maschinen, sonst habe ich nichts zu verzollen.
Zollbeamter Haben Sie eine Dieselerklärung?*

* Drivers going into eastern Europe usually tell German custom officials how much fuel they have in their tank. In this way they can avoid being taxed on whatever fuel they have on their return over the border into Germany.

Fahrer	Bitte schön.
Zollbeamter	Leider müssen wir Ihr Fahrzeug durchsuchen.
Fahrer	Das gibt's ja nicht! Muß das sein?
Zollbeamter	Tut mir leid. Wir müssen Stichproben machen. Fahren Sie bitte zum Parkplatz dort drüben.
Fahrer	Ach, wie ärgerlich. Ich soll um vierzehn Uhr in Prag sein. Das schaffe ich jetzt nicht mehr. Wie lange dauert das denn?
Zollbeamter	Es dauert höchstens zehn Minuten, bestimmt nicht länger.

Practice

1 Answer in English:

(*a*) Welche Papiere usw. will der Zollbeamte sehen?
(*b*) Wohin fährt der Fahrer?
(*c*) Wieviele Kilometer ist er heute gefahren?
(*d*) Wie ist er nach Rotterdam gefahren?
(*e*) Was hat er im Fahrzeug?
(*f*) Was hat er zu verzollen?
(*g*) Warum muß der Zollbeamte Herrn Roberts Fahrzeug durchsuchen?
(*h*) Wo muß der Fahrer sein Fahrzeug parken?
(*i*) Wie lange dauert die Durchsuchung?
(*j*) Um wieviel Uhr soll der Fahrer in Prag sein?

2 After staying in the Czech Republic you drive over the border into Germany on your homeward journey. What do you say in German?

Zollbeamter	Guten Tag. Ihre Pässe bitte.
Sie	(Show your passports.)
Zollbeamter	Alles in Ordnung. Wohin fahren Sie?
Sie	(Say you are going to Calais. You are getting the ship to England.)
Zollbeamter	Haben Sie etwas zu verzollen?
Sie	(Say you have only two bottles of wine and some coffee.)
Zollbeamter	Leider müssen wir Ihr Auto durchsuchen.
Sie	(Say you find this most annoying. You have to be in Dresden for three o'clock, and you won't make it now.)
Zollbeamter	So lange wird es nicht dauern. Wir brauchen nur ein paar Minuten.

3 You will be travelling by car to Germany and need to understand certain road signs. Match each sentence on the following page with a corresponding sign.

(*a*) Der Verkehr darf nur in eine Richtung fahren.

(*b*) Hier dürfen Sie nicht fahren.

(*c*) Hier dürfen Fahrzeuge über 10 m Länge nicht fahren.

(*d*) Wenn ein Auto von der rechten Seite kommt, müssen Sie halten. (Rechts hat Vorfahrt.)

(*e*) Sie dürfen nicht schneller als 60 km pro Stunde fahren.

(*f*) Sie haben auf dieser Straße Vorfahrt.

(*g*) Straßenbahnhaltestelle.

(*h*) Hier ist das Halten und Parken verboten.

(*i*) Kinder gehen über die Straße.

(*j*) Die Straße wird enger.

1 **2** **3** **4** **5** **6** **7** **8** **9** **10**

Information Wenn man selbst tankt, bekommt man manchmal einen Beleg. Diesen Beleg nimmt man mit zur Kasse, wo man bezahlen muß.

An der Tankstelle

Andrea Brown, a British businesswoman, is driving through Germany to attend a trade fair in Hannover. En route she stops at a petrol station.

Geschäftsfrau	Volltanken, bitte.
Tankwart	Super oder Normal?
Geschäftsfrau	Super, bitte. Und machen Sie bitte auch den Reservekanister voll.
Tankwart	Ja, sofort. Soll ich auch den Ölstand prüfen?
Geschäftsfrau	Danke, nein. Ich habe erst vorgestern nachgesehen. Aber kontrollieren Sie bitte den Reifendruck.
Tankwart	Ich sehe mal nach . . . Der Luftdruck ist in Ordnung. Haben Sie noch einen Wunsch?
Geschäftsfrau	Danke, das ist alles. Was macht das, bitte?
Tankwart	Also, dreißig Liter Super, zweiundvierzig Mark, bitte.
Geschäftsfrau	Ich habe leider nur einen Fünfhundertmarkschein. Können Sie bitte wechseln?
Tankwart	Ja, näturlich.
Geschäftsfrau	Kann ich eine Quittung haben?
Tankwart	Selbstverständlich. Bitte schön.
Geschäftsfrau	Danke schön. Auf Wiedersehen.
Tankwart	Auf Wiedersehen. Gute Fahrt.

Practice

1 Was ist richtig, was ist falsch?

(*a*) Der Tankwart soll den Reservekanister vollmachen.
(*b*) Der Tankwart prüft den Ölstand.
(*c*) Der Reifendruck ist in Ordnung.
(*d*) Die Geschäftsfrau hat kein Kleingeld.

2 Here are some other reasons for stopping at a *Tankstelle* or *Werkstatt*:

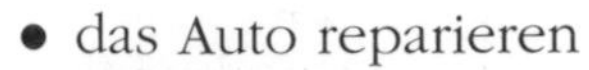

- das Auto reparieren
- die Bremsen prüfen
- den Wagen waschen
- die Reifen wechseln
- den Reifendruck prüfen
- das Wasser nachfüllen

Practise using these expressions in sentences.

Examples Prüfen Sie bitte die Bremsen.
Ich muß das Wasser nachfüllen.
Wir haben die Reifen gewechselt.

3 Get together with a partner and devise a dialogue based on the following situation:

You stop off at a petrol station in Switzerland before travelling back home. Ask the petrol attendant to fill your car up with petrol, check the tyre pressure and oil, and top up the water. When everything is complete, ask what it costs.

Take the part of the petrol attendant. Ask what sort of petrol the customer requires, and tell him how much petrol you have put in. Comment on each of the other tasks as you complete them.

4 Welcher Wagen ist besser?

Technische Daten	**VW Polo**	**Opel Corsa**	**BMW 525i**
Preis	ab DM 18 295,–	ab DM 17 700,–	ab DM 61 400,–
Höchstgeschwindigkeit km/Stunde	147	153	217
Benzinverbrauch 1/100 km bei 90 km/Stunde	4,9 (Normal)	4,7 (Super)	7,2 (Super)
Gewicht (kg)	750	772	1450
Abmessungen:			
Breite (m)	1,58	1,53	1,75
Länge (m)	3,65	3,62	4,72

(*a*) Read the following passage:

Der VW Polo kostet ungefähr 14 485 DM. Er hat eine Höchstgeschwindigkeit von 147 Kilometern und verbraucht 4,9 Liter Normalbenzin pro 100 Kilometer. Er wiegt 750 Kilo und hat eine Länge von 3,65 Metern und eine Breite von 1,58 Metern.

Now write a similar account for the Opel Corsa or the BMW 525i.

(*b*) The following test compares the VW and the Opel.

Der VW ist billiger als der Opel, und er fährt langsamer. Er verbraucht mehr Benzin pro 100 km als der Opel, aber Benzin für den Opel ist teurer als für den VW. Der VW ist nicht so schwer wie der Opel und ist auch etwas länger und breiter als der Opel.

Now compare the BMW with either the VW or the Opel.

(*c*) If you have a car, describe it briefly. Use some of the information on page 136 as guideline.

5 Listening comprehension

(*a*) The job that you have taken in Germany will involve some travel, and you decide to buy a car. You go to the local car salesroom with a German colleague, who makes some comparisons between two types of car. What are the differences?

(*b*) You decide which car to buy. Then your colleague has some further advice. Make notes on what he says.

6

Your colleague plans to take her driving test in Germany. You are helping her to prepare for the theory exam, using the official questions and answers. The answers are not opposite the corresponding questions. Match each question with its appropriate answer.

1. 4. (3 P) Worauf haben Sie sich einzustellen, wenn Sie an diesen Verkehrszeichen vorbeifahren?	Geschwindigkeit anpassen
2. 12. (3 P) Was haben Sie zu tun, wenn Sie sich diesem Verkehrszeichen nähern?	Auf eine Ampel

3. 27. (3 P) Worauf weist dieses Verkehrszeichen zu beachten?		Überholverbote Geschwindigkeitsbe-schränkungen
4. 17. (2 P) Worauf weist dieses Verkehrszeichen hin?		Auf den Anfang einer Autobahn
5. 12 (3 P) Wie verhalten Sie sich bei diesem Verkehrszeichen?		Auf dieser Straße kann Wintersport betrieben werden Die Fahrbahn ist auch bei Schneeglätte nicht gestreut
6. 22. (3 P) Worauf weist dieses Verkehrszeichen hin?		Auf einen Radweg
7. 20. (3 P) Worauf weist dieses Verkehrszeichen hin?		Auf die Autobahnausfahrt 26 – Düsseldorf-Benrath
8. 38. (2 P) Worauf weist die Zahl „26“ in diesem Verkehrszeichen hin?	26 Düsseldorf -Benrath 1000 m	Auf das Ende der Autobahn
9. 44. (2 P) Welche „Streckenverbote“ werden mit diesem Verkehrszeichen aufgehoben?		Sie dürfen nur geradeaus weiterfahren

7 At-sight translation

A German friend has sent you a copy of the following advertisement for a job that he has applied for. Explain to your family in general terms what the advertisement says.

> Ausbildungsplätze für Berufskraftfahrer
>
> In Westeuropa sind wir eine erfolgreiche und moderne Spedition. Qualität und Service haben uns international bekannt gemacht.
>
> Wir brauchen jetzt junge Menschen für interessante Arbeitsplätze zum 1.1.1997 (Mindestalter: 21 Jahre). Wenn Sie Interesse haben, bitte schicken Sie uns Ihren Lebenslauf zusammen mit Lichtbild und Zeugnissen an:
>
> Lohmann Spedition, Dortmunderstr. 7, 48155 Münster Tel. 045021/8030 Fax 045021/2310

8

You are visiting Bad Embach in the car and have to keep stopping to ask the way. Working in pairs, direct each other to different places on the map (below). Remember to distinguish between *fahren* and *gehen.*

You will find the following words and phrases useful:

- die Verkehrsampeln
- der Kreisverkehr
- Entschuldigen Sie bitte

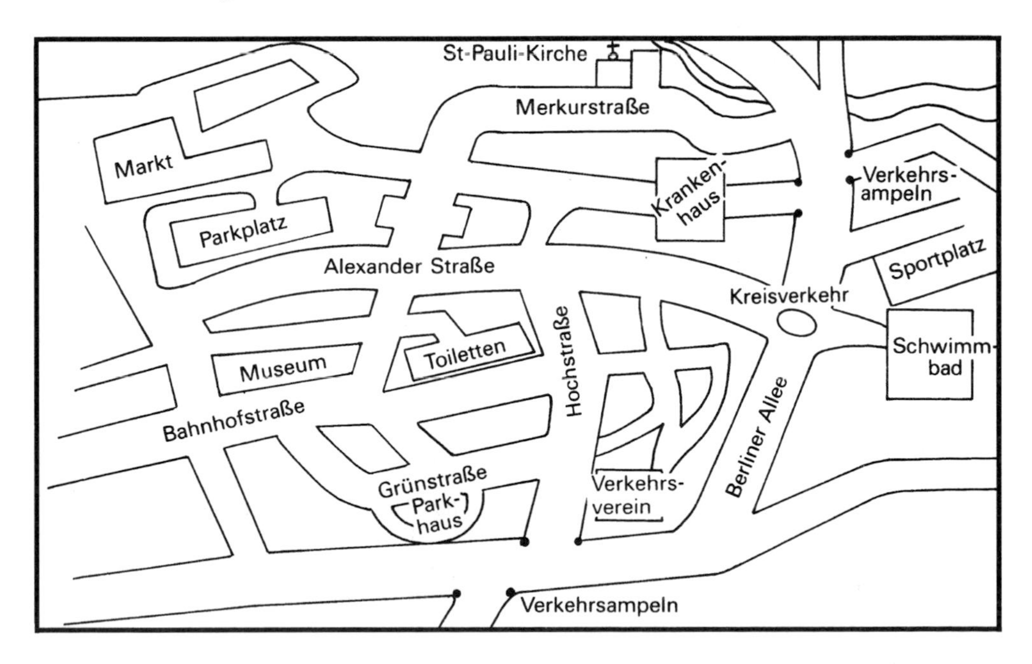

- Wie komme ich am besten zum/zur . . .
- Gibt es hier in der Nähe ein(e) . . .
- Ich bin hier fremd
- Verstehen Sie?
- Sind Sie mit dem Auto?
- Gehen Sie zu Fuß?

9 Listening comprehension

You will hear a conversation between a policeman and a motorist, Herr Kramer, whose car has broken down (*Er hat eine Panne*).

After you have listened to the conversation, complete the phrases in column A with an appropriate phrase from column B.

Column A	*Column B*
Die Batterie ist	in der nächsten Straße.
Herr Kramer hat	dem Polizisten seinen Führerschein.
Die Werkstatt ist	wenn er innerhalb von 30 Minuten nicht zurückkommt.
In der Grünstraße darf	Benzin gekauft.
Herr Kramer zeigt	in Ordnung.
Herr Kramer wird eine Geldstrafe bekommen,	man nicht parken.

Summary

Useful phrases

1	Expressing irritation	Das gibt's ja nicht!
2	Saying you cannot do something anymore	Das schaffe ich nicht mehr
3	Asking for petrol	Volltanken bitte Dreißig Liter Super/Normal Bitte machen Sie den Reservekanister voll
4	Asking for something to be checked	Bitte prüfen Sie den Ölstand Bitte kontrollieren Sie den Reifendruck
5	Saying you have checked something	Ich habe schon nachgesehen
6	Saying that is all	Das ist alles

7	Asking about the cost	Was macht das?
8	Asking if someone can change a banknote	Können Sie wechseln?
9	Asking for a receipt	Kann ich eine Quittung haben?
10	Asking what is wrong	Was ist denn los?

Language forms

1 Further ways of making comparisons

We have already seen in Chapter 4 how to form the comparative. Further ways of making comparisons are shown below.

(a) The comparative and *als*
Als with a comparative means 'than'.

Examples

München ist größer ***als*** *Bremen.*
Munich is bigger than Bremen.

Der VW ist billiger ***als*** *der Opel.*
The VW is cheaper than the Opel.

(b) so . . . wie
means 'as . . . as'.

Examples

Ich bin ***so*** *alt* ***wie*** *Helmut Kohl.*
I am as old as Helmut Kohl.

Snowdon ist nicht ***so*** *hoch* ***wie*** *Everest.*
Snowdon is not so/as high as Everest.

(c) so viel . . . wie
means 'as much/many . . . as'.
Viel usually has endings in the plural but not in the singular.

Examples

Die Russen exportieren nicht ***so viele*** *Autos* ***wie*** *die Japaner.*
The Russians do not export as many cars as the Japanese.

Die Engländer trinken nicht ***so viel*** *Kaffee* ***wie*** *die Deutschen.*
The English do not drink as much coffee as the Germans.

Additional exercises

1 Which of the words in the brackets is the correct answer?

(*a*) Frankfurt ist (größer/kleiner) als Tokio.
(*b*) Trier ist (älter/jünger) als Dortmund.
(*c*) Die Zugspitze ist (höher/niedriger) als Ben Nevis.
(*d*) Goethe hat (früher/später) gelebt als Shakespeare.
(*e*) Eine Straßenbahn fährt (schneller/langsamer) als ein Zug.
(*f*) Ein Mercedes ist (teurer/billiger) als ein Ford Escort.
(*g*) Ein Skiurlaub in Aspen kostet (mehr/weniger) als ein Skiurlaub in Aviemore.

2 True or false?

(*a*) Der Rhein ist so lang wie der Mississippi.
(*b*) Das Opernhaus in Wien ist nicht so alt wie das Opernhaus in Sydney.
(*c*) Dortmund ist nicht so schön wie Tübingen.
(*d*) Esperanto ist so schwer wie Chinesisch.
(*e*) Der Schwarzwald (*Black Forest*) ist so industriell wie das Ruhrgebeit (*Ruhr district*).

3 Complete these sentences with the appropriate facts.

(*a*) In Belgien hört man nicht so viel Französisch wie in ________.
(*b*) Ein Vauxhall Nova kostet nicht so viel wie ein ________.
(*c*) Die Firma Siemens hat nicht so viele Arbeitnehmer wie die Firma ________.
(*d*) Die Österreicher exportieren nicht so viel Wein wie ________.
(*e*) Von Hamburg nach München braucht man mit der Bahn so viel Zeit wie von ________ nach ________.

Kapitel 10

Stadtbesichtigung und Freizeit

Spaziergang durch die Stadt

During a business trip to a trade fair in Düsseldorf, Karen Clark, the Sales Director of a British company, is given a tour of the city by her opposite number, Hedwig Stingl, from the German company she has been visiting.

Die Altstadt, Düsseldorf

Stingl Sind Sie zum ersten Mal in Düsseldorf?

Clark Ja.

Stingl Möchten Sie heute die Stadt besichtigen? Heute nachmittag haben wir bestimmt etwas Zeit.

Clark Ja, gern. Düsseldorf soll sehr schön sein.

Stingl Ja, das stimmt. Es soll eine der schönsten Städte Europas sein. Wollen Sie zuerst die Königsallee sehen? Sie ist Düsseldorfs bekannteste und eleganteste Straße.

Clark Das wird bestimmt interessant.

Stingl Nachher könnten wir in der Altstadt ein bißchen spazierengehen. Dort gibt es allerlei Interessantes - einen großen Marktplatz, Spezialgeschäfte, Antiquitätenläden, Kirchen, Kneipen, angenehme Restaurants, alte Gebäude und so weiter.

Clark Ich glaube, in dieser Stadt langweilt man sich nie.
Stingl Und dann müssen wir einen Spaziergang am Rheinufer machen, wenn wir noch Zeit haben.

Practice

1 Answer the following questions:

(*a*) Wie oft schon ist Karen Clark in Düsseldorf gewesen?
(*b*) Was wissen Sie über die Königsallee?
(*c*) Wo genau in der Altstadt kann man einkaufen?
(*d*) Was machen Karen Clark und ihre Kollegin in der Altstadt? Und später?
(*e*) Was wissen Sie über Düsseldorf von diesem Dialog?
(*f*) An welchem Fluß liegt Düsseldorf?

2 You are on a business trip in Vienna. Your host invites you to visit the sights. What do you say in German?

Gastgeber Sind Sie zum ersten Mal in Wien?
Sie (Say yes, you are.)
Gastgeber Möchten Sie die Stadt besichtigen? Wir haben heute Zeit.
Sie (Say yes, you would like to.)
Gastgeber Möchten Sie zuerst die Ringstraße sehen? Sie ist Wiens eleganteste Straße und hat viele imposante Gebäude.
Sie (Say yes, and then you would like to see the river.)
Gastgeber Die Donau ist ja sehr schön. Dann könnten wir zum Prater fahren. In diesem Park befindet sich das Riesenrad, das größte der Welt.
Sie (Say it is very impressive. You saw it in the film *The Third Man*.)

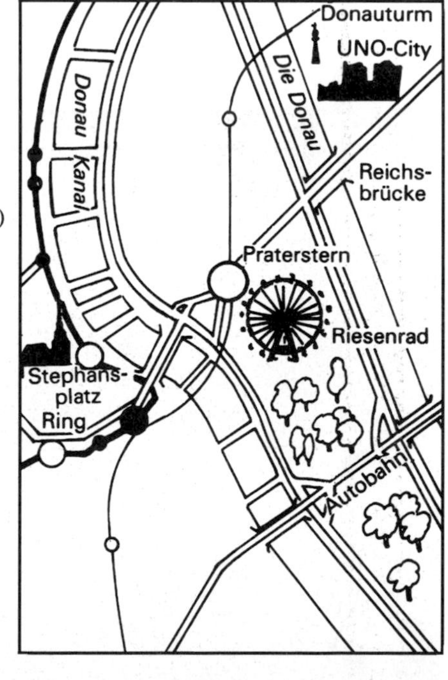

3 You are in Düsseldorf with friends and want to go on a river trip. You have found the following leaflet, but as your friends do not understand German, you must answer their questions.

(*a*) Do the boats run all the year round?
(*b*) What are the furnishings like?
(*c*) Will we get decent food and drink?
(*d*) What age groups are there likely to be on board?
(*e*) Does the leaflet sound welcoming?
(*f*) Is there a choice of excursions?

> Eine Fahrt auf dem Rhein ist immer wieder ein Erlebnis – nicht nur für die Kinder. Und dieses Vergnügen sollten Sie auf keinen Fall versäumen, wenn Sie in Düsseldorf sind.
>
> Die schmucken Passagierschiffe der Rheinbahn sind komfortabel eingerichtet. Wenn Sie Hunger oder Durst haben, dann finden Sie an Bord Bars und Restaurants.
>
> Von Ostern bis Ende September können Sie mit uns fahren. Nehmen Sie an einer unserer zahlreichen Ausflugsfahrten teil, z.B. nach Königswinter mit dem Drachenfels oder nach Zons, einer kleinen Römerstadt am Rhein.
>
> Fahren Sie mit uns. Wir freuen uns, Sie als Gast an Bord zu haben.

Ein Dampfer auf dem Rhein

Im Stadtzentrum

Michael Newby is entertaining a visitor from Germany, and today he is showing him around London. After hearing the conversation, answer the questions that follow.

Newby Wenn Sie Lust haben, können wir heute Londoner Sehenswürdigkeiten besichtigen.

Gast Ja, gern.

Newby Sind Sie zum ersten Mal in London?

Gast Als Kind war ich einmal mit meinen Eltern hier, aber ich kann mich nicht so genau daran erinnern. Wir hatten kein Auto und mußten immer zu Fuß gehen. Meine Schwester studierte damals nicht weit von London.

Newby Dann gibt es viele Möglichkeiten. Möchten Sie lieber eine Stadtrundfahrt machen oder ein bestimmtes Stadtviertel kennenlernen?

Gast Als Geschäftsmann interessiere ich mich besonders für die City. Die möchte ich unbedingt sehen, wenn's geht.

Newby Das geht schon. Wir können ruhig den ganzen Tag dort verbringen. Möchten Sie mit dem Bus oder mit dem Auto fahren?

Gast Was empfehlen Sie?

Newby Vom Bus aus kann man viel besser sehen. Wir können nämlich im Doppeldecker oben sitzen.

Gast Also gut. Fahren wir mit dem Bus.

Practice

1 Answer the following questions:

(*a*) Was weiß der Gast über seinen letzten Besuch in London?
(*b*) Was möchte der Gast lieber machen? Warum?
(*c*) Wieviel Zeit haben Newby und sein Gast?
(*d*) Warum nehmen sie den Bus?
(*e*) Wann war er zum letzten Mal in London?
(*f*) Ist er zum letzten Mal mit dem Wagen gekommen?

2 **Listening comprehension**

While sitting in a café you overhear two German-speaking tourists talking at a table nearby. They cannot agree on where to go next. Note down the woman's suggestions and her partner's comments.

3 Get together with a partner and make up a conversation along these lines:

(*a*) You propose taking a German visitor to see the sights of your town. Ask your visitor if he or she would like to do this, and whether they are there for the first time. Ask which is preferable, a tour of the town or looking at a particular tourist attraction. Then ask whether they would prefer to go by bus, car or on foot.
(*b*) Take the part of a German being entertained by an English host. Tell him or her you would prefer a tour of the town and would like to go by car, as you can travel further and see more that way.

4 While on a language course in Düsseldorf you are taken on a conducted bus tour of the area. The next day you are provided with a summary of the guide's introduction, but there are gaps for you to fill with reflexive verbs.

Use the following reflexive verbs to fill the gaps.

- sich über etwas freuen – to be glad about, take pleasure in something
- sich interessieren für – to be interested in
- es sich bequem machen – to make oneself comfortable
- sich entspannen – to relax
- sich wohlfühlen – to feel at ease
- sich befinden – to be
- sich auf etwas freuen – to look forward to something
- sich bedanken – to thank someone
- sich verlieben in – to fall in love with

- sich langweilen – to be bored
- sich amüsieren – to have fun
- sich setzen – to sit down

Guten Tag, meine Damen und Herren

Willkommen an Bord

Wir machen heute eine schöne Rundreise der Stadt Düsseldorf und seiner Umgebung. Sie __________ __________ jetzt in einem Düsseldorfer Ausflugsbus. Bitte __________ Sie __________, und __________ Sie es __________ __________. Heute nachmittag __________ Sie __________ bestimmt nicht. Sie werden __________ über unsere elegante Stadt __________. Wir haben für jeden Geschmack etwas, zum Beispiel wenn Sie __________ für Geschichte __________, wird unser Schloß Benrath Ihnen sicher gefallen. Wenn Sie aber für das Einkaufen schwärmen, werden Sie __________ im neuen Einkaufszentrum __________.

Fast jeder Besucher __________ __________ in unsere schöne Stadt am Rhein. Ich persönlich__________ __________ auf einen Bummel durch die Altstadt mit ihren vielen Restaurants, Boutiquen, Kneipen und Straßenkünstlern. Ich sehe, wir haben auch Kinder an Bord. Ihr werdet __________ auch nicht __________. Im Rheinstadion, auf dem Wochenmarkt und auf der Kirmes werdet ihr __________ gut __________. Dann können wir __________ vor unserer Rückkehr zur Stadtmitte beim Kaffeetrinken etwas __________. So, meine Damen und Herren, ich __________ __________ für Ihre Aufmerksamkeit und wünsche Ihnen noch einen schönen Nachmittag.

5 While in Düsseldorf you decide to go on a cultural tour of the city. The tour is advertised in the publicity material opposite. You ask the guide the following questions. What does he answer?

(*a*) Über wieviele Museen verfügt Düsseldorf?
(*b*) Wo kann man eine Glassammlung sehen?
(*c*) Wo kann man etwas über das Leben von Heinrich Heine erfahren?
(*d*) Wie lange dauert die Führung durch die Altstadt?
(*e*) Wieviel kostet das vorgeschlagene Programm?

Finally the guide asks you a question:

(*f*) Wie möchten Sie das Programm variieren, wenn Sie in nächster Zeit nach Düsseldorf fahren?

Düsseldorf

Eine Stadt lädt ein

Invitation from a city

Düsseldorf – die (Kultur-)Stadt lädt ein

Vor fast 300 Jahren . . .
. . . machte eine Medici mit ihrem Gemahl Jan Wellem Düsseldorf zum Zentrum der schönen Künste . . .
heute . . .

- verfügt die Stadt über nicht weniger als 18 Museen . . .
- beherbergt die Kunstsammlung Nordrhein-Westfalen die größte Paul-Klee-Sammlung . . .
- findet man im Schloß Jägerhof das drittgrößte Goethe-Museum der Welt . . .
- dokumentiert das Hetjensmuseum, das Deutsche Keramikmuseum, 8000 Jahre Keramikkunst aus allen Erdteilen . . .
- bietet das Kunstmuseum im Ehrenhof eine der schönsten und reichhaltigsten Glassammlungen weltweit . . .
- gilt das Heinrich-Heine-Institut in der Karlstadt, das sich dem Leben und Werk des berühmtesten Düsseldorfer Sohnes widmet, als Zentrum der Heine-Forschung . . .
- besucht man mit Schloß Benrath eines der schönsten spätbarocken Lust- und Gartenschlösser . . .
- zieht die „Deutsche Oper am Rhein“ in jeder Spielzeit mit Musik und Tanz Tausende in ihren Bann . . .
- haben die Inszenierungen des Düsseldorfer Schauspielhauses eine weltweite Fan-Gemeinde . . .
- bringt das Fernsehen die scharfzüngige Ironie des Düsseldorfer „Kom(m)ödchens“ in nahezu jedes Wohnzimmer . . .

Um Ihnen detaillierte Einblicke in dieses „Heute“ zu vermitteln, haben wir für Sie das nachfolgende „Kulturpackage“ ausgearbeitet:

Program:
14.00 Uhr
Sie beginnen die Entdeckungsreise durch das kulturelle Leben Düsseldorfs mit einem kultur-historischen Rundgang durch Altstadt und Karlstadt.

16.00 Uhr
Besuch der Kunstsammlung Nordrhein-Westfalen. Erleben Sie die bedeutendsten Künstler unseres Jahrhunderts in einer einmaligen Zusammenstellung.

18.30 Uhr
Gemütliches Abendessen in einer der traditionsreichen Brauereigaststätten im Herzen der Düsseldorfer Altstadt.

Leistungen:
- zweistündige Führung durch die Altstadt mit sachkundiger Erklärung
- Eintritt in die Kunstsammlung NRW
- 3-Gang-Menü in einer Brauereigaststätte

Preis:
DM99,–p. P., günstige Gruppenpreise auf Anfrage

(auch dieses Programm kann entsprechend Ihren individuellen Wünschen variiert werden)

6 While waiting at the tourist office for information you overhear five instructions. Match each instruction with one of the following places of interest:

(*a*) das Kino
(*b*) die Kunstgalerie
(*c*) das Schwimmbad
(*d*) das Theater
(*e*) das Museum.

7 Listening comprehension

You are visiting a company in Germany and have been invited along to a social evening which takes the form of a quiz. Listen to the quizmaster reading out the final ten questions. Use the following words to help you to write down the answers.

(*a*) Nordrhein – meist
(*b*) Bayern – groß
(*c*) Bremen – klein
(*d*) Händel – berühmt
(*e*) Zugspitze – hoch
(*f*) Rhein – lang
(*g*) Sylt, Nordeney – bekannt
(*h*) Augsburg – alt
(*i*) ICE (Intercity Express) – schnell
(*j*) Kuckucksuhren – beliebt

Example Nordrhein-Westfalen hat die meisten Einwohner.

Then listen to the correct answers on the tape.

8 Sustained speaking/writing

Describe the scene in this picture, orally first, then in writing, giving as much information as possible.

9 Your company is holding a three-day conference for representatives of its European subsidiary companies, and you are helping to organise entertainment during the daytime for the representatives' partners. Your boss dictates a letter to the German subsidiary company giving an outline of possible activities. The cassette contains an extract from the letter. Listen to it and write it down.

10 Translation

You are working for an international organisation in Switzerland and have been asked to translate into English a leaflet to be issued to foreigners coming to work in Switzerland.

> Touristiche Informationen hören Sie über Telefonnummer 120, Wetterberichte über Nummer 162. Teletext und Videotext informieren ebenfalls laufend über das Neuste. Nützliche Rufnummern: Pannenhilfe 140, Polizei 117, Feuerwehr 108, Straßenzustand 163. Diese und weitere Nummern können Sie in allen offiziellen Telefonbüchern auf den blauen Seiten finden. Ladenöffnungszeiten: Montag bis Freitag in der Regel 08.00–18.30 Uhr, am Samstag meistens bis 16.00 Uhr. Auf den wichtigen Bahnhöfen sind Lebensmittel-Automaten installiert. Allgemeine Feiertage sind: Neujahr, Ostern, Auffahrt, Pfingsten und Weihnachten. Der 1. August ist Nationalfeiertag. Über kantonale und lokale Feiertage geben die örtlichen Verkehrsbüros Auskunft. Service inbegriffen gilt in allen Restaurants. Ein Bedienungsgeld ist für Gepäckträger, an Tankstellen mit Kundendienst und in einigen Städten für Taxichauffeure üblich.

Adapted from a text published by the Swiss National Tourist Office

11

In pairs talk about what you like doing in your free time.

Example Am Samstag muß ich arbeiten, aber ich möchte lieber Golf spielen.

12 Listening comprehension

The representative of a British company is in Recklinghausen on a business visit. While there, she is given a tour of the town. Listen to the conversation, then complete the gaps below.

This is the representative's ____________ visit to Recklinghausen, but she has been to the Ruhr District ____________ times before. During the afternoon she is going to see ____________.

Recklinghausen is a ____________ town with many interesting ____________. It is no longer a typical ____________. The ____________ building is St Peter's church. It dates from the ____________ century. The baroque style Engelsburg is now a ____________. There are a few half-timbered houses. In one of them there is a ____________.

Apart from ____________ and art galleries, Recklinghausen has a festival theatre. The Planetarium is another ____________. 40 000 people ____________ it annually. For animal lovers there is the ____________.

Marktplatz mit Propstei-Kirche St. Peter, Recklinghausen

Summary

Useful phrases

1	Inviting someone to see the town/sights	Möchten Sie die Stadt/ Sehenswürdigkeiten besichtigen/ sehen? Wollen Sie die Königsallee sehen? Möchten Sie zuerst die Ringstraße sehen?
2	Expressing acceptance	Ja, gern Das wird bestimmt interessant Sehr gerne
3	Making a suggestion	Nachher könnten wir ein bißchen spazierengehen Dann könnten wir zum Prater fahren
4	Expressing agreement	Ja, das stimmt Meine ich auch
5	Inviting someone to express a preference	Möchten Sie lieber eine Stadtrundfahrt machen oder ein bestimmtes Stadtviertel kennenlernen?

6 Stating possibility	Das geht schon
7 Asking for a recommendation	Was empfehlen Sie?
8 Welcoming someone	Willkommen in . . .

Language forms

1 The imperfect (simple past) tense

This is often used as an alternative to the perfect tense, particularly in written German. It is the tense commonly used in telling stories and relating incidents and in saying what happened on a regular basis.

(a) Regular (weak) verbs
The imperfect is formed by removing *en* from the infinitive and adding the appropriate endings.

kaufen (to buy)

ich kauf*te* (I bought/used to buy/was buying)	wir kauf*ten*
du kauf*test*	ihr kauf*tet*
Sie kauf*ten*	Sie kauf*ten*
er/sie es kauf*te*	sie kauf*ten*

Note Where the stem ends in *t* or *d*, add *e* between the stem and the ending. This makes the word easier to say.

Examples
arbeiten ──► *ich arbeit**ete*** (I worked, I used to work, I was working)
erwarten ──► *wir erwart**eten*** (we expected, we used to expect, we were expecting)

(b) Irregular (strong) verbs
These verbs have their own individual stems to which are added the following endings (note that *ich* and *er/sie/es* do not have an ending):

kommen (to come)

ich kam (I came/used to come/was coming)	wir kam*en*
du kam*st*	ihr kam*t*
Sie kam*en*	Sie kam*en*
er/sie/es kam	sie kam*en*

(c) Mixed verbs
Mixed verbs have their own individual stems but add regular endings.

Examples
denken (to think) ich dach*te*, du dach*test*, er dach*te*, etc.

erkennen (to recognise) ich erkann*te*, du erkann*test*, er erkann*te*, etc.

2 Reflexive verbs

These are verbs whose subject and object are the same person or thing.

Example I wash myself.
subject *object*

The object of a reflexive verb is known as a *reflexive pronoun*. The German reflexive pronouns are:

singular	*plural*
ich ➤ mich (myself)	wir ➤ uns (ourselves)
du ➤ dich (yourself)	ihr ➤ euch (yourselves)
Sie ➤ sich (yourself)	Sie ➤ sich (yourselves)
er ➤ sich (himself, itself)	sie ➤ sich (themselves)
sie ➤ sich (herself, itself)	
es ➤ sich (itself)	

Examples

sich interessieren für (to be interested in, literally: to interest oneself for)

Als Geschäftsmann interessiere ich ***mich*** *für die City.*
As a businessman I'm interested in the City.

sich setzen (to sit down, literally: to seat oneself)

Bitte setzen Sie ***sich***.
Please sit down.

In the perfect tense, the reflexive pronoun follows the auxiliary verb.

Example

sich erinnern an (to remember, literally: to remind oneself of)

Ich habe ***mich*** *an seinen Namen nicht erinnert.*
I didn't remember his name.

3 Dependent infinitive clauses

These express what is wished, expected, intended, hoped for, etc.

Examples

We hope *to travel to Spain this year*
He intends *to go to the conference.*

In German the verb in these clauses is placed at the end and preceded by *zu*. In written German this clause is separated from the preceding clause by a comma.

Examples

Wir hoffen, ***dieses Jahr nach Spanien zu fahren****.*
We hope to travel to Spain this year.

Er hat die Absicht, ***zur Konferenz zu gehen****.*
He intends to go to the conference.

4 The superlative

The superlative is formed in English by adding *est* to an adjective, or by linking it with 'most'.

Example
This is the *most successful* company in Germany with the *highest* exports.

In German the superlative is formed by adding *st* to an adjective. If the adjective ends with *s, t, h* or *z*, then its superlative is formed by adding *est* to make the word easier to say.

Examples

*Das ist der erfolgreich****ste*** *Betrieb in Deutschland.*
That is the most successful company in Germany.

*Die Tagung in Hannover ist die interessant****este*** *des Jahres.*
The conference in Hannover is the most interesting of the year.

If an adjective has an umlaut in the comparative, it also has an umlaut in the superlative.

Examples
alt ➜ *älter* ➜ *älteste*
groß ➜ *größer* ➜ *größte*

As in the comparative, some adjectives do not follow the regular pattern in the superlative.

Examples
gut ➜ *besser* ➜ *beste/am besten*
hoch ➜ *höher* ➜ *höchste/am höchsten*
viel ➜ *mehr* ➜ *meiste/am meisten*

5 Towns/cities used as adjectives

The letters *er* are added to the name of a town or city when it is used adjectivally. This ending remains the same irrespective of the case of the word that follows.

Examples

Ich lese die ***Frankfurter*** *Allgemeine Zeitung.*
I read the Frankfurter Allgemeine newspaper.

Ich esse gern ***Wiener*** *Schnitzel.*
I like to eat Viennese veal cutlet.

*Man fährt schnell mit der **Londoner** U-Bahn.*
You travel fast with the London underground.

Additional exercises

1 Re-write the statements below in the imperfect tense.

(*a*) Ich fahre heute mit der Bahn nach Rom.
(*b*) Der Zug fährt pünktlich ab.
(*c*) Ich genieße die Reise.
(*d*) Das Wetter ist sehr schön.
(*e*) Im Zug esse ich Wiener Schnitzel.
(*f*) Ich lerne viele freundliche Leute kennen.
(*g*) Sie sprechen kein Deutsch.
(*h*) Ich muß Italienisch sprechen.
(*i*) Ich frage den Schaffner: „Wie lange noch bis Rom?"
(*j*) Er antwortet: „Nur noch eine Stunde".

2 Complete the sentences below with the verb in brackets in the imperfect tense.

(*a*) Wir ___ gestern abend ins Kino. (gehen)
(*b*) Der Film ___ sehr lustig (*funny*). (sein)
(*c*) Wir ___ oft. (lachen: *to laugh*)
(*d*) Nach dem Film ___ wir eine Wurst (kaufen).
(*e*) Die Wurst ___ sehr gut (schmecken).
(*f*) Wir ___ mit der Straßenbahn nach Hause. (fahren).
(*g*) Wir ___ nicht weit vom Kino. (wohnen)
(*h*) Nach zehn Minuten ___ die Straßenbahn ___. (anhalten)
(*i*) Ich ___ : „Das war ein schöner Abend". (sagen)

3 Complete each of the following sentences with a reflexive pronoun.

(*a*) Bitte setzen Sie ____.
(*b*) Der Film war furchtbar. Wir langweilten ____.
(*c*) Sie interessiert ____ für Mathematik.
(*d*) Das Kind freut ____ über das Spielzeug.
(*e*) Wir freuen ____ auf den Urlaub.
(*f*) Erinnerst du ____ an mich?
(*g*) Klosterneuburg befindet ____ nicht weit von Wien.
(*h*) Er bedankt ____ für Ihren Brief.
(*i*) Ich langweile ____ nie in London.
(*j*) Sie setzten ____ an den Tisch.

4 Answer the following questions with a full sentence.

(*a*) Der höchste Berg in Österreich ist die Zugspitze, der Großglockner oder der Eiger?.
(*b*) Welcher Fluß ist der längste: der Rhein, die Elbe oder die Donau (*Danube*)?
(*c*) Welche Gegend ist die schönere: das Ruhrgebiet, der Schwarzwald oder die Alpen?
(*d*) Welche Stadt ist die älteste: Welwyn Garden City, Milton Keynes oder York?
(*e*) Welcher Fußballklub ist der berühmteste: Lincoln City, Real Madrid oder FC Tirol?
(*f*) Der kürzeste Monat ist April, August oder Februar?
(*g*) Womit fährt man am schnellsten: mit der Bahn, mit dem Flugzeug oder mit dem Schiff?
(*h*) Wo lernt man Deutsch am besten: in der Schule, zu Hause oder in Deutschland?
(*i*) Was hört man in Kanada am meisten: Englisch oder Französisch?
(*j*) Welcher Wein ist der teuerste: Liebfraumilch, Champagner oder Chianti?

5 What are the following?

(*a*) die Frankfurter Buchmesse
(*b*) die Wiener Sängerknaben
(*c*) das Hamburger Abendblatt
(*d*) der Kölner Dom
(*e*) die Bremer Stadtmusikanten
(*f*) das Brandenburger Tor

Kapital 7–10

Zusätzliche Aufgaben

1 While in Germany you have to go to the doctor, as you are not feeling well. Answer the receptionist's questions:

(*a*) Wie ist Ihr Name bitte?
(*b*) Wie schreibt man das?
(*c*) Ihre Staatsangehörigkeit?
(*d*) Und Ihre Adresse in Deutschland? (*Think of one.*)
(*e*) Haben Sie Ihren Krankenschein? (*You have your E111.*)
(*f*) Darf ich das mal sehen? (*Offer it to the receptionist.*)

2 You are travelling to a business appointment in Schwerin when your car breaks down on the E26 Autobahn between Hamburg and Schwerin. Fortunately you are able to call on the help of a breakdown service.

(*a*) Phone the service, stating that your car has broken down and explaining exactly where you are; ask them to be as quick as possible as you have an important appointment. Give them your mobile phone number: 0171 8204146.

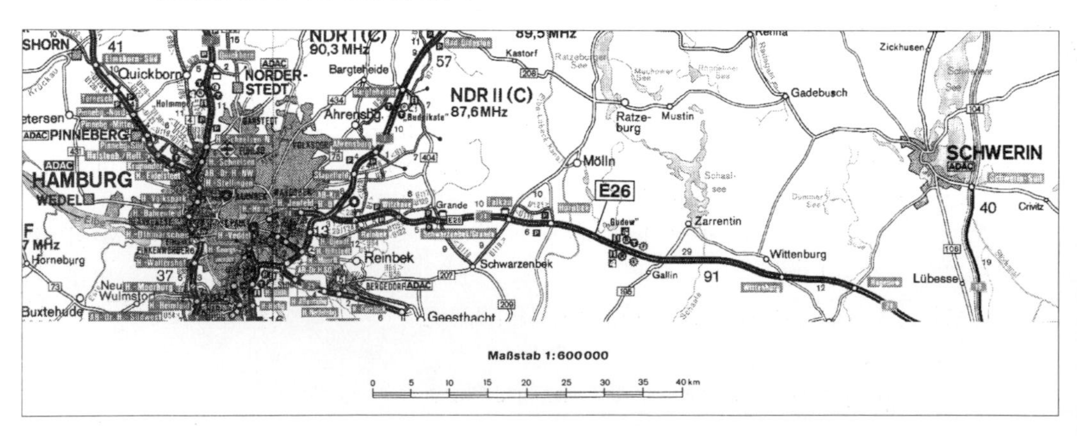

(*b*) Then phone the office where you have an appointment. Leave your message on the answerphone, explaining what has happened, and how long you have been there. Say that you will be about two hours late and that you will phone again when you know more.

3 You are in the centre of a town you know well. A German-speaking motorist stops to ask in halted English the way to a car park. You seize the opportunity to speak in German. Explain how to get to one of the town's car parks. Try to include words like *kleiner* (smaller), *billiger* (cheaper), *größer* (larger), *schneller* (quicker).

Useful vocabulary: *der Parkplatz, das Parkhaus, das Kleingeld, die Tiefgarage.*

4 You are driving through Austria on your way to Switzerland to attend a German language course. Among the literature supplied in advance is this short text on Austria.

Die Republik Österreich

Österreich ist einer der kleineren europäischen Staaten. Seit vielen Jahren bleibt die Einwohnerzahl bei etwa 7,5 Millionen mit zirka achtzig Einwohnern pro Quadratkilometer. Österreich ist zu 90 Prozent katholisch und zu sechs Prozent evangelisch. Die restlichen vier Prozent gehören zu anderen Gruppen. Von Westen nach Osten sind es 560 Kilometer mit einer maximalen Entfernung von Norden nach Süden von nur 280 Kilometern. Nördlich von Österreich liegt Deutschland und südlich Italien. Im Westen liegt die Schweiz.

What does the text say about the following:

(*a*) Austria's size

(*b*) The proportion of inhabitants per km^2

(*c*) Church membership
(*d*) Distances between North, South, East and West
(*e*) The countries surrounding Austria.

5 While on your course you are given the following text about Switzerland with questions to answer. Read the text, then answer the questions in German.

Die Schweiz

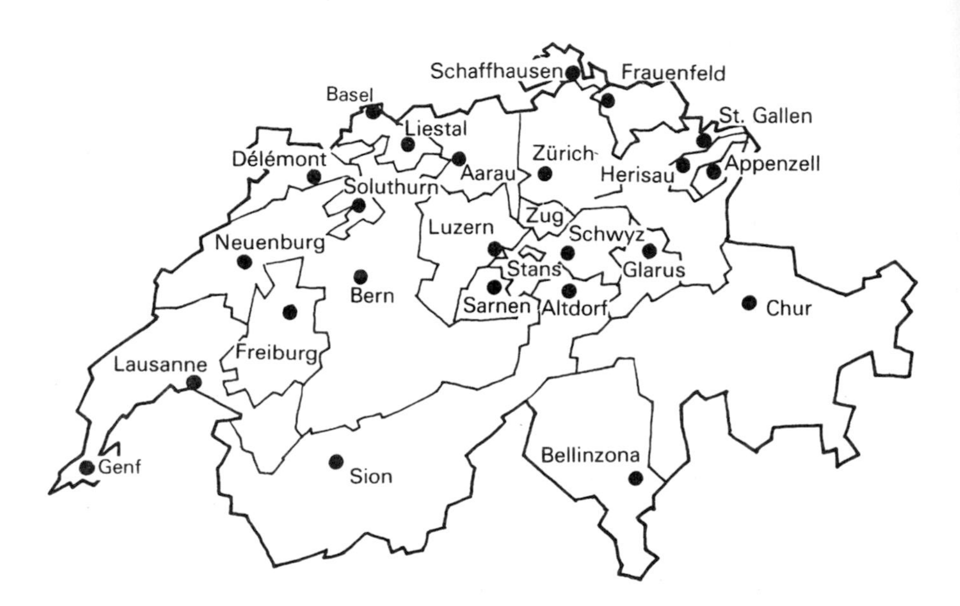

Die Schweiz liegt mitten in Europa und hat als Nachbarländer Deutschland, Österreich, Italien und Frankreich. Die meisten Städte der Schweiz sind nicht sehr groß (Zürich hat 357 000 Einwohner, dann kommt Basel mit 178 000 Einwohnern).

Ein modernes Verkehrsnetz (Autobahn, andere Straßen und Bahn) verbindet die 3000 Gemeinden und Städten. Es gibt auch fünf Flughäfen: in Zürich, Genf, Basel, Bern und Lugano.

Industrie und Handel sind in der Schweiz sehr wichtig. An der Spitze der Exportliste stehen Maschinen, Filmapparate, und chemische und pharmazeutische Produkte. Andere wichtige Ausfuhrgüter (Exportgüter) sind Textilien, Uhren und Lebensmittel.

(*a*) Wieviele Einwohner hat die Schweiz?
(*b*) Wieviele Nachbarländer hat die Schweiz?
(*c*) Wie heißen sie?
(*d*) Ist die Hauptstadt, Bern, eine große oder eine kleine Stadt?

(*e*) Warum ist das Verkehrsnetz wichtig?
(*f*) Wie kann man innerhalb der Schweiz reisen?

6 (*a*) You are entertaining some German-speaking people. Tell them about the area where you live, or an area that you know well.
(*b*) Present what you have prepared to the rest of the class.

7 You are looking for a German friend's car in a car park. While searching you see these number plates. How do they read?

(*a*) NE MH 4130
(*b*) D EZ 8296
(*c*) B CP 7504
(*d*) HB RN 6359
(*e*) M SE 7287
(*f*) F AS 4310

8 You are shopping in a supermarket with a German friend, and are comparing different brands of goods, before deciding which to buy.

Example Dieser Wein ist billig, dieser ist billiger, aber dieser ist am billigsten.

Useful vocabulary: *das Paket, die Flasche, die Tafel, die Tube, das Karton, die Dose, der Beutel, teuer, gut, interessant, wenig, viel, gut schmecken, kosten.*

9 Listening comprehension

You are staying with a friend who wants to take you on a sightseeing tour. What is he suggesting you do?

10 Listening comprehension

Your colleague is interested in buying a new car. She phones the dealer who answers her questions over the phone. You listen in to the conversation.

(*a*) What does it cost?
(*b*) What weight is it?
(*c*) What is the maximum speed?
(*d*) Its length?
(*e*) Its width?
(*f*) Number of cylinders?
(*g*) Tyre pressure: At the front? At the rear?
(*h*) Petrol tank capacity?

11 The company where you are working plans to hold a conference at the *Kurhalle* in Triberg. Among the events there will be speeches, films, and group seminars. About 300 people are expected. Why is the *Kurhalle* suitable? What are the catering facilities?

Das 'neue' Kurhaus – der festliche Rahmen für viele Anlässe
Das Kurhaus ist Tribergs gesellschaftlicher und kultureller Mittelpunkt. Ein großer und ein kleiner Saal sowie verschiedene Nebenräume bieten zahlreiche Möglichkeiten, Veranstaltungen in freundlicher Atmosphäre ganz individuell auszurichten. Dia- und Filmvorführungen sind hier auch möglich. Als Kommunikationszentrum bieten wir damit die Möglichkeit für Tagungen von 50–700 Personen, sowie Konferenzen, Seminare, Schulungen, Begegnungen und Jubiläen. Unsere Informationsstelle im Kurhaus gibt Ihnen gerne alle nötigen Auskünfte. Fordern Sie unsere Tagungsmappe an:
Kurverwaltung Triberg, Postfach 1334, 78098 Triberg, Tel (0 77 22) 8 12 30, Fax (0 77 22) 8 12 36

12 **Listening comprehension**

Peter Vögtle works as a representative for an Austrian food manufacturer. Listen to the interview, then answer the questions in German.

(*a*) Woher kommt er, und wo arbeitet er?
(*b*) Warum findet er seine Arbeit interessant? (drei Gründe)
(*c*) Welche Sprachen kann er?
(*d*) Wieviel Urlaub bekommt er?
(*e*) Was macht er oft im Urlaub?
(*f*) Was macht er nächstes Jahr? Warum? Wann genau?
(*g*) Sucht er im Moment einen neuen Job? Warum (nicht)?
(*h*) Wieviele Stunden pro Woche arbeitet er ungefähr, wenn er nicht unterwegs ist?

13 Carry out interviews with a partner along the lines of Exercise 12, and report back to the rest of the class.

14 The German headquarters of the company that you work for has asked you to write a few lines about yourself, your hobbies and your work for possible inclusion in the staff magazine. Tell the rest of the class what you have written.

15 During a week-long conference which you are helping to organise, there will be a trip to London, mainly for sight-seeing purposes. Plan this trip in outline, ready to send to the German-speaking participants.

16 (a) A German-speaking colleague is part of a group visiting your company for a few days from 2–5 June, and although you are quite busy, you wish to invite your colleague to your home. You and your colleague are trying to fix a time.
Your diary:

Monday	**Thursday** am meetings with German group pm publicity presentation + cinema?
Tuesday Reception for German group Dinner for German group	**Friday** German group departs 8.00
Wednesday Meeting + tour of factory/research Evening class (exam preparation)	**Saturday**

(*b*) Imagine you are a German visiting a UK company. Try to fix a time when you can visit a UK colleague's home.
Your diary:

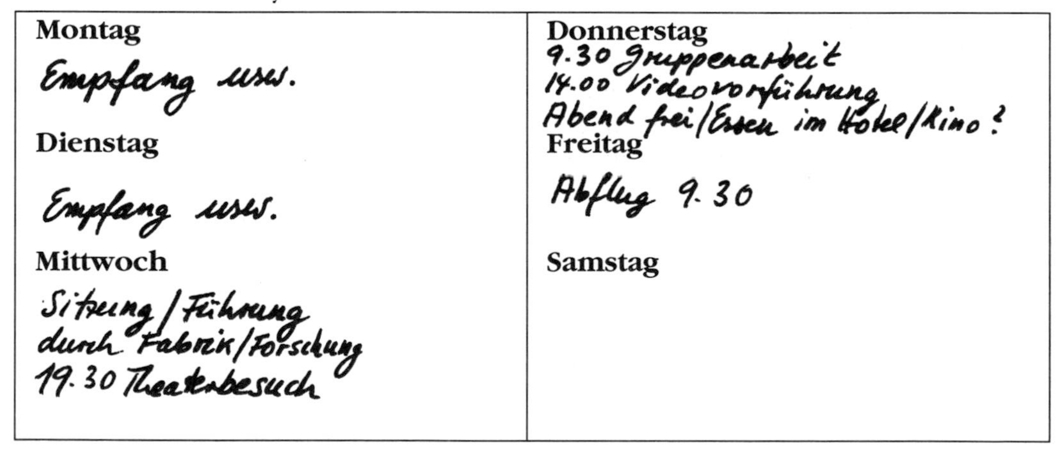

Montag Empfang usw.	**Donnerstag** 9.30 Gruppenarbeit 14.00 Videovorführung Abend frei/Essen im Hotel/Kino?
Dienstag Empfang usw.	**Freitag** Abflug 9.30
Mittwoch Sitzung/Führung durch Fabrik/Forschung 19.30 Theaterbesuch	**Samstag**

17 Your boss is busy and keeps thinking of ways in which you can help him. What have you got to do?

18 While attending a German course, you learn about the imperfect tense/simple past. There is a word search on page 164 to help you learn the verb forms of the following verbs: *können, machen, wissen, tun, gehen, sein, fahren, müssen, essen, werden.*

M	P	K	Ö	N	N	T	E
U	A	G	H	J	E	N	O
S	F	C	I	G	N	I	G
S	Q	D	H	A	C	M	N
T	A	T	B	T	L	Y	E
E	E	X	R	C	E	Z	D
K	R	H	D	A	R	B	R
S	U	W	E	S	O	A	U
F	V	E	T	S	S	U	W

Glossary of grammatical terms

How to use this glossary

1 In some cases, definitions or explanations will be given using other items in the glossary. Should the items used in this way present difficulty, they should also be looked up.

2 As the definitions or explanations are in English, examples are given in English unless a German example is more suited in a particular instance (e.g. compound verbs).

accusative This is the form in which the object of a verb is expressed. The form also occurs after certain prepositions.

adjective A word used to described something (e.g. big, small)

adverb Adverbs modify other words by giving a sharper focus to their meaning. For example, they can give information relating to manner, degree, intensity, etc.
An adverb can modify a verb by saying how the action is done (e.g. quickly); it can modify another adverb (e.g. *very* quickly); it can modify an adjective (e.g. *extremely* clever); it can modify a preposition (e.g. *just* behind the door).
An adverb can also answer the question 'when' (e.g. now, then, sometimes).

auxiliary verb A verb that is used to help in the formation of a tense (e.g. I *will* go; she *has* gone); a mood (e.g. I *would* go, she *might* go); or the passive (e.g. you *were* seen, they *got* hurt).

case The form in which a noun, pronoun or adjective is expressed to show its relationship to other words in a sentence.

clause A block of words that contains a subject, and information about that subject.

comparative The form used of adjectives or adverbs to show a higher degree of a particular quality (e.g. cleverer, smaller, more sensible, more quickly).

compound verb A verb formed by the combination of two other verbs (e.g. *kennen* + *lernen* ⟶ *kennenlernen*).

dative The case used to express the indirect object of a verb. This form also occurs after certain prepositions and verbs.

definite article The word 'the' used to refer to specify a particular instance of something (e.g. *The* man over there).

demonstrative adjective Indicates which person or thing is referred to (e.g. this/that).

demonstrative pronoun Indicates the person or thing referred to in a more emphatic way than a personal pronoun (e.g. *this one*, *that one*, *the one who*). Examples in German include *derjenige* or *der*, *diejenige* or *die*.

dependent infinitive clause A clause containing an infinitive, which expresses the content of what is hoped, wished, expected, etc. (e.g. We hope *to go tomorrow*, She expects *to pass the exam*.)

direct object See **object**.

feminine Female.

future tense The tense that expresses what is going to happen or is expected to happen (e.g. They *will* stay in tonight).

gender The classification of words according to sex, i.e. masculine (male), feminine (female), neuter (sexless). In German, gender is not always determined by an inherent male, female or neuter quality.

genitive The case that expresses possession (e.g. the owner *of* the company/the company'*s* owner).

imperative Expresses a command (e.g. Go away!).

imperfect tense Also known as the simple past tense. It is the tense that expresses what happened in the past on a regular basis (e.g. He *used* to play for Arsenal). It is also used to relate an action in progress in the past (e.g. They *were* playing). It is often used in written German as an alternative to the perfect tense in story-telling or when relating incidents.

indefinite article The word 'a/an' used when something is not specified (e.g. 'I bought *a* book' as opposed to 'I bought *the* book by Jones').

indefinite pronoun A pronoun that does not designate a specific person or thing (e.g. any, some, one). In German the word *einer/eine/eines* is used as an indefinite pronoun (e.g. *einer der Bewerber* means 'one of the applicants').

indirect object See **object**.

infinitive The name of a particular verb (e.g. to run, to jump, etc).

interrogative adjective Asks the question 'which?'

irregular verb Also known as a strong verb. It is a verb that does not follow the usual rules of formation either because it has a different stem or because it has different endings to regular verbs.

main clause Also known as a simple sentence. It is a block of words that communicates a complete thought or message (e.g. He plays the piano).

masculine Male.

modal verb One that expresses the degree of pressure or freedom a person experiences when doing something. Modal verbs include the idea of possibility, willingness and compulsion (e.g. can, may, want, ought, should, must).

negation/the negative Expressing that something is not the case. Use of the word 'not' is the most frequent means of forming the negative.

neuter Sexless, i.e. neither masculine (male) nor feminine (female).

noun A word used to name or identify persons, places or things.

nominative The case that expresses the subject of a verb.

object There are two kinds of object: the *direct object* which receives the action of a verb (e.g. He wrote *the letter*); the *indirect object* which is the person or thing that does not receive the action of a verb but is nevertheless affected by the verb (e.g. He sent *the company* a fax).

past participle The form of the verb showing that an action has been finished or that a change of state has occurred (e.g. We have *closed* the deal; I have *been* ill).

perfect tense Denotes that an action that took place in the past was completely finished (e.g. I have read the book). In English it is formed with 'has/have' plus a past participle: in German it is formed with the verbs *haben* or *sein* plus a past participle.

personal pronoun A word standing in place of a subject or object (e.g. 'Michael Newby speaks German' becomes '*He* speaks *it*').

plural More than one. The opposite of 'singular'.

possessive adjective Shows whose something is (e.g. my, your, his book).

prefix An element placed at the beginning of a word to form a new word, but with a meaning connected with the original word (e.g. *after*thought, *re*consider).

preposition A word that shows a relationship between persons or things in time or space (e.g. She works *for* Siemens; The file is *on* your desk).

present tense The tense that expresses what is happening now (e.g. *It's snowing*) or what happens on a regular basis (e.g. *I go* to the Frankfurt Book Fair every year).

pronoun A word used to replace a noun so as to avoid repetition of the noun (e.g. 'Jane lives in Essen and *she* likes it there' instead of 'Jane lives in Essen and Jane likes it there').

reflexive pronoun The object of a reflexive verb (myself, yourself, himself, herself, etc.).

reflexive verb A verb of which the subject and object are the same (e.g. *I* wash *myself*).

regular verb A verb that always obeys rules of formation relating to stem and ending, e.g. *machen*.

sentence The complete expression of a message or thought in the form of a statement, a command, a question, or an exclamation.

separable verb A German verb whose prefix separates from the rest of the verb when no other verb is present in the sentence (e.g. ausgehen ⟶ Ich *gehe* heute abend *aus*).

simple past tense See **imperfect tense**.

singular Denoting one person or thing. The opposite of 'plural'.

stem The part of the verb onto which endings are attached.

strong verb See **irregular verb**.

subject The element in the sentence which the sentence is about, e.g. **Wolfgang Schüßler** ist Student in Berlin.

subordinate clause A clause with incomplete meaning (e.g. When the computer breaks down; If I go). Extra information is needed to make full sense of the clause (e.g. When the computer breaks down, I call the engineer).

subordinating conjunction A word linking two clauses and introducing a subordinate clause (e.g. if, when, although, because).

superlative Expresses the highest degree of a quality (e.g. cleverest).

tense The form of a verb that indicates whether an action is in the past, present or future.

verb A word used to express an action (e.g. he *runs*), a state (e.g. I *am*) or an occurrence (e.g. it *happens*).

weak verb See **regular verb.**

Irregular verbs

The following is a list of the principal parts of irregular verbs occurring in *Working with German Coursebook 1.*
*verbs taking *sein* in the perfect tense

Infinitive	3rd Person Singular Present	3rd Person Singular Imperfect	Past Participle
befinden (sich)	befindet	befand	befunden
beginnen	beginnt	begann	begonnen
bekommen	bekommt	bekam	bekommen
besitzen	besitzt	besaß	besessen
bestehen	besteht	bestand	bestanden
bieten	bietet	bot	geboten
binden	bindet	band	gebunden
bleiben*	bleibt	blieb	geblieben
brennen	brennt	brannte	gebrannt
bringen	bringt	brachte	gebracht
denken	denkt	dachte	gedacht
dürfen	darf	durfte	gedurft
empfehlen	empfiehlt	empfahl	empfohlen
entsprechen	entspricht	entsprach	entsprochen
erhalten	erhält	erhielt	erhalten
erkennen	erkennt	erkannte	erkannt
erscheinen*	erscheint	erschien	erschienen
essen	ißt	aß	gegessen
fahren*	fährt	fuhr	gefahren
finden	findet	fand	gefunden
fliegen*	fliegt	flog	geflogen
geben	gibt	gab	gegeben
gehen*	geht	ging	gegangen
gelten	gilt	galt	gegolten
genießen	genießt	genoß	genossen
geschehen*	geschieht	geschah	geschehen
gewinnen	gewinnt	gewann	gewonnen
haben	hat	hatte	gehabt
halten	hält	hielt	gehalten
heben	hebt	hob	gehoben
heißen	heißt	hieß	geheißen
helfen	hilft	half	geholfen
kennen	kennt	kannte	gekannt
kommen*	kommt	kam	gekommen
können	kann	konnte	gekonnt

Infinitive	3rd Person Singular Present	3rd Person Singular Imperfect	Past Participle
lassen	läßt	ließ	gelassen
liegen	liegt	lag	gelegen
mögen	mag	mochte	gemocht
müssen	muß	mußte	gemußt
nehmen	nimmt	nahm	genommen
rufen	ruft	rief	gerufen
schlafen	schläft	schlief	geschlafen
schließen	schließt	schloß	geschlossen
schreiben	schreibt	schrieb	geschrieben
sehen	sieht	sah	gesehen
sein*	ist	war	gewesen
sinken*	sinkt	sank	gesunken
sitzen	sitzt	saß	gesessen
sollen	soll	sollte	gesollt
sprechen	spricht	sprach	gesprochen
stehen	steht	stand	gestanden
steigen*	steigt	stieg	gestiegen
tragen	trägt	trug	getragen
treffen	trifft	traf	getroffen
treiben	treibt	trieb	getrieben
trinken	trinkt	trank	getrunken
tun	tut	tat	getan
verbinden	verbindet	verband	verbunden
verlieren	verliert	verlor	verloren
verraten	verrät	verriet	verraten
verstehen	versteht	verstand	verstanden
waschen	wäscht	wusch	gewaschen
werden*	wird	wurde	geworden
werfen	wirft	warf	geworfen
wissen	weiß	wußte	gewußt
wollen	will	wollte	gewollt
ziehen	zieht	zog	gezogen

Vocabulary list

*irregular verb

A

ab (*dat*) from
das **Abendessen, –** supper
aber but
abfahren* (*sep*) to set off, to leave
die **Abfahrt, –en** departure
die **Abfrage, –n** enquiry
abgehen* (*sep*) to hand in
abheben* (*sep*) to take out (money from bank)
abholen (*sep*) to meet (at station)
die **Abmessung, –en** dimension
die **Abreise, –n** departure
der **Absender, –** sender
Abstand gewinnen* to distance onself
die **Abteilung, –en** department
abziehen* (*sep*) to deduct
die **Adresse, –n** address
aktuell current
akzeptieren to accept
alle all
alles everything
Allerheiligen All Saints' Day
Allerseelen All Souls' Day
allerlei all sorts of
allgemein general
der **Alkohol, –e** alcohol
alphabetisch alphabetical
als than, as
also therefore, well, right, OK
also gut OK then
alt old
der **Amerikaner, –** American (man)
die **Amerikanerin, – nen** American (woman)
die **Ampel, –n** traffic lights
amüsieren (*refl*) to enjoy oneself
an (*acc/dat*) at
die **Ananas, –** pineapple
anbieten* (*sep*) to offer
das **Andenken, –** souvenir
andere other
anerkennen* (sep) to recognise
der **Anfang, ¨–e** beginning
die **Anfrage, –n** request, enquiry
das **Angebot, –e** offer, quote
angenehm pleasant
der **Angestellte, –n** clerk
das **Anmeldeformular, –e** registration form
ankommen* (*sep*) to arrive
die **Ankunft, ¨–e** arrival
anpassen (*sep*) to adjust
anprobieren (*sep*) to try on
anregen (*sep*) to stimulate
die **Anspruchsbescheinigung, –en** certiticate of entitlement
antiallergisch anti-allergic
der **Antiquitätenladen, ¨–** antique shop
der **Apfel, ¨–e** apple
das **Apfelkompott** stewed apple
der **Apfelsaft** apple juice
die **Apotheke, –n** dispensing chemist's shop
der **Apotheker, –** chemist
der **April** April
arabisch Arabian
die **Arbeit, –en** work
arbeiten to work
der **Arbeiter, –** worker
der **Arbeitgeber, –** employer
der **Arbeitnehmer, –** employee
das **Appartement, –s** apartment
der **Architekt, –en** architect
die **Architektur** architecture
ärgerlich annoying
der **Arzt, ¨–e** doctor
ärztlich medical
Ashermittwoch Ash Wednesday
atmen to breathe
die **Attraktion, –en** attraction
auch also
auf (*acc/dat*) on, on to
aufbewahren (*sep*) to store
aufbrauchen (*sep*) to use up
der **Aufenthalt, –e** stay
die **Auffahrt** Ascension Day

die **Aufgabe, –n** task
aufheben* to lift
die **Auflösung, –en** solution
die **Aufmerksamkeit** attention
das **Auge, –n** eye
der **Augenblick, –e** moment
die **Augentropfen** (*pl*) eyedrops
der **August** August
aus (*dat*) from, of
der **Ausbildungsplatz, –̈e** position with on-the-job training
die **Ausfahrt, –en** exit
der **Ausflugsbus, –se** excursion bus
die **Ausflugsfahrt, –en** excursion
die **Ausfuhrgüter** (*pl*) export goods
ausfüllen (*sep*) to fill in
ausgeben* (*sep*) to spend (money)
die **Auskunft, –̈e** information
das **Ausland** abroad, overseas
auslösen (*sep*) to operate, release
ausreichend sufficient
außen outside
außer except
außerhalb (*gen*) outside
die **Aussicht** view
das **Auto, –s** car
mit dem Auto by car
die **Autobahn, –en** motorway
der **Autofocus** automatic focus
der **Automat, –en** automatic machine

B
das **Bad, –̈er** bath
die **Bahn, –en** train
mit der Bahn by train
der **Bahnhof, –̈e** station
bald soon
ballaststoffreich full of roughage
der **Balkon, –s** balcony
die **Bank, –en** bank
das **Bankett, –e** banquet
die **Banknote, –n** bank-note
bankrott machen to go bankrupt
der **Bann, –e** charm, spell
die **Bar, –s** bar
die **Barabholung** access to cash
das **Bargeld** cash
barock baroque
basteln to do handicrafts
die **Batterie, –n** battery
der **Bauchtanz, –̈e** belly dance
die **Bauernstube, –n** snug, quaint bar; Tyrolean bar
der **Baum, –̈e** tree
bayerisch Bavarian
beachten to watch out for
bedanken (*refl*) to thank, be grateful
der **Bedarf** need
der **Bedienerschlüssel,–** key
der **Bedienung-Service** table service
die **Bedienungsanleitung, –en** operating instructions
das **Bedienungsgeld, –er** tip, service charge
bedeutend significant
beherbergen to house
befinden* (*refl*) to be (situated)
beginnen* to begin
die **Begleichung, –en** settlement, payment
bei (*dat*) at, near
das **Bein, –e** leg
beinahe almost
das **Beispiel, –e** example
zum Beispiel for example
bekannt familiar
der **Bekannte, –n** acquaintance
die **Bekleidung** clothing
bekommen* to get, to have
der **Beleg, –e** voucher, slip
Belgien Belgium
der **Belgier, –** Belgian (man)
die **Belgierin, –nen** Belgian (woman)
beleidigt offended
die **Belichtung** exposure
benötigen to need
benutzen to use
der **Benzinverbrauch** petrol consumption
die **Beratung** advice, consultation
die **Berechnung, –en** charge
bereit ready
der **Berg, –e** mountain
der **Beruf, –e** career, profession
der **Berufskraftfahrer, –** professional lorry driver
berühmt famous
berühren to touch
beschaffen to obtain
beschäftigen to employ
die **Bescheinigung, –en** certificate
die **Beschränkung, –en** limit
besichtigen to look round, visit
besitzen* to have, possess

besonders especially
besser better
die **Besserung** improvement
bestehen* **aus** (*dat*) to consist of
bestellen to order
bestimmt certainly
der **Bestimmungsort, –** destination
der **Besuch, –e** visit
zu Besuch kommen to visit
Besuch haben to have visitors
besuchen to visit
der **Betrag, ¨–e** total
betreiben* to take place (winter sports)
der **Betrieb, –e** company
der **Betriebsingenieur, –e** works engineer
der **Betriebsrat** works council
das **Bett, –en** bed
der **Beutel, –** bar
bevor before
die **Bewegung, –en** movement
bewirken to do
bezahlen to pay
beziehungsweise or
das **Bier, –e** beer
das **Bild, –er** picture
der **Bildschirm, –e** screen
billig cheap
binden* to bind, tie
die **Birne, –n** pear
bis (zum, zur) until
bitte please
bitte schön/sehr it's a pleasure, you're welcome
blau blue
bleiben* to stay
bleifrei lead-free
der **Blitz, –e** flash
die **Blume, –n** flower
das **Blumenhaus, ¨–er** flower shop
der **Blumenkohl, –e** cauliflower
die **Bluse, –n** blouse
der **Bluthochdruck** high blood pressure
an Bord on board
die **Boutique, –n** boutique
die **Branche, –n** branch, area
brauchen to need
die **Brauerei, –en** brewery
breit wide
die **Breite, –n** width
die **Bremse, –n** brake
brennen* to burn
der **Brief, –e** letter
der **Briefeinwurf** letter-box in post office
der **Briefkasten, ¨–** postbox
die **Briefmarke, –n** postage stamp
die **Brieftasche, –n** wallet
bringen* to bring
der **Brite, –n** British (man)
die **Britin, –nen** British (woman)
das **Brot, –e** bread
das **Brötchen, –** bread roll
das **Buch, ¨–er** book
zu Buche schlagen to be bad
buchstabieren to spell
der **Bummel, –** stroll
die **Bundeskegelbahn** skittle alley (to official German dimensions)
das **Bundesland, ¨–e** federal state (Germany), federal province (Austria)
das **Bundesparlament** federal parliament
die **Bundespost** federal postal service
der **Bundesrat** upper house (Parliament)
die **Bundesrepublik Deutschland** Germany
bürgerlich plain, homely
das **Büro, –s** office
der **Bus, –se** bus
mit dem Bus by bus
die **Butter** butter

C

ca. (circa) approximately
der **Campingplatz, ¨–e** camp-site
das **Café, –s** café
der **Champignon, –s** mushroom
die **Chefsekretärin, –nen** head secretary
die **Chemikalien** (*pl*) chemicals
chemisch chemical
die **Christi Himmelfahrt** Ascension Day
die **Codierung** coding
der **Computer, –** computer

D

Dänemark Denmark
danken to thank
danke schön thank you very much
dann then
der **Darm, ¨–e** bowel
darüber across
daß· that
das **Datum, Daten** date

die **Delikatesse, –n** delicacy
dauern to last
denken* to think
denn because, then
das **Deutsch** German (language)
der **Deutsche, –n** German (man)
die **Deutsche, –n** German (woman)
die **Devise, –n** foreign currency
der **Dezember** December
dezent subdued, discreet
die **Diät, –en** diet
der **Dialog, –e** dialogue, message
dick fat
dieser this
direkt direct, straight
die **Diskette, –n** disk
die **Disko, –s** disco
der **Dolmetscher, –** interpreter
der **Dom, –e** cathedral
der **Doppeldecker, –** double-decker bus
das **Doppelzimmer, –** double room
dort there
dort drüben over there
die **Dose, –n** tin
drei three
das **Drittel, –** third
drittgrößte third largest
die **Drogerie, –n** non-dispensing chemist
drüben over (there)
drücken to press
duften to be scented
duftend aromatic
der **Durchfall** diarrhoea
durchgehend non-stop, the whole time
durchschlafen* to sleep through the night
durchsuchen to search (through)
die **Durchwahl, –en** direct dialling
dürfen to be allowed
der **Durst** thirst
die **Dusche, –n** shower

E

ebenfalls also, likewise
die **Ecke, –n** corner
das **Ei, –er** egg
eigen (its) own
eigentlich schon yes, I am actually; yes, I do actually
der **Eigentümer, –** proprietor
eignen (*refl*) **für** to be suitable for
einbeziehen* (*sep*) to include
eilig in a hurry
der **Einblick, –e** insight
eingerichtet furnished
einfach single, simple
eingebaut built–in
einige some, several
einkaufen (*sep*) to buy
das **Einkaufen** shopping
der **Einkaufsleiter,–** senior buyer (man)
die **Einkaufsleiterin, –nen** senior buyer (woman)
die **Einkaufsstadt, ¨–e** shopping centre (literally town)
das **Einkaufszentrum, –en** shopping centre
das **Einkommen, –** income
der **Einlieferungsschein, –** certificate of posting
einlösen (*sep*) to cash
das **Einmachen** bottling (fruit)
einmal one (literally 'once')
einmalig unique
einige several
das **Einmarkstück, –e** one-mark coin
einnehmen to eat and drink, partake of; to take
eins one
einsteigen* (*sep*) to get into
einstellen (*refl*) to watch out for
eintauschen (*sep*) to exchange
der **Eintritt** entrance (fee)
einwerfen* (*sep*) to put, to post
der **Einwohner, –** inhabitant
die **Einwohnerzahl, –en** number of inhabitants
das **Einzelzimmer, –** single room
das **Eis, –e** ice, ice-cream
das **Eisen** iron
elegant elegant
elektrisch electric
der **Elektroniker, –** electronics engineer
elektronisch electronic
elf eleven
die **Eltern** (*pl*) parents
der **Empfänger, –** recipient
die **Empfangshalle, –n** reception area
empfehlen* to recommend
das **Ende, –n** end
eng narrow

der **Engländer, –** Englishman
die **Engländerin, –nen** English woman
englisch English
entfernt away
die **Entdeckung, en** discovery
die **Entfernung, –en** distance
enthalten* to include, to contain
entlang (*acc*) along
die **Entleerung** emptying, evacuation
entschuldigen to excuse
entspannen (*refl*) to relax
die **Entspannung** relaxation
entsprechen* to correspond to
entsprechend according to
entweder . . . oder . . . either... or
entwerten to cancel, to stamp
er he, it
die **Erbse, –n** pea
die **Erbsensuppe, –n** pea soup
der **Erdbeerjoghurt** strawberry yoghurt
die **Erdnuß, ¨–sse** peanut
der **Erdteil, –e** part of the earth
erfolgreich successful
erforderlich essential
das **Erdgeschoß** ground floor
erhalten* to get, to receive
erhältlich available
erinnern (*refl*) **an** (*acc*) to remember
die **Erkältung, –en** cold, chill
erkennen to recognise
die **Erklärung,–en** explanation, description
das **Erlebnis, –se** experience
erledigen to settle
ermöglichen to make possible
die **Ernährung** nutrition, nourishment
die **Ernte, –n** harvest
erscheinen* to appear
die **Erste Hilfe** first aid
erste first
erstmals firstly
der **Erwachsene, –n** adult
erwarten to expect
es it
das **Essen, –** meal
essen* to eat
essen gehen* to go out for a meal
die **Eßgewohnheit, –en** eating habits
etwa about, around
etwas some, something, somewhat
europäisch European
die **Europäische Union** European Union
evangelisch Protestant
das **Exemplar, –e** copy
explosionsartig like an explosion
exportieren to export
die **Exportleiterin, –nen** export manager (woman)
die **Exportliste, –n** list of exports
die **Exportgüter** (*pl*) exports

F

die **Fabrik, –en** factory
der **Fachhandel** specialist trade
fachlich specialist
das **Fachwerkhaus, ¨–er** half-timbered house
fähig able, capable
die **Fahrbahn, –en** roadway
fahren* to go (by transport), to leave
der **Fahrer, –** driver
die **Fahrkarte, –n** ticket
die **Fahrkartenausgabe, –n** ticket-office
der **Fahrplanauszug, ¨–e** extract from travel timetable
der **Fahrpreis, –e** travel cost
der **Fahrschein, –e** ticket
der **Fahrstuhl, ¨–e** lift
die **Fahrt, –en** journey
das **Fahrzeug, –e** vehicle
falsch wrong
die **Familie, –n** family
der **Familienname, –n** surname
fangfrisch freshly caught
das **Farbbild, –er** colour picture
der **Farbfernseher, –** colour television
das **Faß, ¨–er** cask
fast almost
fehlen to be the matter
der **Feiertag, –e** public holiday
der **Februar** February
der **Fehler,–** mistake
die **Feinmechanik** precision engineering
die **Fensterbank, ¨–e** window seat
die **Ferienwohnung, –en** holiday flat
das **Fernsehen, –** television
fernsehen* (*sep*) to watch television
die **Festplatte, -en** hard disk
der **Festsaal** party room
das **Festspiel, –e** festival
fett fat
die **Feuerwehr** firebrigade
der **Film, –e** film
finden* to find

die **Firma, Firmen** firm, company
fix und fertig complete
die **Fläche, –n** area
die **Flasche, –n** bottle
das **Fleisch** meat
fliegen* to fly
der **Flug, ¨–e** flight
der **Flughafen, ¨–** airport
die **Flugkarte, –n** air ticket
folgend following
fördern to assist
das **Formular, –e** form
die **Forschung, –en** research
der **Fotoartikel, –** photographic accessories
Frankreich France
der **Franzose, –n** Frenchman
die **Französin, –nen** French woman
französisch French
die **Frau, –en** wife, woman, Mrs (or Miss/Ms in titles)
frei free
die **Freizeitshalle, –n** recreation room
freuen (*refl*) to be pleased
freuen (*refl*) **auf** (*acc*) to look forward to
der **Freund, –e** friend (male)
die **Freundin, –nen** friend (female)
freundlich friendly
frisch fresh
frischgepreßt freshly squeezed
der **Frisiersalon, –s** hairdresser's
der **Friseur, –e** hairdresser
der **Fronleichnam** Corpus Christi
das **Frühstück, –e** breakfast
frühstücken to have breakfast
fünf five
funktionieren to work, to operate
für (*acc*) for
führen to lead, to display
der **Führerschein, –e** driving licence
die **Führung, –en** guided tour
der **Füllstoff, –e** fibre (which makes you feel full)
der **Fuß, ¨–e** foot
zu Fuß on foot
die **Fußgängerzone, –n** pedestrian precinct

G

die **Gabel, –n** fork
der **Gang, ¨–e** course
die **Gänseleber, -n** goose liver
ganz whole, complete
ganzjährig all year round
der **Garagenhof, ¨–e** parking area
gar nicht not at all
das **Gartencenter,–** garden centre
das **Gartengerät, –e** garden implement
das **Gartenschloß ¨–sser** castle with large grounds
der **Gast, ¨–e** guest
der **Gasthof, ¨–e** pub
die **Gaststätte, –n** pub
geben* to give
das **Gebäude, –** building
gebrauchen to use
gedeckt laden
geeignet suitable
gefallen* to please
gegen (*acc*) against, in return for
gegenüber (*dat*) opposite
die **Gegend, –en** area
die **Gegenwart** present (time)
das **Gehackte** minced beef
die **Geheimzahl, –en** secret number
gehen* to go (on foot)
gehören (zu) (*dat*) to belong to
gelb yellow
das **Geld, –er** money
das **Geldautomat, –en** cash dispenser
der **Geldwechsel, –** bureau de change
gelten to be applicable
der **Gemahl, –e** spouse
die **Gemeinde, –n** community
gemischt mixed
das **Gemüse** (*pl*) vegetables
gemütlich cosy
genau exactly
genauso just as
genießen* to enjoy
genußvoll enjoyable
geöffnet open
das **Gepäck** luggage
der **Gepäckträger, –** porter
gepflegt cultivated, seasoned (wine)
geradeaus straight on
das **Gericht, –e** dish (food)
gering low, small
gern(e) I'd like to, of course, gladly
gern geschehen it's a pleasure
gesamt entire
der **Gesamtbetrag, ¨–e** total amount
das **Gesamteinkommen, –** total income
das **Geschäft, –e** shop

der **Geschäftsführer, –** managing director
der **Geschäftsmann, –leute** businessman
die **Geschäftsreise, –n** business trip
die **Geschäftstelle, –n** bank/where you have an account
geschehen* to happen
das **Geschenk, –e** present
die **Geschichte, –n** history
geschlossen closed
der **Geschmack, ¨–e** taste
die **Geschwindigkeit, –en** speed
gesondert separate
gesund healthy
gestern abend yesterday evening
die **Getränkekarte, –n** wine list
das **Gewicht, –e** weight
gewürzt spiced
gezuckert sweetened
das **Glas, ¨–er** glass
gleich right away, just
gleichfalls likewise
das **Gleis, –e** track, platform
golden golden
die **Grenze, –n** border
Griechenland Greece
der **Griff, –e** handle
der **Grill** barbecue
die **Grippe** flu
groß large
Großbritannien Great Britain
die **Größe, –n** size
grün green
die **grüne Versicherungskarte, –n** green card (insurance)
ins Grüne in the country
die **Gruppe, –n** group
günstig favourable
gut good, well
die **Güteklasse, –n** quality
die **Güter** (*pl*) goods

H

haben* to have
halb half
Halbpension half-board
die **Hälfte, –n** half
die **Halsschmerzen** (*pl*) sore throat
die **Hand, ¨–e** hand
etwas zur Hand haben to have available
der **Handel** trade
Handel treiben to trade
der **Handelspartner, –** trading partner
die **Handelsstadt, ¨–e** commercial town
die **Haselnußcreme** hazelnut spread
häufig frequent
der **Hauptbahnhof, ¨–e** main station
der **Hauptexport, –e** main export
das **Hauptgericht, –e** main course
hauptsächlich mainly
die **Hauptstadt, ¨–e** capital city, town
das **Haus, ¨–er** house
zu Hause at home
der **Haushaltsartikel, –** household item
der **Heilbutt** halibut
Heilige Drei Könige Epiphany
der **Heimarbeiter, –** home worker
heißen* to be called
helfen* to help
das **Hemd, –en** shirt
herrlich magnificent, splendid
die **Herrenbekleidung** menswear
die **Herrschaften** (*pl*) ladies and gentlemen
herstellen (*sep*) to produce
die **Herstellung** production
herunter down
das **Herz, –en** heart
herzlichen Dank thank you very much indeed
heute today
heute früh this morning
heute nachmittag this afternoon
hier here
hierher here (movement)
die **Hilfe, –n** help
der **Himbeerjoghurt, –s** raspberry yoghurt
hingegen on the other hand
hin und zurück there and back, return
hinter behind
hinunter down, along
hinüber across
hinweisen (*sep*) **auf** to indicate, point to
hoch high
die **Höchstgeschwindigkeit, –en** maximum speed
die **Hochstraße, –n** flyover road
Holland Holland
holländisch Dutch
der **Honig** honey
hören to hear
die **Hose, –n** pair of trousers
das **Hotel, –s** hotel

das **Hotel garni** bed and breakfast hotel
das **Hotelzimmer, –** hotel room
der **Hund, –e** dog
der **Hunger** hunger
der **Husten** cough
der **Hustenreiz** irritation of the throat

I

ich I
die **Idee, –n** idea
ihr her, its
Ihr your
immer always
immer noch still
importieren to import
in (*acc/dat*) in, into
die **Industrie, –n** industry
industriell industrial
die **Industriestadt, ⸚e** industrial town
der **Ingenieur, –e** engineer
die **Information, –en** information
informieren to inform
der **Inhalt, –e** contents
inklusive (*gen*) including
innen inside
innerhalb (*gen*) within
installieren to install
das **Instrument, –e** instrument
die **Inszenierung, –en** production (theatre)
interessant interesting
das **Interesse, –n** interest
interessieren (*refl*) **für** to be interested in
der **Ire, –n** Irishman
die **Irin, –nen** Irish woman
irisch Irish
Irland Ireland
Italien Italy
der **Italiener, –** Italian (man)
die **Italienerin, –nen** Italian (women)
italienisch Italian

J

die **Jagd** hunt
das **Jahr, –e** year
das **Jahresende, –n** end of the year
das **Jahrhundert, –e** century
jährlich per year, annually
der **Januar** January
jeder every
jederzeit at any time
jetzt now
die **Jugendherberge, –n** youth hostel
der **Juli** July
der **Junge, –n** boy
der **Juni** June

K

der **Kabeljau, –s** cod
der **Kaffee** coffee
das **Kaffeetrinken** coffee break
der **Kalender, –** calendar
die **Kamera, –s** camera
die **Kammer, –n** house, chamber (parliament)
der **Kanadier, –** Canadian (man)
die **Kanadierin, –nen** Canadian (woman)
kantonal canton (adj)
der **Karfreitag** Good Friday
die **Karotte, –n** carrot
das **Kartoffelpüree** mashed potatoes
der **Käse** cheese
die **Kassette, –n** cassette
katholisch Catholic
kaufen to buy
das **Kaufhaus, ⸚er** department store
der **Kaufmann, –leute** business man
der **Käse** cheese
die **Kasse, –n** cash desk
kaum hardly
die **Kegelbahn, –en** skittle alley
kein(e) no
kennen* to know
kennenlernen (*sep*) to get to know, to meet
der **Kilometer, –** kilometer
das **Kind, –er** child
die **Kinderbekleidung** children's wear
die **Kirche, –n** church
die **Kirmes, –sen** fair, funfair
die **Klasse, –n** class
das **Kleid, –er** dress
die **Kleidung** clothing
klein small
das **Kleingeld** loose change
knackig crisp
knapp just under
die **Kneipe, –n** pub
kochen to cook
das **Kochsalz** cooking salt
koffeinfrei decaffeinated
der **Kofferraum, ⸚e** boot
der **Kollege, –en** colleague (man)
die **Kollegin, –nen** colleague (woman)

der **Komfort** comfort
komfortabel comfortable
kommen* to come
kompakt compact
die **Kongreßstadt, –¨e** town where conferences are held
können* to be able to
das **Konto, –s** account
der **Kontostand, –¨e** balance
kontrollieren to check
der **Kopf, –¨e** head
der **Kopfsalat, –e** lettuce
der **Kopfschmerz, –en** headache
kosten to cost
kräftigen to strengthen
krank ill
der **Krankenschein, –e** medical insurance record card
das **Krankenhaus, –¨er** hospital
die **Krankheit, –en** illness
der **Kreditkarte, –n** credit card
der **Kreisverkehr** roundabout
die **Kreuzung, –en** crossroads
kriegen to get
die **Küche, –n** kitchen, cuisine
der **Kuchen, –** cake
der **Kühlschrank, –¨e** fridge
der **Kunde, –n** customer
der **Kundendienst** customer service
die **Kunst, –¨e** art
kunstvoll artistic(ally)
der **Kurs, –e** exchange rate
das **Kursbuch, –¨er** timetable
die **Kurzwaren** (*pl*) haberdashery

L

die **Ladenöffnungszeit, –en** shopping hours
die **Lage, –n** situation
der **Lagerverwalter, –** warehouse manager, supervisor
das **Land, –¨er** country, province, state
auf dem Land in the country, in farming
der **Landtag, –e** provincial assembly
der **Landeshauptmann, –¨er** head of government of a province
lang long
die **Länge, –n** length
langfristig in the long term
langsam slow(ly)
langweilen (*refl*) to be bored
laufend constantly
die **Lebensart** way of life
die **Lebensmittel** (*pl*) foodstuffs, provisions
der **Lebensmittelautomat, –en** food dispenser
leben to live
das **Leben, –** life
lebendig lively
der **Lebenslauf, –¨e** curriculum vitae
die **Leberwurst** liver sausage
ledig single, unmarried
die **Leerung, –en** emptying
leger casual
die **Legitimation, –en** proof of identity
der **Lehrer, –** teacher
der **Lehrling, –e** apprentice
leider unfortunately
die **Leistung, –en** performance, ouput
leistungsfähig efficient
lernen to learn
die **Leute** (*pl*) people
das **Licht, –er** light
das **Lichtbild, –er** photograph
lieb welcome (literally 'dear')
lieber rather
die **Liebe** love
liefern to deliver
liegen* to be, to lie
die **Liegewiese, –n** area of grass for sunbathing
das **Lineal, –e** ruler
links on the left, to the left
der **Liter, –** litre
der **Lkw–Fahrer, –** lorry driver
der **Löffel, –** spoon
der **Lohn, –¨e** wage
lokal local
lösen to buy (a ticket)
der **Luftdruck, –¨e** pressure (in tyres)
Lust haben to want
das **Lustschlöß, –¨sser** country seat
Luxemburg Luxemburg
das **Luxushotel, –s** luxury hotel

M

machen to make, to amount to
das **Magazin, –e** magazine
der **Magenschmerz, –en** stomach-ache
das **Magenweh** stomach–ache
mager lean
der **Mai** May
der **Maifeiertag** May Day

das **Mal, –e** time
man one
manchmal sometimes
der **Mann, –̈er** husband, man
die **Mariä Empfängnis** Immaculate Conception
die **Mariä Himmelfahrt** Assumption
die **Mark, –stücke** mark (currency)
das **Markenheftchen, –** book of stamps
der **Markt, –̈e** market
der **Marktplatz, –̈e** market–place
der **März** March
die **Marmelade** jam
die **Maschine, –n** machine, machinery
der **Matjes(hering, –e)** salted herring
maximal maximum
mehr more
mehrere several
mehrfach multiple
die **Mehrwertsteuer** (MwSt.) value added tax
die **Meile, –n** mile
mein my
meinen to think
meist most
meistens mostly
der **Mensch, –en** person
das **Menü, –s** menu
merken to see, to notice
die **Messe, –n** trade fair
das **Messer, –** knife
die **Metallwaren** (*pl*) metal goods
die **Metzgerei, –en** butcher's
die **Milch** milk
mild mild, slightly
die **Million, –en** million
das **Mindestalter,** minimum age
mindestens at least
die **Minute, –n** minute
die **Mischung, –en** minute
mit (*dat*) with
der **Mitarbeiter, –** work colleague, employee
mitbringen* (*sep*) to bring
mitkommen* (*sep*) to come along
mitnehmen (*sep*) to take
das **Mittagessen, –** midday meal
die **Mittagspause, –n** lunch break
mitten in (*acc/dat*) in the middle of
modern modern
die **Möbel** (*pl*) furniture
die **Mode** fashion
das **Modehaus, –̈er** fashion house
mögen to like, to want to
die **Möglichkeit, –en** possibility
möglichst if possible
der **Moment, –e** moment
der **Monat, –e** month
das **Motiv, –e** motif, picture
motorisieren to motorise
müde tired
der **Mund, –̈er** mouth
die **Münze, –n** coin
der **Münzeinwurf** slot
der **Münzwechsler, –** change machine (money)
das **Museum, Museen** museum
die **Musikabteilung, –en** music department
die **Muskel, –n** muscle
der **Muttertag** Mother's Day
müssen to have to

N

der **nach** to
das **Nachbarland, –̈er** neighbouring country
nachfüllen (*sep*) to top up
nachher afterwards
nachlassen (*sep*) to abate
der **Nachmittag, –e** afternoon
die **Nachricht, –en** news
nachsehen* (*sep*) to check
die **Nachspeise, –n** dessert
nächste next
die **Nacht, –̈e** night
der **Nachtisch, –e** dessert
nachts at night
die **Nähe** vicinity
in der Nähe near here
nähern (*refl*) to approach
nahezu almost
die **Nahrung** food
der **Name, –n** name
die **Nase, –n** nose
der **Nationalfeiertag, –e** national public holiday
der **Nationalrat** lower chamber (parliament)
natürlich naturally
neben (*acc/dat*) next to, besides
das **Nebenzimmer, –** adjoining room
nehmen* to have, to take
der **Nerv, –en** nerve
das **Nettoeinkommen, –** net income
neu new, fresh

neuartig new–style
das **Neujahr** New Year
neun nine
nicht mehr no longer
nichts nothing
nicht wahr? isn't it? won't they? etc.
nie never
noch even, still
noch etwas? anything else?
noch nie not yet, never before
Nordamerika North America
der **Norden** the north
das **Normal(benzin)** two-star petrol
normalerweise normally
der **Notruf, –e** emergency telephone number
der **November** November
nur only
nützlich useful

O

ob whether
oben upstairs, on top
der **Ober, –** waiter
die **Oberfläche, –n** surface
oberhalb (*gen*) above
das **Objektiv, –e** lense
Obstsalat, –e fruit salad
die **Ochsenschwanzsuppe, –n** oxtail soup
oder or
ofenfrisch oven-fresh
offen by the glass, open
öffentlich public
öffentliche Verkehrsmittel public transport
offerieren to offer
offiziell official
öffnen to open
die **Öffnungszeit, –en** opening time
der **Ohrenschmerz, –en** earache
oft often
das **Ohr, –en** ear
das **Öl, –e** oil
der **Ölstand** oil level
der **Oktober** October
die **Oper, –n** opera
der **Orangensaft, ¨–e** orange juice
der **Ort, –e** place
örtlich local
der **Osten** the east
das **Ostern** Easter
Österreich Austria
der **Österreicher, –** Austrian (man)
die **Österreicherin, –nen** Austrian (woman)

P

paar a few
ein paarmal a few times
die **Packung, –en** packet, pack
das **Paket, –e** parcel
die **Pannenhilfe** breakdown assistance
das **Parfüm, –s** perfume
die **Parfümerie, –n** perfumery
die **Panne, –n** breakdown
das **Papier, –e** paper, documents
parken to park
das **Parkhaus, ¨–er** multistorey car park
der **Parkplatz, ¨–e** car park
das **Parkverbot** 'no parking'
der **Paß, Pässe** passport, travel pass
das **Passagierschiff, –e** passenger-ship, boat
passen to fit
passieren to happen
die **Person, –en** person
das **Personal** personnel, staff
der **Personalausweis, –e** identity card
der **Personalchef, –s** head of personnel
persönlich personal
der **Pfannkuchen, –** pancake
das **Pfeffersteak, –s** spicy steak
das **Pfingsten** Whitsuntide
der **Pfirsich, –e** peach
die **Pflanze, –n** plant
pflanzlich organic
der **Pförtner, –** porter
das **Pfund** pound (sterling)
pharmazeutisch pharmaceutical
das **Pilsener, –** lager
die **Pkw–Unterstellung** accommodation for private cars
die **Planung** planning
die **Pokelwaren** pickled foods
die **Polizeiwache, –n** police station
die **Pommes frites** (pl) chips
der **Pool, –s** pool
das **Porto, –s** postage, postal charge
Portugal Portugal
das **Porzellan, –e** porcelain
die **Post** post, post office
das **Postamt, ¨–er** post office
das **Postwertzeichen, –** postage stamp

der **Preis, –e** price
prima superb
das **Privatzimmer, –** rented room in private house
pro per
die **Probiermöglichkeit, –en** opportunity to sample
das **Produkt, –e** product
die **Produktion** production, manufactured goods
der **Produktionsleiter, –** production manager
das **Programm, –e** programme
der **Programmierer, –** computer programmer
das **Prozent** per cent
der **Pullover, – (Pulli, –s)** pullover

Q
der **Quadratkilometer, –** square kilomerer
die **Qualität, –en** quality
der **Quellstoff, –e** fibre (which swells in your stomach)
die **Quittung, –en** receipt

R
das **Radio, –s** radio
der **Radiowecker, –** radio alarm clock
der **Radweg, –e** cycle path
rasch quick, speedy
die **Räumlichkeit, –en** capacity, space, premises
die **Rechnung, –en** bill
recht haben to be right, correct
rechts on the right
rechtzeitig punctually
in der Regel in general, as a rule
reich rich
reichhaltig plentiful, comprehensive
die **Reihenfolge, –n** order
der **Reifendruck, ¨–e** tyre pressure
der **Reis** rice
die **Reise, –n** journey
das **Reisebüro, –s** travel agent
die **Reiseländer** (*pl*) tourist countries
der **Reisende, –n** traveller
der **Reisepaß, –pässe** passport
der **Reisescheck, –s** traveller's cheque
die **Reklamation, –en** complaint
relativ relatively
die **Religion, –en** religion
religiös religious
reparieren to repair
der **Reservekanister, –** spare can
reservieren to reserve
das **Restaurant, –s** restaurant
restlich remaining
das **Rezept, –e** prescription
die **Rezeption** reception
rheinisch Rhenish
richtig correct, that's right, really
die **Richtung, –en** direction
das **Rinderfilet, –s** fillet steak
das **Rindfleisch** beef
roh raw
die **Rohkost** raw food
die **Rolle, –n** role, part
die **Rolltreppe, –n** escalator
das **Romanisch** Romansch
die **Römerstadt, ¨–e** Roman town
rostfrei stainless
die **Röstkartoffel, –n** roast potato
rot red
der **Rotkohl** red cabbage
der **Rotwein, –e** red wine
der **Rücken, –** back
die **Rückkehr** return
rückwärts backwards
rufen* to call
die **Rufnummer, –n** telephone number
der **Ruhetag, –e** closed (literally 'day of rest'), day off
ruhig quiet, calm, easily
das **Ruhrgebiet** Ruhr area
rund approximately
die **Rundreise, –n** round trip

S
sachkundig expert
saftig succulent
der **Salat, –e** salad
die **Salzkartoffel, –n** boiled potato
die **Sammlung, –en** collection
samstags on Saturdays
satt full, satisfied
der **Sauerbraten** stewed pickled beef
die **S–Bahn** local train
schaffen to manage
die **Schallplatte, –n** record
der **Schalter, –** counter
scharf hot, spiced
scharfzüngig sharp-tongued
schauen to look
die **Scheibe, –n** slice

der **Schein, –e** note (money)
der **Schellfisch, –e** cod
die **Schere, –n** scissors
das **Schieferdach, ¨–er** slate roof
schicken to send
das **Schiff, –e** ship
die **Schiffstour, –en** boat trip
der **Schinken, –** ham
der **Schinkenspeck** bacon
der **Schlaf** sleep
schlafen* to sleep
das **Schlaraffenland** fool's paradise
schlecht bad
schließen* to close
schmal narrow
schmecken to taste
der **Schmerz, –en** pain
das **Schmerzmittel, –** pain-killer
die **Schneeglätte, –n** snowy surface
die **Schneidwaren** (*pl*) cutting implements
schnell quickly
das **Schnitzel, –** cutlet
der **Schnupfen** cold, sniffle
die **Schmucksachen** (*pl*) jewellery
das **Schneidegerät, –e** cutting implement
schon already
schön good, nice, pleasant
die **Schönheit** beauty
der **Schrank, ¨–e** cupboard
schreiben* to write
die **Schreibwaren** (*pl*) stationery
der **Schuh, –e** shoe
die **Schule, –n** school
schwärmen to be enthusiastic
schwarz black
das **Schweinefleisch** pork
das **Schweineschnitzel, –** pork cutlet
die **Schweiz** Switzerland
der **Schweizer, –** Swiss (man)
Schweizerin, –nen Swiss (woman)
schweizerisch Swiss
schwer difficult, heavy
die **Schwerindustrie, –n** heavy industry
der **Schwermaschinenbau** heavy engineering
das **Schwert, –er** sword
das **Schwimmbad, ¨–er** swimming-pool
sechs six
sehen* to see
die **Sehenswürdigkeit, –en** sights, places of interest
sein to be
seit (*dat*) since
seitdem since then
die **Seite, –n** side, page
die **Sekretärin, –nen** secretary
selber, selbst myself yourself etc.
die **Selbstbedienung** self-service
selbstverständlich of course
Service inbegriffen service included
setzen (*refl*) to sit down
sicher of course, certainly, safe
Sie you
sie she, it
das **Silber** silver
das **Silvester** New Year
sinken* to sink
die **Sitznische, –n** corner seat
so so
sofort straight away
sogar even
sogennant so-called
der **Sohn, ¨–e** son
sonst otherwise, apart from that
sonstig other
die **Spedition, –en** forwarding agent
der **Speicherplatz, ¨–e** memory (computer)
die **Spitze, –n** top, head
die **Sprache, –n** language
der **Sommer** summer
die **Sorte, –n** sort
sortieren to sort
das **Sparbuch, ¨–er** savings book
die **Sparkasse, –n** savings bank
spät late
die **Speisekarte, –n** menu
die **Spezialität, –en** speciality
spielen to play
das **Spielzeug** toy
die **Spielwaren** (*pl*) toys
der **Spieß, –e** spit
die **Spirituosen** (*pl*) spirits
die **Spitze, –en** top, head
der **Sportartikel, –** sports item
der **Sportplatz, ¨–e** sportsground
der **Sprachraum, ¨–e** area where a language is spoken
sprechen* to speak
die **Sprechstundenhilfe, –n** doctor's receptionist
sprühen to spray
der **Staat, –en** state

die **Staatsangehörigkeit, –en** nationality
das **Stadion, Stadien** stadium
die **Stadt, ¨–e** town, city
der **Stadtbereich, –e** the town area
die **Stadtbesichtigung, –en** tour of a town
die **Stadtmitte, –n** town centre
der **Stadtplan, ¨–e** town map
der **Stadtrand, ¨–er** outskirts
die **Stadtrundfahrt, –en** tour of the city
das **Stadtviertel** part of town
der **Stahl, ¨–e** steel
ständig continuously
stattfinden* (*sep*) to take place
stehen* to stand
der **Stein, –e** stone
stempeln to stamp
die **Stenotypistin, –nen** shorthand-typist
der **Stern, –e** star
die **Stichprobe, –n** random check
stimmen to be right
der **Stock, –werke** storey, floor
die **Straße, –n** street
die **Straßenbahnhaltestelle, –n** tram stop
der **Straßenkünstler, –** street artist
der **Straßenzustand, ¨–e** condition on roads
der **Strauß, ¨–e** bouquet
auf der Strecke bleiben to come to grief
das **Streckenverbot, –e** traffic restriction
streuen to grit
die **Stube, –n** room
das **Stück, –e** each, piece, play
der **Student, –en** student (male)
die **Studentin, –nen** student (female)
studieren to study
die **Stunde, –n** hour
suchen to look for
der **Sucher, –** viewfinder
Südafrika South Africa
der **Süden** the south
südlich (gen) to the south
das **Super(benzin)** four-star petrol
die **Suppe, –n** soup
süß sweet
die **Süßigkeit, –en** sweets
das **Symbol, –e** symbol

T

die **Tablette, –n** pill
der **Tafelapfel, ¨–** eating apple
der **Tag, –e** day
am Tag during the day
der **Tag der deutschen Einheit** Day of German Unity
täglich daily
der **Tagungsraum, ¨–e** conference room
tanken to refuel
die **Tankstelle, –n** petrol station
der **Tankwagen, –** petrol lorry
der **Tankwart, –e** petrol pump attendant
die **Tasche, –e** case
das **Taschenbuch, ¨–er** paperback
die **Tasse, –n** cup
die **Tastatur, –en** set of push-buttons
die **Taste, –n** push-button, key
die **Tastennummer, –n** number of push-button, key
die **Tastenreihe, –n** row of push-buttons, keys
der **Taxichauffeur, –e** taxi driver
der **Taxifahrer, –** taxi driver
der **Taxi-Ruf** number for calling a taxi
der **Tee** tea
der **Teil, –e** part
teilweise partially
das **Telefon, –e** telephone
das **Telefonbuch, ¨–er** telephone directory
telefonieren to phone
der **Telefonist, –en** **telephonist (male)**
die **Telefonistin, –nen** telephonist female)
die **Telefonnummer, –n** telephone number
die **Telexnummer, –n** telex number
der **Termin, –e** appointment
teuer expensive
die **Textilien** (*pl*) textiles
die **Textilindustrie, –n** textile industry
das **Theater, –** theatre
tiefgekühlt frozen
der **Tierfreund, –e** animal lover
tippen to type
der **Tisch, –e** table
das **Tischtennis** table tennis
der **Toast** toast
die **Tochter ¨–** daughter
die **Toilette, –n** toilet
die **Tomate, –n** tomato
die **Torte, –n** tart, flan
touristisch tourist (*adj*)
die **Tradition, –en** tradition
tragen* to take, to carry
trampen to hitchhike
treffen* to meet

die **Treppe, –n** stairs
das **T-Shirt, –s** T-shirt
tun to make, to do
türkisch Turkish
typisch typical

U

die **U-Bahn** underground train
über (*acc/dat*) via, about, over
übermorgen day after tomorrow
über Nacht overnight
überall everywhere
der **Überholverbot, –e** 'no overtaking'
übermitteln to transmit
übernachten to stay, to spend the night
üblich usual
übrig left over, remaining
übrigens moreover
die **Uhr, –en** clock
die **Uhrzeit, –en** time
um (*acc*) at, around
der **Umgang** use
die **Umrechnungstabelle, –n** conversion table
umsteigen* (*sep*) to change (trains)
der **Umtausch** exchanged goods, customer services
die **Umgebung, –en** surrounding region, area
umwechseln (*sep*) to change (money)
unbedingt certainly
und and
der **Unfall, ⸚e** accident
ungefähr approximately
die **Unkosten** (*pl*) expenses
unser our
die **Unterhaltung** entertainment
die **Unterhaltungsmusik** light, background music
die **Unterkunft, ⸚e** accommodation
unterschreiben* to sign
unterwegs on your way
unverheiratet single, unmarried
der **Urlaub, –e** holiday
usw. (und so weiter) etc.

V

der **Valentinstag** St Valentine's Day
variieren to vary
der **Vegetarier, –e** vegetarian (male)
die **Vegetarierin, –nen** vegetarian (female)
verbinden* to connect
die **Verbindung, –en** connection
verboten prohibited
verbrauchen to consume, to use
verbringen* to spend (time)
in **Verbindung mit** together with
die **Verdauung** digestion
die **Vereinbarung, –en** agreement
verfügen über to have, have access to
die **Verfügung, –en** access
die **Vergiftung, –en** poisoning
das **Vergnügen, –** pleasure
verhalten* (*refl*) to behave
verheiratet married
der **Verkauf, ⸚e** sale
verkaufen to sell
die **Verkaufsbedingung, –en** sales conditions
der **Verkaufsleiter, –** sales manager
der **Verkehr** traffic
die **Verkehrsampel** traffic lights
verkehrsgünstig easily accessible
das **Verkehrsnetz, –e** traffic network
der **Verkehrsverein, –e** tourist office
der **Verkauf, ⸚e** sign
das **Verkehrszeichen, –** road sign
verletzt injured
verlieben (*refl*) to fall in love
verlieren* to lose
vermehren (*refl*) to increase, multiply
vermeiden to avoid
vermitteln to provide
verraten* to give evidence of, show
versäumen to miss
verschieden various
der **Verschluß, ⸚sse** shutter
die **Versicherungskarte, –n** insurance document
versteckt hidden
verstehen* to understand
verstopft blocked
verteilen to distribute
der **Vertreter, –** representative
die **Verwaltung, –en** administration
verwandeln to transform
verwenden to use
verzollen to declare (for customs)
viel much
viele many
vielen Dank many thanks

vielleicht perhaps
vielleicht doch perhaps I will after all
vielmals very much (literally many times)
vier four
voll full
der **Volkstrauertag** day of national mourning
vollautomatisch fully automatic
das **Vollkornprodukt, –e** wholemeal food
die **Vollmilch** full-cream milk
die **Vollpension** full-board
volltanken *(sep)* to fill up (with petrol)
von (*dat*) from, of
vor (*acc/dat*) before, ago
die **Voraussetzung, –en** requirement, prerequisite
vorbei past
die **Vorfahrt** right of way
vorgestern the day before yesterday
vorhanden available
vorläufig provisionally
vormittags in the morning
der **Vorname, –n** first, Christian name
vorne over there, in front
vorrätig in stock
die **Vorspeise, –n** hors-d'oeuvre
vorwärts forwards
vorziehen* (*sep*) to prefer

W

der **Wagen, –** car
die **Wahl, –en** choice
wählen to choose, to make a choice, to elect
wahr true (see 'nicht wahr')
während (*gen*) during
der **Waliser, –** Welshman
die **Waliserin, –nen** Welsh woman
walisisch Welsh
wann? when?
warm warm
warum? why?
was that, which, what
waschen* to wash
das **Wasser** water
die **Wasserleitung, –en** mains water connection
der **Wechselkurs, –e** exchange rate
wechseln to give change, to exchange (money), to change
die **Wechselstube, –n** bureau de change
der **Weckdienst** (early morning) call service
wehtun* (*sep*) to hurt
Weihnachten (*pl*) Christmas
zweiter Weihnachtstag Boxing Day
weil because
der **Wein, –e** wine
weisen to indicate
weiß white
Weißer Sonntag Low Sunday (first Sunday after Easter when Roman Catholic children take their first communion)
der **Weißwein, –e** white wine
weit far
weiter further
weiterfahren* (*sep*) to continue (by transport)
weitergehen* (*sep*) to continue (on foot)
weiterzahlen (*sep*) to continue paying
welcher? which?
weltbekannt world-famous
weltweit worldwide
wenige a few
weniger less
wenn if
werden* to become
die **Werkstatt, ¨–en** garage (for repairing cars), workshop
das **Werkzeug, –e** tool
der **Wert, –e** value
der **Westen** the west
der **Wetterbericht, –e** weather report
wichtig important
widersprechen to contradict
widmen (*refl*) to devote
wie how, as
wieder again
Auf Wiederhören goodbye (on the telephone)
Auf Wiedersehen goodbye
wiegen* to weigh
das **Wiener Schnitzel** Wiener Schnitzel
wieviel? how much?
wieviele? how many?
das **Wild** game, venison
Willkommen in welcome to
wirklich really, real
wissen* to know
der **Wissenschaftler, –** scientist

wo? where?
die **Woche, –n** week
das **Wochenende, –n** weekend
der **Wochenmarkt, ¨–e** weekly market
wohin? where to?
wohlfühlen (*sep*) (*refl*) to feel at ease
wollen* to want
wunderbar wonderful
der **Wunsch, ¨–e** wish
wünschen to wish
die **Wurst, ¨–e** sausage

Z
die **Zahl, –en** number, figure
zahlen to pay
zählen to count, to include
zahlreich numerous
das **Zahlungsmittel, –** method of payment
die **Zahnschmerzen** (*pl*) toothache
zehn ten
das **Zeichen, –** sign
zeigen to show
die **Zeit, –en** time
die **Zeitbombe, –n** time bomb
die **Zeitschrift, –en** magazine
die **Zeitung, –en** newspaper
das **Zelt, –e** tent
der **Zentimeter, –** centimetre
das **Zentrum, Zentren** centre
das **Zeugnis, –se** certificate
ziehen to pull, draw
das **Ziel, –e** destination
der **Zielbahnhof, ¨–e** destination
ziemlich rather
die **Zigarette, –n** cigarette
das **Zimmer, –** room
der **Zimmernachweis, –e** list of hotels
die **Zimmervermittlung, –en** accommodation bureau
zirca about, approximately
die **Zitrone, –n** lemon
der **Zitronentee** lemon tea
die **Zollauskünfte** (*pl*) customs information
der **Zollbeamte, –n** customs official
die **Zone, –n** zone, region
zu (*dat*) too. to
zuerst first of all
die **Zufahrt, –en** access
zufriedenstellen (*sep*) to satisfy
der **Zug, ¨–e** train
zumachen (*sep*) to close
zunehmend increasingly
zurück back
zusammen together
die **Zusammenstellung, –en** collection
zusätzlich additional
der **Zuschlag, ¨–e** surcharge
zuschicken (*sep*) to send to
zuviel too much
zwei two
zweistündig two-hour
zweite second
di **Zwiebel, –n** onion
zwischen (*acc/dat*) between
zwölf twelve

Transcripts of listening comprehensions and dictations

Chapter 1, exercise 9 (page 10)

- ● Guten Tag, ich heiße Richard Hill.
- ■ Guten Tag, Wilhelm Jaeger aus Hamburg. Woher kommen Sie?
- ● Ich bin Engländer. Ich wohne in Luton, aber ich arbeite in London.
- ■ Bei welcher Firma sind Sie?
- ● Ich bin Verkaufsleiter bei der Firma Stonecraft. Und Sie?
- ■ Ich bin Geschäftsführer der Firma Alsterwerk. Sind Sie zum ersten Mal in Deutschland?
- ● Nein, ich komme sehr oft nach Deutschland.
- ■ Das glaube ich. Sie sprechen nämlich sehr gut Deutsch.
- ● Danke schön.

Chapter 1, exercise 11 (page 11)

(*a*) Ich heiße Thomas Meyer. Ich wohne in Halle und arbeite in Leipzig als Ingenieur bei der Firma Schmidt. Meine Frau und ich haben zwei Söhne und eine Tochter. Ich lerne Englisch bei meiner Firma.

(*b*) Mein Name ist Otto Helm. Ich arbeite hier in London als Deutschlehrer, aber ich komme aus München in Deutschland. Ich bin unverheiratet.

(*c*) Mein Name ist Françoise Laprade. Ich komme aus Straßburg. Das ist in Frankreich. Mein Mann und ich wohnen nicht in Frankreich. Wir wohnen in Luxemburg. Ich bin Dolmetscherin bei der EU. Mein Mann ist Programmierer.

(*d*) Schäfer ist mein Name. Ich komme aus Österreich. Mein Mann ist Amerikaner. Zu Hause sprechen wir Englisch. Wir haben ein Kind – eine Tochter. Sie heißt Sabine. Ich bin Exportleiterin von Beruf und spreche Englisch, Französisch und natürlich Deutsch.

(*e*) Mein Name ist Vogel – V O G E L. Ich bin LKW-Fahrer und komme aus Dresden. Meine Frau Maria, arbeitet als Sekretärin. Sie ist Schweizerin und spricht Deutsch, Italienisch und Französisch. Wir lernen Englisch. Zu Hause sprechen wir Deutsch.

Chapter 2, exercise 1 (page 18)

(*a*)	Wann kommt Herr Schmidt?	Am vierten Mai
(*b*)	Wann fliegt Herr Johnson nach Deutschland?	Am neunten Mai
(*c*)	Wann besuchen Sie die Firma Sasshofer?	Am zweiten Mai
(*d*)	Wann kommen Sie nach Düsseldorf?	Am sechsten Mai
(*e*)	Wann fährt Frau Young nach Mönchengladbach?	Am achten Mai
(*f*)	Wann kommen Sie zu Besuch?	Am fünften Mai

Chapter 2, exercise 5 (page 20)

(*a*) Ich fliege am Samstag, den 17. Oktober, von Paris nach München. Ich bin am Samstag abend in München und fahre direkt zu meinem Hotel. Ich bleibe bis zum 20. Soll ich ein Hotelzimmer reservieren?

(*b*) Ich komme am Montag, den 18. Oktober mit der Bahn. Ich bin um 10.30 in München. Am 21. fahre ich dann nach Nürnberg weiter. Holen Sie mich vom Bahnhof ab oder soll ich ein Taxi nehmen?

(*c*) Hier Richardson. Ich fliege am 18. von Manchester nach London, dann von London weiter. Ich bleibe bis zum 22. Ich bin um 12.30 in München und bei Ihnen um 13.15. Geht das?

(*d*) Hier Haugegaard. Ich fliege am 17. von Dänemark und bin um 11.15 in München. Ich bin zu Mittag bei Schmidt. Am 20. fahre ich nach Frankreich. Kommt Herr Schneider aus der Schweiz?

(*e*) Ich komme nicht von Spanien, sondern von Italien. Ich bin nämlich vom 15. bis zum 17. in Rom. Ich fliege also am 18. von Rom nach München und bin gegen halb eins bei Schmidt. Ich bleibe bis zum Wochenende. Fahren wir am 19. zur Messe oder am 20.?

Chapter 2, exercise 10 (page 22)

Wann kommen Sie zur Messe?
Am vierten Juli
Am zehnten Mai
Am achten August
Am zwanzigsten März
Am neunundzwanzigsten April
Am siebzehnten Januar
Am dritten Juni
Am zwölften Februar
Am einunddreißigsten Oktober
Am ersten Dezember

Chapter 2, exercise 12 (page 23)

Herr Bauer	Guten Tag, Herr Schneider, hier Klaus Bauer. Wie geht es Ihnen?
Herr Schneider	Ach guten Tag, Herr Bauer. Danke gut, und Ihnen?
Herr Bauer	Danke, auch gut. Herr Schneider, ich fahre nächsten Montag nach Düsseldorf zur Messe. Sie auch?
Herr Schneider	Ja, sicher.
Herr Bauer	Also, gut. Ich fliege am Sonntag von München. Wann fahren Sie?
Herr Schneider	Ich fliege am Samstag von Innsbruck. Ich besuche am Wochenende Freunde in Duisburg und fahre dann am Montag mit der Bahn zur Messe.
Herr Bauer	Na, gut. Dann hole ich Sie vom Bahnhof ab. Wann kommen Sie in Düsseldorf an?
Herr Schneider	Um halb neun bin ich in Düsseldorf.
Herr Bauer	Also gut, bis dann. Schönes Wochenende!

Chapter 3, exercise 3 (page 34)

Wie ist Ihre Nummer bitte?

74	16	25
27	43	02
34	54	88
29	48	65
53	52	44
97	65	21
51	0	93
72	2	28

Chapter 3, exercise 2 (page 38)

1

- ● Wann fährt der nächste Zug nach Frankfurt?
- ■ Um 08.30, von Gleis vier.
- ● Fährt der Zug direkt nach Frankfurt?
- ■ Nein, Sie müssen in Stuttgart umsteigen.
- ● Wann kommt der Zug in Frankfurt an?
- ■ Um 11.45.

2

- ● Wann fährt der nächste Zug nach Basel?
- ■ Um 10.25 von Gleis 2.
- ● Fährt der Zug direkt nach Basel?
- ■ Ja, er fährt direkt.
- ● Wann kommt der Zug in Basel an?
- ■ Um 13.08.

3

- ● Entschuldigen Sie bitte, aber wann fährt der nächste Zug nach Heidelberg?
- ■ Er fährt um 12.45 von Gleis 7.
- ● Fährt er direkt nach Heidelberg?
- ■ Nein, Sie müssen in Mannheim umsteigen.
- ● Und wann kommt er in Heidelberg an?
- ■ Um 22.15.

4

- ● Wann fährt der nächste Zug nach Bonn?
- ■ Um 13.37 von Gleis 5.
- ● Muß ich umsteigen?
- ■ Ja. Sie müssen in Frankfurt umsteigen.
- ● Und wann kommt der Zug in Bonn an?
- ■ Um 16.50.

Chapter 3, exercise 5 (page 40)

(*a*) Der nächste Zug nach Berlin fährt um 10.02 ab und kommt um 12.54 in Berlin an. Eine einfache Fahrkarte kostet DM 21,85.

(*b*) Sie wollen nach Wiesbaden? Mal sehen. Ja, Sie fahren um 14.21 nach Fulda. In Fulda umsteigen. Ab Fulda um 16.25. Sie sind in Wiesbaden um 17.10. Einfach kostet das DM44,35.

(*c*) Ein Zug nach Köln heute abend – ja, ab Hannover um 19.35, in Köln um 22.50. Hin und zurück kostet das DM 62,75.
(*d*) Ein Zug nach Hamburg heute nachmittag – Abfahrt 14.07, Ankunft in Hamburg um 15.21. Einfach kostet das DM 18,20.
(*e*) Der letzte Zug nach Leipzig fährt heute abend um 21.04. Sie sind in Leipzig um 0.05. Eine einfache Fahrkarte kostet DM 26,60.
(*f*) Der nächste Zug nach Aachen? Ab Hannover um 9.45. In Köln umsteigen. Sie sind in Köln um 12.10. Ab Köln um 12.35. Ankunft in Aachen um 13.20. Eine Rückfahrkarte kostet DM 74,50.

Zusätzliche Aufgaben, exercise 5 (page 48)

Herr Wagner von der Firma Meyer kommt um 10.15. Er bleibt bis 11.45. Herr Braun erwartet ihn um 11.50. Zu Mittag möchte Frau Rieth die Messe am 16. Mai in Zürich besprechen. Um 13.30 fahren Sie nach Mannheim. Sie müssen nämlich um 14.00 bei der Firma Kohl sein. Es ist jetzt 8.45. Ach ja – in fünf Minuten ruft Frau Eberhard an, die Geschäftsführerin von Kohl.

Zusätzliche Aufgaben, exercise 6 (page 48)

Ingrid Reith R E I T H aus Halle auf Nummer 0 46/4 22 14
Anton Schuster S C H U S T E R aus Leipzig auf Nummer 03 41 47 55 02
Viola Kramer K R A M E R aus Köln – Nummer 02 21/24 86 42
Petra Steinbach S T E I N B A C H aus Hannover – Telefonnummer 05 11/15 23 6
Peter Wissmann W I S S M A N N aus Potsdam – Nummer 03 31/7 44 03
Jürgen Frischmuth F R I S C H M U T H aus Wuppertal – Nummer 02 02/31 16 15

Zusätzliche Aufgaben, exercise 11 (page 49)

Bonn liegt am Rhein und ist als Touristenstadt sehr wichtig. Von Interesse in Bonn sind die Universität, der Dom und das Rathaus; auch interessant sind das Beethovenhaus und die Beethovenhalle (eine Konzerthalle). Bonn ist mit dem Auto, mit dem Zug, mit dem Flugzeug (über Flughafen Köln-Bonn) und sogar mit dem Dampfer auf dem Rhein gut erreichbar.

Chapter 4, exercise 3 (page 53)

Herr Zimmerman reist am Dienstag, dem achtzehnten März, nach Duisburg und fährt gleich zum Hotel Arabella. Er hat im Hotel ein Einzelzimmer mit Bad reserviert. Heinrich Zimmerman ist Deutscher und arbeitet und wohnt in Köln. Seine Adresse ist Bahnhofstraße 40, 5000 Köln 1. Er arbeitet bei der Firma Schumann AG. Er bekommt Zimmer Nummer 75 im vierten Stock und muß im Hotel ein Anmeldeformular ausfüllen und unterschreiben. Sein Paß hat die Nummer F 8206374. Herr Zimmermann hat vor seiner Abreise am Samstag viel zu tun.

Chapter 4, exercise 7a (page 58)

Hotel Hotel Schloß, guten Tag.
Walker Guten Tag, Walker von der Firma Smithdown in Bristol, England.
Hotel Wie kann ich Ihnen helfen?
Walker Ich komme mit einigen Kollegen und Kolleginnen am 12. Juni nach Deutschland und möchte für die Gruppe eine Reservierung machen.
Hotel Zur Zeit haben wir noch Zimmer frei. Was wünschen Sie genau?
Walker Wir sind zu acht. Drei bringen Ihre Partnerinnen bzw Partner mit. Wir brauchen drei Doppelzimmer und zwei Einzelzimmer.

Hotel Und wie lange möchten Sie bleiben?
Walker Drei Tage – vom 12. bis zum 15. Juni.
Hotel Die Zimmer sind alle mit Bad. Geben Sie mir bitte die Namen Ihrer Kollegen.
Walker Ed Roberts, unser Verkaufsdirektor, mit seiner Frau; Mary Baxter, unsere Produktionsleiterin, mit ihrem Mann; Marion Shaw, Roy Stephenson mit seiner Frau, und ich selbst Alan Walker. An einem der Tage muß Herr Roberts ziemlich früh, um 7.00, nach Hamburg fahren.
Hotel Das ist kein Problem.
Walker Was kostet eine Übernachtung bei Ihnen?
Hotel Doppelzimmer DM 145,– bis DM 185,-; Einzelzimmer DM 88,– bis DM 118,–.
Walker Haben Sie auch Konferenzzimmer?
Hotel Ja, für bis zu 20 Personen.
Walker Am 14. brauchen wir eins mit Fax und Telefon. Geht das?
Hotel Ich sehe mal nach und komme auf Sie zurück. Wie ist Ihre Faxnummer bitte?
Walker 01242 660534. Aber bitte erst heute nachmittag. Unsere Faxmaschine ist im Moment nicht in Ordnung.
Hotel Ist gut.
Walker Vielen Dank.

Chapter 4, exercise 11 (page 61)

Tourist Können Sie uns ein nicht zu teures Hotel empfehlen?
Angestellte Wollen Sie ein Hotel in zentraler Lage?
Tourist Nein, lieber ein ruhiges Hotel außerhalb der Stadt.
Angestellte Da gibt es das Parkhotel und den Gasthof Huber. Das Parkhotel ist groß und modern, aber der Gasthof Huber ist billiger.
Tourist Was kostet ein Doppelzimer mit Bad im Gasthof?
Angestellte Eine Übernachtung mit Frühstück, dreißig Mark pro Person.
Tourist Das geht. Hat der Gasthof einen eigenen Parkplatz?
Angestellte Ja, hat er – sogar einen großen.
Tourist Also gut, fahren wir hin. Haben Sie bitte einen Stadtplan?
Angestellte Ja, bitte schön. Und nehmen Sie auch diesen Zimmernachweis mit.

Chapter 5, exercise 4 (page 73)

Schröder So Frau Richter, was möchten Sie?
Richter Für mich – ein Kännchen Kaffee und Toast, Butter und Marmelade – das ist alles.
Schröder Herr Friedrich.
Friedrich Ich möchte Tee, ein Ei, Brötchen, und ein Glas Orangensaft.
Schröder Möchten Sie Tee mit Milch oder Zitrone?
Friedrich Lieber Zitrone.
Schröder Frau Taylor.
Taylor Wo ist die Speisekarte bitte?
Schröder Hier ist sie. Bitte schön.
Taylor Danke, also einen Orangensaft, und ein Erdbeerjoghurt. Zum Frühstück esse ich nicht sehr viel. Ich habe auch gestern abend sehr viel gegessen.
Schröder Herr Weber . . .
Weber Ich nehme eine Tasse Tee mit Milch, und Toast mit Butter und Schinken. Schinken esse ich sehr gern. Es hat gestern wunderbar geschmeckt.
Schröder Frau Schneider.

Schneider	Ich nehme einen Apfelsaft, zwei gekochte Eier, Toast, Butter und Orangenmarmelade und eine Tasse Kaffee.
Schröder	Möchten Sie Käse oder Schinken?
Schneider	Schinken nicht, ich bin Vegetarierin, aber, ja, ich möchte etwas Käse. Edamer bitte.
Taylor	Ich möchte auch eine Tasse Kaffee. Haben Sie koffeinfreien?
Schröder	Einen Kaffee für Frau Taylor. Und ich nehme Orangensaft, Tee, ein Ei, Brötchen, Butter und ein Himbeerjoghurt. Guten Appetit, alle zusammen.

Chapter 5, exercise 11 (page 78)

Newby	Das ist ein sehr gutes Restaurant. Das Essen schmeckt prima. Kommen Sie oft hierher?
Walter	Eigentlich schon. Ich bringe meine Kollegen und Gäste nur hierher.
Newby	Das kann ich gut verstehen. Das Restaurant ist wirklich sehr schön, und es gibt viele interessante Gerichte.
Walter	Ich sehe, daß Sie deutsches Essen gut kennen, Mr Newby.
Newby	Ja, ich bin oft auf Geschäftsreise in Deutschland und Österreich gewesen. Wiener Schnitzel habe ich zum ersten Mal in Linz gegessen. Seitdem esse ich sehr oft Wiener Schnitzel. Übrigens, wie schmeckt Ihnen das Essen in England?
Walter	Gar nicht so schlecht. *Yorkshire Pudding* zum Beispiel ist etwas Einmaliges. Aber ich esse lieber deutsche Küche, weil ich gerne gut gewürzt esse.
Weidmann	Ich finde, das schmeckt mir nicht. Ich esse lieber etwas Süßes. Kuchen und Torten mit Sahne schmecken mir sehr, sehr gut.
Meyer	Das merkt man, Ewald. Was ist denn aus Ihrer Diät geworden?
Weidmann	Herr Ober, die Rechnung bitte!

Chapter 6, exercise 4 (page 94)

A	Ich habe einen Pullover für meinen Mann gekauft – einen schönen blauen, sehen Sie mal. Ich habe nur DM120 dafür bezahlt.
B	Sehr preiswert.
C	Ich habe ein Computer-Magazin gesehen. Hier ist es. Ich habe DM13,75 bezahlt und auch für nächsten Monat ein Exemplar bestellt.
B	Das ist für Sie bestimmt interessant.
D	Ich wollte eigentlich für meine Party ein neues Kleid kaufen, aber ich habe eine Hose und eine Bluse gefunden. Die Hose ist schwarz und die Bluse ist rot. Die Hose hat DM135 gekostet und die Bluse DM220, alles zusammen circa DM350. Ich habe sie anprobiert und sie paßt mir gut.
B	Darf ich mal sehen?
D	Ja, gerne.
E	Ich bin zum Garten-Center gegangen und habe zwei Pflanzen gekauft. Die kleine ist für das Büro. Sie duftet so schön. Die große ist für mein Haus.
B	Was hat die kleine gekostet?
E	DM15
F	Ich habe meine Flugkarte nach Amerika bestellt.
B	Schön, wann fährst du?
F	Im Juni.
B	Fritz, was hast du in der Mittagspause gemacht?
G	Ich habe gearbeitet.

Chapter 6, exercise 9 (page 96)

Gast A Also, gehen Sie die Donaustraße entlang, bis Sie zur Hochstraße kommen. Hier gehen Sie nach links. Auf der rechten Seite sehen Sie dann das Büro. Sehr modern ist es. Dort finden Sie einen Stadtplan und andere Auskünfte über unsere Stadt. Es ist gar nicht weit.

Gast B Ja, also gegenüber dem Hotel ist die Steinstraße. Gehen Sie diese Straße entlang bis zur Kreuzung. Dort müssen Sie dann nach links und dann die zweite Straße rechts nehmen. Sie sehen dann rechts die Firma. Der Geschäftsführer heißt Herr Lange. Er spricht bestimmt Französisch, weil er mit Frankreich und Belgien Geschäftsverbindungen hat.

Gast C Ja, das ist ganz einfach. Vom Hotel sind das nur fünf oder sechs Minuten. Gehen Sie hier links geradeaus bis zur Kreuzung. Dort geht es rechts weiter in die Berliner Allee. Das Geschäft liegt auf der rechten Seite. Wenn sie sehr moderne Bekleidung suchen, kann ich Ihnen ein zweites Geschäft empfehlen. Es heißt Chic. Gehen sie die Berliner Allee hinunter und dann links in den Bonner Weg. Das Geschäft ist dort links an der Ecke.

Gast D Das ist hier im Zentrum. Sehen Sie den Fußgängerüberweg dort drüben? Gehen Sie darüber und dann in die Sankt-Pauli-Straße. Dort geht es rechts weiter bis in die Hochstraße. Gehen Sie dann links noch 200 Meter weiter. Bis der Zug fährt, haben Sie bestimmt noch zwanzig Minuten.

Gast E Einzelzimmer haben wir frei, aber leider keine Doppelzimmer. Ich empfehle Ihnen den Sonnenhof in der Steinstraße auf der linken Seite. Der Inhaber heißt Herr Weismann. Dort sind noch Zimmer frei.

Zusätzliche Aufgaben, exercise 8 (page 104)

(*a*) Meine Damen und Herren. Heute in unserer Lebensmittelabteilung – drei Kilo Äpfel zum Sonderpreis von DM11,50. Sie kaufen zwei Kilo.Wir schenken Ihnen ein drittes. Dieser Sonderpreis gilt nur bis zum Wochenende.

(*b*) Meine Damen und Herren. Von heute bis Samstag bekommen Sie in unserer Möbelabteilung – Tische und Stühle zum Sonderpreis. Ein Stuhl kostet normalerweise DM210. Sie bekommen ihn für DM189. Tische – normalerweise DM1220. Sie bezahlen nur DM1098. Besuchen Sie unsere Möbelabteilung im dritten Stock.

(*c*) Haben Sie Hunger? Dann besuchen Sie unser Restaurant. Bestellen Sie eine Tasse Kaffee oder Tee, dann bekommen Sie dazu ein Stück Apfelstrudel oder Kuchen ganz kostenlos. Oder bestellen Sie ein Hauptgericht und wir geben Ihnen dazu ein Glas Wein oder eine Nachspeise. Dieses Sonderangebot gilt montags und dienstags.

(*d*) Möchten Sie einen Film für Ihre Kamera? Im ersten Stock können Sie zehn Filme zum Sonderpreis von DM75,00 kaufen. Das zahlen Sie normalerweise für acht Filme. Sie bekommen also zwei ganz kostenlos. Am Freitag geht dieses Sonderangebot zu Ende.

Zusätzliche Aufgagen, exercise 9 (page 105)

(*a*) DM 150,57
(*b*) DM 492,21
(*c*) DM 374,09
(*d*) DM 441,75
(*e*) DM 557,33
(*f*) DM 1200,43
(*g*) Genau DM 961,00
(*h*) DM 586,50 und dann noch DM 10,74 — also DM 597,24.
(*i*) DM 234,86
(*j*) DM 820,87

Zusätzliche Aufgaben, exercise 11 (page 105)

Erstens, hier ist ein von Fax Herrn Braun. Er möchte ein Doppelzimmer vom 1. bis zum 8. Juni mit Halbpension.

Dann kommt Ehepaar Kramer. Sie haben angerufen und wollen ein Doppelzimmer vom 15. bis zum 18. Juli. Das ist auch Halbpension, ach nein, sie wollen nur Zimmer mit Frühstück.

Dann noch ein Fax vom Frau Franke. Für Ihre Familie möchte sie zwei Doppelzimmer und ein Einzelzimmer; das sind also die Eltern und drei Kinder, alle unter 14 Jahren, für den 16. Juli, eventuell auch für den 17. Reservieren Sie bitte das Zimmer für zwei Nächte. Die Frankes wollen Halbpension.

Wir hatten auch ein Telefonat von einer Dame, wie heißt sie denn, ach ja Frau Beschel. Sie kommt mit einem fünfjährigen und einem siebenjährigen Kind und möchte ein Familienzimmer vom 3. bis zum 7. August. Das Dreibettzimmer ist zu der Zeit bestimmt frei. Sie wollen Vollpension.

Chapter 7, exercise 3 (page 111)

1
- ● Ich habe seit drei Tagen Halsschmerzen.
- ■ Diese Tabletten sind sehr gut. Sie müssen sie auf der Zunge zergehen lassen und Sie dürfen nicht mehr als acht pro Tag nehmen. Wenn es Ihnen bis zum Wochenende nicht besser geht, müssen Sie zum Arzt gehen.

2
- ● Können Sie mir bitte helfen? Mein Sohn hat seit zwei Tagen Ohrenschmerzen.
- ■ Dann kann ich Ihnen nichts geben. Sie brauchen ein Rezept vom Arzt. Sie dürfen nicht warten. Gehen Sie sofort zum Arzt mit Ihrem Sohn.

3
- ● Haben Sie etwas gegen Husten?
- ■ Husten Sie tags oder nachts?
- ● Meistens am Tag, seit einer Woche.
- ■ Also, diese Tabletten sind sehr gut, aber Sie dürfen sie nicht mehr als sechsmal pro Tag nehmen. Sie müssen auch die Gebrauchsinformation lesen.

4
- ● Mein Mann hat Grippe. Er hat seit gestern Fieber und Kopfschmerzen.
- ■ Dann empfehle ich Ihnen dieses Medikament. Möchten Sie es flüssig oder als Tabletten? Sie können beides haben.
- ● Flüssig bitte. Wie oft muß er das Medikament nehmen?
- ■ Einen 5-mm-Löffel dreimal täglich nach dem Essen.

5
- ● Mein Sohn ist sehr erkältet. Seine Nase ist nachts verstopft.
- ■ Seit wann?
- ● Seit drei Tagen.
- ■ Nehmen Sie diesen Schnupfenspray.
- ● Er kann nicht schlafen. Haben Sie Tabletten?
- ■ Für ein Kind kann ich Ihnen keine Schlaftabletten verschreiben. Der Spray hilft ihm bestimmt.

6
- ● Ich kann seit zwei Wochen nicht schlafen.
- ■ Probieren Sie diese Tabletten. Nehmen Sie gegen 21.00 Uhr zwei Stück. Wenn es nicht besser wird, müssen Sie zum Arzt gehen.

Chapter 7, exercise 6 (page 112)

Ja, guten Tag. Hier Wagner, Herrn Dr. Bennings Sekretärin, von den Wiener Stahlwerken. Gespräch vom achten Januar, acht Uhr zehn. Ich muß Ihnen leider mitteilen, daß Herr Dr. Benning krank ist, und deshalb kann er morgen nicht nach England fliegen. Da er eine Grippe hat, dauert es bestimmt ein paar Tage, bis er wieder gesund ist. Wenn es ihm nächste Woche besser geht, werden wir Sie noch einmal anrufen. Vielleicht können wir dann einen Termin für den 16. oder 17. ausmachen, wenn das Herrn Hall und seinen Kollegen paßt. Wenn das nicht paßt, besucht Dr. Benning am Ende des Monats die Automesse in London und kann dann direkt danach Ihre Firma besuchen, also am 29. oder am 30. Januar. Als Bestätigung dieses Anrufs schicke ich Ihnen auch heute noch ein Fernschreiben. Ich komme dann in zwei Tagen zurück, wenn ich weiß, wie es Dr. Benning geht. Dr. Benning laßt Mr Hall grüßen und bedauert sehr, daß er diese Woche nicht kommen kann.

Chapter 8, exercise 5 (page 122)

Firmenname	**Höchstwert**	**Tiefstwert**
Klein	41	39
Braun	225	216
Interschweiz	779	718
Grün	1130	995
Raster	350	324
Schneider	2038	1975
Doepfner	20400	19500
Hauert	4070	3843
Wehrli	7800	7484
Eicher	6175	6115

Chapter 8, exercise 6 (page 125)

Angestellte Guten Tag. Kann ich Ihnen helfen?

Tourist Ja, bitte. Ich möchte englisches Geld in D-Mark umwechseln. Wie ist denn der Wechselkurs im Moment?

Angestellte DM 2,24.

Tourist Ach, das Pfund sinkt ständig! Vor zwei Jahren war das noch auf DM 2,40. Also, geben Sie mir D-Mark für hundert Pfund. Ich habe fünfzig Pfund Bargeld, und ich will auch fünfzig Pfund Reiseschecks einlösen. Geht das?

Angestellte Ja. Darf ich Ihren Paß sehen?

Tourist Bitte schön.

Angestellte Danke schön. Wollen Sie das Geld in großen Scheinen?

Tourist Ich möchte drei Fünzigmarkscheine, drei Zehnmarkscheine und etwas Kleingeld, bitte.

Angestellte Unterschreiben Sie hier, bitte. So, bitte schön. Den Wechselkurs finden Sie auf der Quittung.

Tourist Vielen Dank. Auf Wiedersehen.

Angestellte Auf Wiedersehen.

Chapter 9, exercise 5 (page 137)

(*a*) Der VW kostet weniger als der BMW. Er ist auch kleiner als der BMW.
Der BMW braucht mehr Benzin als der VW.
Der BMW ist länger und breiter als der VW.
Mit dem BMW können Sie schneller fahren als mit dem VW.
Mit dem VW muß man öfter tanken als mit dem BMW.
Der BMW verbraucht mehr Liter Benzin pro Kilometer als der VW.

(*b*) Benzin vom Supermarkt ist billiger als bei der Tankstelle, aber man muß dafür länger warten.
Zwei kleine Dosen Öl sind teurer als eine große.
Öl ist an der Tankstelle sehr preiswert, aber beim Supermarkt ist es noch preiswerter.
Die Vorderreifen müssen weicher sein als die Hinterreifen. Die Hinterreifen sind also etwas härter.

Chapter 9, exercise 9 (page 140)

Polizist Guten Tag, was machen Sie denn hier? Sehen Sie denn nicht, in der Grünstraße ist Parkverbot.

Herr Kramer Guten Tag. Ja, ich weiß. Es tut mir leid, aber ich habe eine Panne.

Polizist Darf ich bitte Ihre Papiere sehen? . . . So, Herr Kramer, was ist denn los?

Herr Kramei Das weiß ich nicht. Die Batterie ist es bestimmt nicht, weil das Licht noch funktioniert. Benzin ist es auch nicht, weil ich gerade vollgetankt habe.

Polizist Also, was wollen Sie machen? Wollen Sie den ADAC rufen, oder zur nächsten Werkstatt gehen, oder können Sie es selbst reparieren?

Herr Kramet Wo gibt es hier in der Nähe eine Werkstatt?

Polizist Also, gehen Sie bis zur Kreuzung, dann links. Nach ungefähr 30 Metern nehmen Sie wieder die erste Straße links. Aber machen Sie schnell. Die Werkstatt macht um fünf Uhr dreißig zu. Dann ist kein Mensch mehr da. Kommen Sie innerhalb von dreißig Minuten zurück, sonst bekommen Sie eine Strafe von 25 Mark.

Chapter 10, exercise 2 (page 147)

1
- ● Ich möchte schwimmen gehen.
- ■ Ich möchte lieber Tennis spielen. Zum Sportplatz ist es nicht so weit wie zum Schwimmbad.

2
- ● Wir könnten ins Kostümmuseum gehen.
- ■ Das Kostümmuseum ist nicht so interessant wie das Kunstmuseum.

3
- ● Interessierst du dich für die Stadtkirche?
- ■ Ach, sie ist nicht so schön wie der Dom.

4
- ● Gehen wir in die Stadt?
- ■ Nein, dort ist es nicht so ruhig wie hier.

5
- ● Wenn du Lust hast, können wir an einer Ausflugsfahrt mit dem Dampfer teilnehmen.
- ■ Lieber mit dem Bus. Vom Boot aus sieht man nicht so viel wie vom Bus.

6
- ● Wir können ins Kino gehen.
- ■ Lieber ins Theater. Ins Kino zu gehen macht nicht so viel Spaß wie ins Theater zu gehen.

7
- ● Möchtest du dir die Geschäfte ansehen?
- ■ Eigentlich nicht. Sie sind hier nicht so elegant wie zu Hause.

8
- ● Möchtest du noch ein Bier trinken?
- ■ Ja, gerne.

Chapter 10, exercise 6 (page 150)

(*a*) Sie ist in der Steinstraße. Dort sehen Sie viele Bilder, besonders von Nolde.
(*b*) Es liegt in der nächsten Straße. Im Moment ist eine sehr gute Ausstellung von Antiquitäten zu sehen.
(*c*) Ja, gleich hier um die Ecke. Es ist von acht Uhr morgens bis zehn Uhr abends geöffnet. Der Eintritt ist nur drei Mark 50, und das Wasser ist warm.
(*d*) Das finden Sie in der Münchener Straße. Der Film soll sehr interessant sein, und die Musik ist auch sehr gut, glaube ich.
(*e*) Es ist gegenüber dem Stadtpark. Diese Woche können Sie ein Stück von Shakespeare auf Deutsch sehen.

Chapter 10, exercise 7 (page 150)

(*a*) Welches Land hat die meisten Einwohner?
(*b*) Wie heißt das größte Land Deutschlands?
(*c*) Wie heißt das kleinste Land Deutschlands?
(*d*) Nennen Sie einen der berühmtesten deutschen Komponisten.
(*e*) Wie heißt der höchste Berg?
(*f*) Wie heißt der längste Fluß?
(*g*) Wie heißen die bekanntesten Badeinseln?
(*h*) Nennen Sie eine der ältesten Städte.
(*i*) Welche Zugverbindung ist die schnellste zwischen zwei Großstädten?
(*j*) Was sind die beliebtesten Souvenirs aus dem Schwarzwald?

(*a*) Nordrhein-Westfalen hat die meisten Einwohner.
(*b*) Mit 70 554 Km^2 ist Bayern das größte Land.
(*c*) Mit 404 Km^2 ist Bremen das kleinste Land.
(*d*) Einer der berühmtesten deutschen Komponisten ist Händel.
(*e*) Die Zugspitze ist der höchste Berg.
(*f*) Der Rhein ist der längste Fluß.
(*g*) Die bekanntesten Badeinseln sind Sylt und Norderney.
(*h*) Eine der ältesten Städte ist Augsburg.
(*i*) Der ICE ist die schnellste Zugverbindung.
(*j*) Die beliebtesten Souvenirs aus dem Schwarzwald sind Kuckucksuhren.

Chapter 10, exercise 9 (page 150)

Während der dreitäigigen Konferenz versuchen wir, den Gästen ein abwechslungsreiches und interessantes Programm zu bieten. Das Programm ist noch nicht fertig, aber für Folgendes wird die Gruppe sich bestimmt interessieren: Busausflüge, Stadtbesichtigung, Führung durch eine Modefabrik, Theaterbesuch, Zeit zum Einkaufen, und so weiter. Unsere Dolmetscher und Dolmetscherinnen werden natürlich immer zur Hand sein. Genauere Information schicken wir Ihnen in zwei bis drei Wochen zu.

Chapter 10, exercise 12 (page 151)

Gastgeber Willkommen in Recklinghausen. Sind Sie zum ersten Mal hier?
Vertreterin Im Ruhrgebiet war ich schon viermal, aber in Recklinghausen selbst noch nie.
Gastgeber Möchten Sie heute nachmittag Sehenswürdigkeiten besichtigen?
Vertreterin Sehr gerne. Recklinghausen soll eine schöne Stadt sein.
Gastgeber Ja, es ist heute eine moderne Stadt mit vielen interessanten Gebäuden. Als Handels-, Einkaufs- und Kongreßstadt ist es nicht mehr die typische Industriestadt von früher.
Vertreterin Gibt es noch alte Gebäude?
Gastgeber Eigentlich nur wenige. Recklinghausens ältestes Gebäude ist die Kirche St. Peter. Sie ist aus dem zwölften Jahrhundert. Die barocke Engelsburg ist jetzt ein Hotel. Auch gibt es hier ein paar Fachwerkhäuser. In einem davon befindet sich eine interessante Kunstgalerie.
Vertreterin Ich habe gehört, daß Recklinghausen dem Besucher viel zu bieten hat.
Gastgeber Ja, das stimmt. Wir haben außer Museen und Kunstgalerien das Ruhrfestspielhaus. Hier finden die berühmten Ruhrfestspiele statt. Das Planetarium ist auch eine große Attraktion. 40 000 Personen besuchen es jährlich. Und für Tierfreunde gibt es den Zoo.
Vertretern Eine lebendige Stadt, also. Ich glaube, daß man sich hier kaum langweilen kann!
Gastgeber Meine ich auch. Ich hoffe, Sie werden Ihren ersten Besuch in unserer Stadt so richtig genießen.

Zusätzliche Aufgaben, exercise 9 (page 161)

(*a*) Wenn du Lust hast, können wir ins Theater gehen.
(*b*) Wenn das Wetter gut ist, können wir einen schönen Ausflug machen.
(*c*) Wenn du daran Interesse hast, können wir ins Museum gehen.
(*d*) Wenn du großen Hunger hast, können wir essen gehen. Ich kenne ein gutes Restaurant.
(*e*) Wenn wir nicht genug Geld haben, müssen wir zur Bank gehen.
(*f*) Wenn wir Zeit haben, können wir später im neuen Einkaufszentrum einkaufen gehen.
(*g*) Wenn du dich ausruhen möchtest, können wir später ausgehen.
(*h*) Wenn du deine Flugkarte bestellen möchtest, kannst du das heute machen.
(*i*) Wenn du zu müde bist, können wir mit dem Bus fahren.
(*j*) Wenn du dich hinsetzen willst, können wir hier etwas trinken.

Zusätzliche Aufgaben, exercise 10 (page 161)

● Außerdem möchte ich noch einiges wissen.
■ Ja, bitte schön.
● Können Sie den Preis bestätigen?
■ Diesen Monat DM43 575,–, ab nächsten Monat DM44 363,–
● Und das Gewicht?
■ Moment mal. Das Gewicht ist 1250 kg.
● Und seine Höchstgeschwindigkeit?
■ Maximal 190 Stundenkilometer.
● Jetzt einige Abmessungen: Erstens die Länge.
■ 3,62 Meter.
● Die Breite?
■ 1,54 Meter.
● Reifendruck?

- ■ Vorne 26, hinten 28.
- ● Und letzens die Benzinvollmenge?
- ■ 85 Liter. Kommen Sie doch nochmals vorbei. Das Auto haben wir im Moment hier.

Exercise 12 (page 162)

Interviewer Woher kommen Sie, Herr Vögtle?
Vögtle Ich komme aus der Schweiz, aber ich arbeite in Österreich.
Interviewer Was machen Sie in Österreich?
Vögtle Ich arbeite für eine schweizerische Firma. Sie heißt Schärf. Wir produzieren Lebensmittel, zum Beispiel Kekse, Kuchen usw.
Interviewer Wie lange arbeiten Sie schon dort?
Vögtle Seit drei Jahren.
Interviewer Finden Sie Ihre Arbeit interessant?
Vögtle Ja, ich interessiere mich sehr für meine Arbeit. Erstens, weil meine Firma sehr gut ist. Man erwartet sehr viel von uns, aber dafür sind wir sehr gut bezahlt, und wir bekommen auch genug Urlaub im Jahr. Zweitens, weil meine Kollegen und Kolleginnen sehr freundlich sind. Aber das Schönste ist, daß ich die Gelegenheit habe, im Ausland zu wohnen, und ins Ausland zu fahren, zum Beispiel nach Italien, Frankreich und Deutschland. Ich habe auch die Gelegenheit, Fremdsprachen zu sprechen. Es macht mir wirklich Spaß.
Interviewer Welche Sprachen sprechen Sie eigentlich?
Vögtle Deutsch ist meine Muttersprache. Dann spreche ich noch Französisch, Italienisch und etwas Englisch. Das lerne ich noch.
Interviewer Und wieviel Urlaub bekommen Sie im Jahr?
Vögtle Sechs Wochen.
Interviewer Wo verbringen Sie normalerweise Ihren Urlaub?
Vögtle Meistens in der Schweiz, weil es zu Hause so schön ist. Wir können auch die Familie besuchen, Mutter, Vater usw. Diesen Sommer aber, vom 19. bis zum 26. Juli fahren wir hoffentlich nach England, weil ich English sprechen möchte.
Interviewer Wie lange bleiben Sie noch in Österreich?
Vögtle Ich weiß es nicht. Zur Zeit möchte ich keine neue Arbeit suchen. Ich fühle mich sehr wohl in Österreich und habe auch mehr Freunde hier als in der Schweiz.
Interviewer Wie lange arbeiten Sie pro Tag?
Vögtle Das ist schwer zu sagen – meistens von 8.00 Uhr bis 17.00 oder 18.00 Uhr mit einer halben Stunde Mittagspause. Wenn ich unterwegs bin, kann das viel länger sein.

Exercise 17 (page 163)

(*a*) Holen Sie Herrn Kurmeyer vom Bahnhof ab.
(*b*) Werfen Sie diese Briefe in den Briefkasten ein.
(*c*) Füllen Sie diese Formulare aus.
(*d*) Rufen Sie die Firma Siebert an.
(*e*) Schicken Sie diese Pakete ab.
(*f*) Lösen Sie bitten das französische Geld ein.
(*g*) Ich kann Frau Rowolds Brief nicht finden. Gehen Sie bitte meine Papiere durch.
(*h*) Bringen Sie bitte mein Auto zur Tankstelle.
(*i*) Sehen Sie bitte nach, ob das Auto Wasser und Öl braucht.
(*j*) Kommen Sie bitte um 16.00 Uhr zurück. So, Sie haben alles gemacht. Sie dürfen jetzt nach Hause gehen. Amüsieren Sie sich gut heute abend.